Eco-Alchemy

Eco-Alchemy

*Anthroposophy and the History
and Future of Environmentalism*

Dan McKanan

UNIVERSITY OF CALIFORNIA PRESS

University of California Press, one of the most
distinguished university presses in the United States,
enriches lives around the world by advancing scholarship
in the humanities, social sciences, and natural sciences. Its
activities are supported by the UC Press Foundation and
by philanthropic contributions from individuals and
institutions. For more information, visit www.ucpress.edu.

University of California Press
Oakland, California

Library of Congress Cataloging-in-Publication Data

Names: McKanan, Dan, 1967 – author.
Title: Eco-alchemy : anthroposophy and the history and
    future of environmentalism / Dan McKanan.
Description: Oakland, California : University of
    California Press, [2018] | Includes bibliographical
    references and index.
Identifiers: LCCN 2017028629 | LCCN 2017035244 (ebook) |
    ISBN 9780520964389 (epub) | ISBN 9780520290051
    (unjacketed cloth : alk. paper) | ISBN 9780520290068
    (pbk. : alk. paper)
Subjects: LCSH: Environmentalism—Philosophy. |
    Anthroposophy.
Classification: LCC GE195 (ebook) | LCC GE195 .M44 2018
    (print) 2018 | DDC 363.7001—dc23
LC record available at https://lccn.loc.gov/2017028629

Manufactured in the United States of America

26 25 24 23 22 21 20 19 18
10 9 8 7 6 5 4 3 2 1

CONTENTS

ACKNOWLEDGMENTS

This book is the fruit of more than twenty years of interaction with the anthroposophical movement, and I have accumulated many debts over the decades. I am grateful to farmer John Peterson for introducing me to biodynamics when I purchased an Angelic Organics share in the summer of 1995, and to the people of Camphill Village Minnesota for welcoming me into their community in the summers of 1999, 2000, and 2001. I especially thank Laura Briggs, Bill Briggs, and Lois Smith, as well as the late Trudy Pax and Jan Zuzalek, for their sustained enthusiasm for my research over the years. There is not space here to name every person who has extended hospitality to me and my family during research visits to other anthroposophical initiatives, but I would highlight some who have been especially generous in facilitating our travel and extending my network of interviewees: Guy Alma, Jan Bang, Thea Maria Carlson, Mark Finser, Gene Gollogly, Diedra Heitzman, Jonas Hellbrandt, Beth Ingham, Robert Karp, Jens-Peter Linde, Maria Lyons, Steve Lyons, Robert McDermott, Angelika Monteux, Richard Neal, Tobias Pedersen, Martin Ping, Andrew Plant, Rachel Schneider, Steffen Schneider, Hannah Schwartz, Claus Sproll, Bodo von Plato, Sherry Wildfeuer, and Helen Zipperlen. Several of these people have also provided detailed feedback on my ideas and chapter drafts, as have Michael Babitch, David

Schwartz, and Stephen Usher. I also wish to thank the dozens of students who have accompanied me on field trips to anthroposophical initiatives, sharing their observations and insights along the way.

I am especially grateful to Harvard Divinity School for granting me a sabbatical leave in 2013–14, and for providing the research funding that supported several of my visits to anthroposophical initiatives. My most extensive research trip, in the summer of 2013, was made possible by a grant from Harvard's Center for the Study of World Religions, which also supported my travel during the subsequent sabbatical year. I appreciate the sustained enthusiasm of Frank Clooney and Corey O'Brien during that year. I am also grateful for the consistent support and professionalism of my editor at the University of California Press, Eric Schmidt, for the generous feedback I received from the press's anonymous peer reviewers, and for comments and criticisms shared by attendees, when I presented portions of this research at the Communal Studies Association, at the Association for the Study of Esotericism, at the American Academy of Religion, and at Harvard.

My deepest gratitude, as always, is to my fellow travelers in both life and anthroposophical research, Tammy and Oriana McKanan. They have accompanied me on almost every adventure, and their perceptive observations and uncanny insights have improved every page of this book.

INTRODUCTION

The Ecology of Environmentalism

Today's environmental movement is a vast ecosystem that includes farmers and teachers, monkey-wrenching activists and pragmatic politicians, pagans and Protestants, toddlers playing on the beach and elders planning a green burial. All are united by an awareness that their individual destinies are caught up with the health of natural systems at the local, global, and cosmic levels. Human beings have always evolved in symbiosis with wheat and cattle and intestinal bacteria; environmentalists are human beings who are becoming conscious of our interdependence. This consciousness is changing what we eat, how we treat plants and animals, where we live, and how we travel. Environmental consciousness is also changing our culture: the stories we tell, the ways we teach and learn, our outer rituals and innermost beliefs.[1]

One context in which ecological evolution is taking place is within the spiritual communities and practical initiatives inspired by Rudolf Steiner, an early twentieth-century Austrian teacher, whose interests ranged from education to agriculture to "how to know higher worlds." Students of Steiner's spiritual science, also known as anthroposophy (from the Greek words for "human" and "wisdom"), are active in every corner of the environmental movement, from organic farming to environmental education to holistic scientific research. At Temple-Wilton

Community Farm in New Hampshire, farmers Lincoln Geiger, Anthony Graham, and Andrew Kennedy use Steiner's "biodynamic" methods to nurture the health of their soil, plants, and animals. They draw on Steiner's social teachings to cultivate a community of neighbors who support the farm economically and share in its bounty. The system of "community supported agriculture" that they and other biodynamic farmers introduced in 1986 has spread to more than six thousand farms in the United States and thousands more worldwide.[2] One hundred miles north, the residents of Heartbeet Lifesharing, half of whom have developmental disabilities, use similar methods to nurture their farm and community. By partnering with cheesemakers, restauranteurs, and seed savers, they have sparked a good food revolution in rural Hardwick, Vermont.[3]

Across the Atlantic in Ireland and Norway, intentional communities that, like Heartbeet, are part of the Steiner-inspired Camphill movement, have led their nations' turn to sustainable technologies such as biomass and biogas energy production, natural wastewater treatment, and green building. The Water Research Institute in Maine, the Nature Institute in rural New York, the Mandaamin Institute in Wisconsin, and their many counterparts in Europe, continue the holistic scientific research begun by Steiner's students a century ago. Financing for such initiatives, and for many environmental enterprises not directly inspired by Steiner, flows from anthroposophical banks such as GLS in Germany and Triodos in the Netherlands, multibillion dollar institutions that pioneered the concept of "green banking." Persons who wish to learn more about these initiatives turn to such anthroposophical publications as *Lilipoh* in the United States and *New View* in Great Britain. And those who wish to launch an environmental career can do so at Rudolf Steiner College in California, Threefold Educational Center in New York, Emerson College in England, an apprenticeship program on a biodynamic farm, or the Anthroposophical Society's spiritual center in Switzerland, known as the Goetheanum. This book will tell the stories of these and many other people and organizations.

This book will also explore the hidden symbioses between the anthroposophical movement and apparently unrelated expressions of environmental commitment. The organic gardens established by the San Francisco Zen Center inspired a host of restaurants devoted to local, vegetarian food, and they nudged American diets toward a healthier balance. They are rightly seen as an expression of Buddhist ecology, yet the charismatic gardener who designed them called himself a "child of Rudolf Steiner."[4] Another model of Buddhist environmentalism is Bhutan's "Gross National Happiness" project, one of whose architects, Ha Vinh Tho, encountered Steiner's ideas at a Camphill community. Several environmental initiatives, such as Stonyfield Yogurt and *Orion* magazine, that began within the anthroposophical movement have claimed new identities and new niches within the ecology of environmentalism. Even Rachel Carson, widely recognized as the activist responsible for the expansion of the environmental movement in the 1960s and 1970s, drew much of the source material for *Silent Spring* from a lawsuit filed by biodynamic farmers Marjorie Spock and Polly Richards.[5]

As these examples suggest, anthroposophy's most visible contribution to environmentalism has been biodynamic agriculture, a spiritual and alchemical form of farming that prepared the way for the organic movement of the twentieth century. In arguing that anthroposophy is integral to the story of environmentalism, I am also arguing for the centrality of agriculture, and challenging the assumption that concern for wild nature is what defines environmentalism. To be sure, wilderness preservation has a rich history, as do movements combating industrial pollution and human overpopulation. But when we place exclusive emphasis on the ways humans have sinned against the environment, and on concomitant attempts to defend nature from people, we reinforce the notion that humans are intrinsically alienated from nature. Organic agriculture, by contrast, lifts up the possibility that humans can be fully at home in nature, contributing actively to ecosystems in which myriad organisms thrive together.

In recent decades, scholars, activists, and religious communities have embraced organic agriculture as part of a multifaceted environmental strategy that also includes wilderness restoration, work against environmental racism, and efforts to heal the planet's carbon-induced fever.[6] Theologian Norman Wirzba and biblical scholar Ellen F. Davis have shown that the biblical and liturgical traditions of Judaism and Christianity presuppose an "agrarian" worldview whose wisdom remains relevant today.[7] Around the world, sustainable farming practices are proliferating at Gandhian ashrams in India, Buddhist monasteries in Thailand, indigenous villages in Peru, and Israeli kibbutzim.[8] Here in the United States, Native American reservations have renewed traditional cultivation practices, Buddhist and Roman Catholic monastic communities have revived the tradition of growing their own food, and Jewish and Christian congregations have planted gardens and hosted community supported farms. In seeking to connect ancient wisdom to contemporary concerns, some of these people have bypassed the first half of the twentieth century, tracing the roots of organics no further back than the spiritual poetry of Wendell Berry in the 1970s. In this study, I hope to introduce spiritual food activists to the deeper historical and spiritual sources of their commitments.

At the same time, I do not want to suggest that anthroposophy's contribution to environmentalism is limited to agriculture. Biodynamics is the center of the story, but its periphery is as wide as anthroposophy itself. Even manifestations of anthroposophy that seem unrelated to the environment have ecological significance. The best known of Steiner's initiatives is the international network of Waldorf Schools, which spread to four continents in the half century after Steiner's death, and today number a thousand schools and two thousand kindergartens.[9] Seasonal celebrations and farm immersions are integral to the Waldorf curriculum, and many Waldorf graduates pursue environmental careers. The Camphill network of intentional communities, which includes Heartbeet and one hundred other villages and schools, seeks primarily to honor the human dignity of persons with and without developmental disabilities. It has created exemplary "ecovillages" characterized by clean energy, natural wastewater treatment, organically inspired architecture, and biodynamic farming. More broadly, anthroposophy's celebration of the "wisdom of humanity" allows it to balance artistic and cultural commitments with reverence for nature. Long before environmentalists renewed devotion to Mother Earth, Steiner taught that our planet is a single organism with a spiritual personality, and his followers honor both "Anthropos" and "Gaia" in their meditations and actions.

This balancing act may be anthroposophy's greatest gift to the environmental movement. Anthroposophy is a holistic worldview that seeks to achieve harmony through creative work with the polarities of human and nature, matter and spirit, macrocosm and microcosm. It draws on alchemy, which built its understanding of the physical world on the polarities of hot and cold, wet and dry, that which dissolves and that which coagulates.[10] An admirer of the alchemists, Steiner offered a balanced, threefold view of the human being, in which "soul" connects and mediates between "spirit" and "body." He also urged his students to find a middle path between the demons Ahriman, who seeks to bind us to the material world, and Lucifer, who tempts us to ungrounded spiritual flight.

Environmentalism, similarly, is a movement that seeks to restore harmony between humanity and nature by helping humans model our behavior on the rhythms of natural systems. Anna Bramwell, whose comprehensive history of *Ecology in the Twentieth Century* shapes my analysis, argues that this movement coalesced around 1920, through the confluence of "an anti-mechanistic, holistic approach to biology" and the view that certain resources are inherently limited and must be conserved. She further argues that ecology retained a German cultural cast, even as it took hold in Britain and the United States, and that it was "a new political category in its own right," aligning only temporarily and awkwardly with liberal, conservative, socialist, and fascist traditions. Anthroposophy shared these traits, and thus it is unsurprising that it has been a vital part of the story from the beginning.[11]

Anthroposophy consistently confounds observers who seek to impose dichotomous categories onto environmentalism. Those who see environmentalism as one strand of the postsixties Left must contend with the fact that important leaders of the Nazi Party had great enthusiasm for Steiner's approach to agriculture, though rarely for Steiner himself. Conversely, those who see Nazi environmentalism as evidence of an antihumanist "ecofascism" must recognize that Steiner's spiritual science of humanity also led to advocacy on behalf of persons with disabilities, skepticism about eugenics and the need for population control, and the intriguing teaching that the shedding of Christ's blood on Golgotha dissolved national and ethnic distinctions while revitalizing the soil. Observers who try to place anthroposophy on one or the other side of various polarities—West versus East, modern science versus antimodern magic, the political left versus right—invariably leave out something important. Anthroposophy also confounds Bron Taylor's otherwise helpful distinction between "dark green" and "light green" forms of spirituality, with the former ascribing inherent value (or divinity) to nature and the latter advocating for environmental practices as a means to human betterment.[12] Steiner taught such an intimate link between humanity and the cosmos that his students typically engage in "dark green" behaviors (for example, honoring the inherent dignity of cows by refusing to remove their horns) for seemingly "light green" reasons.

Anthroposophy's creative work with polarities invites all environmentalists to broaden our vision and escape ideological monocultures. As I discovered over the course of dozens of interviews, students of Steiner have a remarkable capability to broaden the definition of "ecology" to include education, health, the creative use of money, and ritual celebrations. They are breaking down the imaginary distinctions that cause people to imagine they must choose between jobs and the environment, between sustainability and social justice, or between endangered species and the human family.

In sum, I hope to show one cannot fully understand the environmental movement today without taking into account anthroposophy's multifaceted contributions. Yet I am not claiming a privileged place for anthroposophy within environmentalism. I personally am a Unitarian Universalist, and I could perhaps make a parallel case for Unitarian Universalist environmentalism, incorporating the nature philosophies of Emerson and Thoreau, the wilderness preservation initiatives of nineteenth-century ministers Edward Everett Hale and Thomas Starr King, the jurisprudence of William O. Douglas, and the denomination's recent decision to divest from fossil fuels. The story I will tell in these pages is just one of many that constitute the epic of environmentalism.

I write from a personal commitment to environmentalism, understood as a social movement that seeks to respect natural systems, and to ecology, understood as a way of knowing that stresses interconnection. At the same time, my stance is neutral with regard to the spiritual practices and worldview that are unique to anthroposophy. My personal experience does not equip me to render a judgment for or against the uniqueness of Rudolf Steiner's spiritual insights, or for or against the "truth" of his picture of the world. My judgment that environmentalism has been enriched by anthroposophy is pragmatic, focused on the effects of anthroposophically inspired initiatives. My approach is thus a blend of what anthropologists would call the "emic" and "etic" perspectives in scholarship: I have an emic, or insider's, approach to environmentalism and an etic, or outsider's, approach to anthroposophy. Both approaches have value, and other important dimensions of the phenomena I discuss here might be revealed by scholars working from other vantage points.

My research methods are a hybrid of textual, historical, and ethnographic approaches. I first encountered anthroposophy in the summer of 1995, when I purchased a weekly share in the Angelic Organics community supported farm. Four years later, as a fledgling professor in central Minnesota, I began spending a portion of each summer at Camphill Village Minnesota to conduct the research that led to my earlier book *Touching the World: Christian Communities Transforming Society*.[13] Since that time I have visited anthroposophical initiatives in the United States, Canada, the United Kingdom, Ireland, Iceland, Norway, and

Switzerland, and have conducted formal interviews with hundreds of individuals associated with these initiatives. I have read widely but not exhaustively in the works of Steiner and his students. My picture of anthroposophy is broad but has been shaped by my personal location: I know the Camphill and biodynamic movements much better than Waldorf schooling or anthroposophical medicine; I understand anthroposophy in the Anglo-American world better than in German-speaking territories or the Global South; and I know more about spirituality and social movements than about agriculture or biology. Readers who finish this book with a desire to learn more would do well to seek out texts that highlight other contexts for anthroposophical striving.

An adequate epic of environmentalism must be thoroughly ecological, treating each story in relation to everything else. To say that anthroposophy has a unique place in the history of environmentalism is not to deny that other spiritual traditions have made essential contributions. Just as earthworms and cows and nitrogen-fixing bacteria and humans are all integral to the story of a farm, the story of environmentalism cannot be fully understood without anthroposophy. What's more, the stories of biodynamic farmers, community supported agriculture customers, and Waldorf school students are all integral to the story of anthroposophy, and are all worthy of careful study alongside the germinating ideas of Rudolf Steiner. In the pages that follow, I will begin with Steiner and move quickly to the ways anthroposophy has evolved in symbiosis with an energetic and global environmental movement. In reconstructing the story, I draw on my training in history and the academic study of religion, but also attend to the ways anthroposophy's holistic methods of inquiry can aid in the telling of its story. The result, I hope, will make its own contribution to the continual evolution of environmentalism.

Seed

Rudolf Steiner's Holistic Vision

This is not, primarily, a book about Rudolf Steiner. It is a book about environmental initiatives inspired by Steiner that accents events that occurred decades after his death. In my view, Steiner is worth studying because his students have built an interconnected global network of schools, farms, intentional communities, clinics, innovative businesses, and other "initiatives" that bring healing energies to both nature and society. That network has experienced its most dramatic growth in the years since 1970, and it encompasses far more people than are members of the Anthroposophical Society. Most of the people who have been touched by anthroposophical initiatives have never read a word of Steiner's writings; many have never even heard of Steiner. Yet their story begins with the "seed" of Steiner's teachings. Like Marxism or Lutheranism, anthroposophy is a movement whose founder played an oversized role. One would be hard pressed to identify any practice in any anthroposophical initiative that does not correspond to something that Steiner wrote or said. This is not to say that Steiner's influence cannot be exaggerated. It *is* exaggerated when students of Steiner give him credit for all of anthroposophy's virtues and blame themselves for its faults, and when anthroposophy's critics blame the movement for every disturbing thing that Steiner ever said. This exaggeration stems from the volume of Steiner's writings and lectures and the dizzying array of his interests. Though no one could hope to "master" all this material, it would be foolish to argue that anthroposophy is more than Steiner without first looking squarely at Steiner himself.[1]

The double point I am making can be illustrated by considering Steiner's comments about actual seeds. Modern scientists, Steiner observed, believed that seeds contained genetic instructions for growing into particular plants. He agreed that, at the time of planting, a seed possesses "the highest complexity attained within the Earth-domain." But once in the soil, he continued, the seed "disintegrates ... into cosmic dust." At this chaotic moment, the plant is created by forces that stream in from "the entire surrounding Universe." The parent plant simply placed the seed in the right position to receive those cosmic influences.[2] This unusual approach to genetics has been partly validated by research on "epigenetics," which shows that genes cannot build organisms by themselves, but only through complex interactions with the environment. Few epigeneticists would go as far as Steiner, but in any case my point is metaphorical. Anthroposophy has become an important part of the "ecology of environmentalism" because the "seed" of Steiner's influence has, especially since 1970, been disintegrating into chaos. The process has been painful for Steiner's most devoted students, but it has allowed creativity to flow in from surrounding cultural networks. And yet, because the seed was well placed, plants continue to sprout bearing the image of Steiner's teachings.

STEINER'S ESOTERIC, EVOLUTIONARY, AND REFORMIST TEACHINGS

Just what were those teachings?[3] Many of Steiner's admirers regard him as triply unique: uniquely deep in his clairvoyant access to the "akashic" record of consciousness; uniquely broad in his capacity to connect spiritual insights to the riches of science and culture; and uniquely practical in his application of spirituality to the challenges of education, agriculture, and other professions. Many students find that Steiner's teachings repay a lifetime of study. But as these students often acknowledge, the emphasis on Steiner's uniqueness has not always served anthroposophy well. It can be dispiriting to imagine that one's devoted meditative practice will not reveal as many secrets of the universe as can be found on the pages of Steiner's books. Yet Steiner actually urged his followers to rely first on their own experiences, and only secondarily on what he offered as "indications." "The fear of every anthroposophist," observed Andrew Plant, a longtime participant in the Camphill movement, "is to say 'Steiner said' more than twice in a year," for every time we say it "we betray him."[4] This sentiment is echoed and violated in many anthroposophical conversations. The emphasis on uniqueness also betrays Steiner by decontextualizing him, obscuring the ways he related to his own milieu and how he might be related in fresh ways to new contexts. Steiner taught that the way to understand a phenomenon is to place it in the widest possible context, and so I offer here a contextual interpretation of Steiner himself.[5]

Rudolf Steiner participated in three currents of western culture, each of which he gave a distinct stamp. He was, first, a bearer of Western esoteric traditions who sought to express those traditions in modern and scientific terms. Esoteric traditions, which are a hidden undercurrent of mainstream religiosity, characteristically affirm spiritual correspondences between the universe and human consciousness, describe nature as a living reality, and initiate participants into lineages of spiritual practice. Many also affirm belief in reincarnation and cultivate alternative healing practices. Steiner's esoteric genealogy includes the Hermeticists, Platonists, Gnostics, and Manichees of antiquity; the Cathars and Templars of the Middle Ages; the Rosicrucians, alchemists, and Swedenborgians of early modernity; and the Buddhist, Hindu, and Zoroastrian traditions that Europeans rediscovered in the nineteenth century. His comments on these traditions drew on publicly accessible texts and his own clairvoyant experience. He consistently affirmed that he did not teach anything on the basis of ancient authority, but confirmed everything with his own spiritual research. In many respects, his esoteric teaching mirrored that of the Theosophical Society (founded in 1875 by Helena Blavatsky and Henry Steel Olcott), whose German section he led from 1904 to 1912. Along with the Theosophists, Steiner prepared the way for the "New Age" movement that sprang up half a century after his death.[6]

Steiner was determined to translate esoteric teachings into the scientific vocabulary he had learned as a student in a technical high school (rather than a humanistic Gymnasium) and at the Vienna Institute of Technology. He broke with the Theosophical Society because he refused to see Eastern wisdom as superior to that of the West, and he had little affinity with the antimodernism of other early twentieth-century esoteric currents, notably the "traditionalism" of René Guenon. Instead, he called for an esotericism that honored modernity's stress on individual freedom, repeatedly warning that "old instincts" are "no longer competent to deal with the demands of modern mankind."[7] Acknowledging the value of secrecy in past esotericisms, Steiner also affirmed that its time had passed: "In our time knowledge cannot be retained in limited circles."[8]

The second current of Western culture in which Steiner participated was evolutionary thought. Nineteenth-century scholars saw all phenomena—especially those of geology, biology, and history—in terms of evolutionary processes rather than of the stable laws favored by Enlightenment scientists such as Isaac Newton. Darwinian evolution was one of several fruits of this impulse, and Steiner was deeply interested in all the new sciences. He had a love-hate relationship with Ernst Haeckel, the leading exponent of Darwinian evolution in the German-speaking world and the scientist who coined the term *ecology*. Steiner loved the way Haeckel forced his contemporaries to think in terms of processes, but hated his tendency to reduce all processes to material causes. For Steiner, biological and cultural transformations derived ultimately from spiritual sources. His vision built on the idealistic philosophies of his German predecessors Fichte, Schelling, and Hegel, and was in many ways parallel to the views of his non-German contemporaries Henri

Bergson, Alfred North Whitehead, and Teilhard de Chardin. (Steiner acknowledged the influence of Bergson, but Whitehead and Teilhard produced their most relevant works after Steiner's death.)

Steiner's evolutionism was shaped decisively by Johann Wolfgang von Goethe, whose scientific writings Steiner edited shortly after finishing his schooling. The great poet was also an idiosyncratic scientist, who counseled disciplined but subjective observation of holistic phenomena rather than atomizing experimentation. He was one of the first to propose that species had "metamorphosed" over time. In part because of his affinity for Goethe, Steiner never accepted the "materialistic" details of Darwinism, but offered a spiritual alternative. Accepting the sequence of physical events described by Darwin, he recognized "within that sequence ... the activity of *spiritual impulses*." Indeed, "he realized that the human spirit is older than all other living beings.... We did not develop from [other organisms] but left them behind and severed them from ourselves so that our physical form could attain the image of our spirit."[9] Such claims set Steiner apart from Bergson, Whitehead, and Teilhard, all of whom sought to *expand* the Darwinian paradigm to include spirit, without directly challenging its materialism.

The third cultural current in which Steiner participated was the impulse to social reform that gave birth to socialism, anarchism, the Protestant social gospel, and Catholic social teaching. Sympathizing with many of these, Steiner insisted that inner spiritual transformation was the key to institutional change. Before his career as a spiritual teacher, he publicly condemned the anti-Semitic persecution of Alfred Dreyfus, participated in gatherings sponsored by the poet and reformer Ludwig Jacobowski, gave lectures at a workers' college sponsored by the Socialist Party, and identified himself as an "individualist anarchist." As a Theosophical leader, he lambasted those Theosophists who imagined that spiritual ideas are good "for the inner life of the soul" but "worthless for the practical struggle of life."[10] Later, in the wake of the First World War, he developed a distinctive social philosophy known as "threefolding," which he attempted to implement through political organizing and the creation of cooperative enterprises. His policy prescriptions—to distinguish more clearly between the economic, political, and cultural spheres; and to eliminate wage labor in favor of a system in which people freely work for the benefit of others—echoed those of the utopian socialists and individualist anarchists. But in keeping with his evolutionary philosophy, Steiner insisted that no social strategy could "hold good for all time." Rejecting all forms of coercion, he suggested that "universal welfare is only attainable through a world-conception that shall lay hold upon the souls of all men and fire the inner life."[11] Steiner's emphasis on interiority might be compared to that of Ralph Waldo Emerson, who stood aloof from activism but inspired his friends to embrace abolitionism, women's rights, and socialism. It is no accident that the anthroposophical college near London is named for Emerson.

In distinguishing the esoteric, evolutionary, and reformist dimensions of Steiner's thought, I do not mean to impose a sharp distinction between these dimensions or to suggest that Steiner was the only person to unite them. The Theosophical Society, within which Steiner first articulated his esoteric worldview, also had an evolutionary and reformist vision. Goethe had esoteric interests. Many social reformers drank from the wells of Goetheanism and theosophy. But by Steiner's time, the currents were diverging. In 1920 the Communist Party was the ascendant expression of social reform, and it was hostile to esotericism and disconnected from evolutionary science. University science departments were controlled by Darwinian materialists, who were hostile to the other two currents. Esotericism was turning toward the strident antimodernism of the Guenonian traditionalists, who were usually apolitical and occasionally reactionary. Steiner was one of the few teachers who anticipated the reintegration of evolutionary, esoteric, and reformist currents that would occur with the New Age movement of the 1970s.

Still, anthroposophy was never separate from the broader network of spiritualities that traced their roots to theosophy. Much ink has been spilled debating the degree of Steiner's dependence on his theosophical predecessors, just as much ink has been spilled over the alleged plagiarisms of theosophy's founder, Madame Blavatsky.[12] Steiner explained the appearance of plagiarism by saying that his clairvoyant perceptions came "without names," forcing him to turn to "older accounts of spiritual matters for ways to express these still nameless things in words."[13] Personally, I lack the clairvoyant gifts needed to judge this explanation.

Anthroposophy is unique in one respect: no other daughter of theosophy has inspired a comparable array of educational, agricultural, medical, social, and artistic initiatives. Yet those initiatives reflect concerns that were widely shared by individual theosophists and esotericists. In any anthroposophical initiative, one can find practitioners of other esoteric spiritualities, who are proportionately more numerous than mainstream Christians or secularists. From the beginning, spiritually eclectic individuals helped anthroposophical initiatives grow and spread. The uniqueness of anthroposophy may thus rest in the way Steiner integrated his spiritual teachings with reformist practice, while other spiritual seekers held these elements more loosely together.

ANTHROPOSOPHY AND ITS INITIATIVES: SELF-REINFORCING AND SELF-DISPERSING

Steiner's integration of spirituality and reform was reflected in the organizational structure of the anthroposophical movement, which has always been characterized by a polarity between the Anthroposophical Society and the initiatives. The society was founded by students of Steiner in December 1912, shortly after his break with theosophy. Steiner directed the construction of the society's headquarters, known as the Goetheanum, in Dornach, Switzerland. At the Christmas Conference of 1923, he refounded the society under his direct leadership. By that time, Steiner's students had created several distinct entities intended to put his ideas into practice. The most significant initiatives were the Waldorf School in Stuttgart, created in 1919 to educate the children of employees at a cigarette factory, and The Coming Day, a network of cooperative businesses that was destroyed in the economic turmoil after the First World War. The decision to refound the society was partly motivated by Steiner's sense that anthroposophists had failed to find the right balance between anthroposophy and its initiatives. Currently, the society has approximately fifty thousand members, a number that has not changed significantly since the turn of the twenty-first century, while thousands of initiatives continue to grow and proliferate.

The polarity of society and initiatives has helped the anthroposophical movement to maintain a creative balance between what I will call "self-reinforcing" and "self-dispersing" tendencies. A self-reinforcing spirituality, as I define it, expects a high level of commitment from its adherents and seeks to regulate multiple dimensions of their lives. It may demand a large investment of time or money; it may impose detailed rules related to diet and dress; it may encourage members to socialize primarily with one another. Such spiritualities may have limited appeal, but they effectively conserve and recycle the resources brought by adherents, enabling future growth. The Church of Jesus Christ of Latter-day Saints is a well-known example of a self-reinforcing spiritual movement.

A self-dispersing spirituality, by contrast, seeks to disseminate itself as broadly as possible by making minimal demands on adherents— indeed, one might hesitate to call them adherents. Typically, it touches only one dimension of life, allowing people to connect to it regardless of their practices in other spheres. Practitioners do not experience themselves as members of a corporate body so much as seekers or customers. Astrology, as it is practiced in the contemporary West, exemplifies the self-dispersing pattern: vast numbers of people connect with it in a superficial way, or even use it as a primary framework for meaning making, without coalescing into a movement. Multiple self-dispersing spiritualities may relate to one another in a "milieu" of seekers, who share a desire for alternatives to religious and scientific orthodoxies.

My distinction between these spiritual styles is shaped by Colin Campbell's distinction between sectarian (what I call self-reinforcing) and cultic (what I call self-dispersing) forms of practice, and by his suggestion that the latter constitute a "cultic milieu." I have chosen not to use Campbell's terms, even though I find his analysis helpful, because the term *cult* is often used in a sense diametrically opposed to Campbell's—that is, to designate a spiritual group that is pathologically self-reinforcing, sacrificing the freedom of its members for the benefit of the group or its leader. I also prefer to avoid the emotionally loaded language of "cult" and "sect" because neither self-reinforcing nor self-dispersing spiritualities are inherently problematic. Yet self-reinforcing spiritualities always carry the risk of authoritarianism, just as self-dispersing spiritualities may fall prey to consumerism.[14]

Ecologically, one might compare a self-reinforcing spirituality with a redwood tree, and a self-dispersing spirituality with a dandelion. The redwood exerts a dominant influence in a few specialized environments, absorbing water and shedding foliage in ways that invite a symbiotic community into existence. The dandelion, by contrast, spreads its seeds as widely as possible, allowing it to interact more superficially with nearly all species that live in temperate climates.

The Anthroposophical Society, and especially its "First Class" of fully committed members, exhibits many self-reinforcing qualities: members do intense spiritual work together, and often view themselves as karmically bound together across multiple lifetimes. Anthroposophical initiatives, by contrast, function in a self-dispersing manner: anyone, regardless of worldview, may enroll in a Waldorf school or purchase a biodynamic product. At the same time, the initiatives contribute to the self-reinforcing quality of the society, for they allow members to organize all aspects of their lives—education, nutrition, medicine, religious ritual, and artistic practice—along anthroposophical lines. Before 1970, members of the Anthroposophical Society controlled virtually all initiatives and often steered them in a self-reinforcing direction. Since 1970, the movement has tilted in a self-dispersing direction, as nonmembers of the society have played an important role in expanding the initiatives.

One consequence of the polarity between anthroposophy's self-reinforcing and self-dispersing qualities is that students of Steiner have strong feelings about the terminology they use to identify themselves. Some use *anthroposophist* to designate committed practitioners and members of the Anthroposophical Society. Others refuse to use this term, either because they think it expresses a lofty ideal to which they can only aspire, or because it sounds sectarian or clubbish—though they may concede that students of Steiner are prone to sectarianism or clubbishness! Some have proposed *anthroposopher* as an alternative that reflects the evolving character of anthroposophical striving, but it has not been widely embraced. Since the objections are of recent vintage, I have sometimes used the term *anthroposophist* to describe deceased members of the Anthroposophical Society, but have otherwise preferred *student of Steiner, student of anthroposophy, or member of the Anthroposophical Society.* These terms imply personal commitment and *not* a merely intellectual interest in Steiner's ideas. I should also note that I sometimes use anthroposophy as shorthand for the anthroposophical movement (encompassing both society and initiatives), while many others would use it only to designate the "evolving body of knowledge" that has been achieved in relation to a spiritual personality known as Anthroposophia.[15]

Steiner's most commonly cited definition of anthroposophy is "a path of knowledge aiming to guide the spiritual element in the human being to the spiritual in the universe."[16] These words were echoed when I asked participants in contemporary initiatives to describe "the major ideas and practices of anthroposophy." Echoing the name *anthroposophy*, many stressed Steiner's view of what it means to be *human.* Some pointed out the evolutionary character of Steiner's view of humanity; others called attention to Steiner's threefold view of the human being as body, soul, spirit, or his fourfold account of the interrelationship of our physical body, etheric body (the life force we have in common with plants), astral body (common to all animals), and uniquely human "I," or "ego." Others emphasized Steiner's teaching about the spirit, describing anthroposophy as a path that brought matter and spirit together. Many described anthroposophy as a *free* spiritual path, in some cases suggesting that it should not be conflated with Steiner's teaching, since "there are other ways of describing it today and unfolding it and discovering it."[17] And many suggested that what truly sets anthroposophy apart is its practicality. Mark Finser, one of the founders of RSF Social Finance, quoted the verse used at the opening of the first Waldorf school, which continues to be used to open RSF board meetings: "Seek the really practical material life, but seek it in such a way that it does not numb you to the spirit that works within it."[18]

THE BIRTH OF BIODYNAMICS

One way that students of anthroposophy "seek the really practical material life" is through a system of agriculture that Steiner introduced in a 1924 course of lectures. These lectures were given less than a year before Steiner's death, which meant that Steiner did not have time to elaborate his teaching or give it a name. Farmers began to refer to "biological-dynamic agriculture" three years later, and in English this was shortened to "bio-dynamics" and then "biodynamics." (For convenience, I use the formulation that is current today.) Biodynamics represents Steiner's last initiative—though also one that grew rapidly in the decade or two after his death. It was not so much the apex of Steiner's thought as a depth to which he turned after previous attempts at social transformation had ended in disappointment. Five years earlier, he had launched a campaign to persuade postwar Central Europe to embrace a "threefold social order," in which distinct institutions would carry responsibility for economic, political, and cultural life. This provoked violent opposition from fascists and socialists, and may have been a factor in the 1922 burning of Steiner's first Goetheanum. Around the same time, the networks of cooperative businesses intended to usher in a threefold society were bankrupted by Germany's postwar hyperinflation. In the face of these failures, Steiner intensified his interest in education and nutrition, both of which he saw as ways to nurture humanity for social and spiritual development. When his student Ehrenfried Pfeiffer asked him why anthroposophy had borne so little fruit, Steiner replied that "Nutrition as it is to-day does not supply the strength necessary for manifesting the spirit in physical life."[19]

During the early 1920s, Steiner was in conversation with two groups of farmers—farm managers who worked for anthroposophical businesses in southwestern Germany, and aristocratic members of the Anthroposophical Society with significant estates in the eastern territory of Silesia (then part of Germany, now part of Poland). One individual bridged these two groups: Count Carl von Keyserlingk managed eighteen Silesian estates but also consulted with Steiner regarding the agricultural enterprises of the business network known as The Coming Day.[20] These farmers called his attention to the declining quality of European soils: fields that had once produced crops thirty years in a row now had to be left fallow after only five. Steiner's students who worked in the medical and veterinary fields reported an increase in animal diseases. And Steiner's students who were pursuing university degrees in the natural sciences, among them Ehrenfried Pfeiffer and Günther Wachsmuth, were eager for Steiner to spell out the connections between his teachings—especially about the etheric forces found in living beings—and biological science.

Initially, Steiner responded to such inquiries in piecemeal fashion. On one occasion, he told Pfeiffer that plants could not be diseased per se, but always suffered "from diseased conditions in their environment"; on another, he shared ideas about plant breeding with farmer Ernst Stegemann. In the fall of 1923, Steiner taught Pfeiffer and Wachsmuth to make a homeopathic preparation that would eventually be known as "500." They collected cows' horns, filled them with manure, buried them in the fall, and dug them up in the spring. Steiner diluted the contents of the horns in a pail of water, used Pfeiffer's walking stick to demonstrate an energetic stirring technique, and explained how the dilution should be sprayed over the garden. As Pfeiffer recalled, "Such was the momentous occasion marking the birth-hour of a world-wide agricultural movement."[21]

Only a handful of people experienced this lesson, and Steiner had not explained the rationale underlying his seemingly bizarre instructions. Meanwhile, Count Keyserlingk was so eager to host a lecture series on agriculture that he sent his nephew to camp on Steiner's doorstep in Dornach until he agreed to come east. Accordingly, between June 7 and

16, 1924, Steiner offered a cycle of eight lectures in which he explained how (in Pfeiffer's words) "to reunite the plant, viewed as a system of forces under the influence of cosmic activities, with nature as a whole."[22] These were accompanied by a series of youth lectures intended to instill both "fidelity to the earth" and "courage to traverse the world of the stars," as one participant put it. Members of the Christian Community (a religious initiative rooted in anthroposophy) found the course to be a fitting prelude to their first celebration of Saint John's Day, which Steiner had recast as a Christian version of the summer solstice, on the grounds that Christ himself was a spiritual being associated with the sun. "The Pagan festival of the summer solstice with its fires and flames as we had loved it in our youth, was now to return in its Christian form."[23]

Steiner's Agriculture Course was the first systematic articulation of an approach to agriculture that rejected chemical fertilizers and pesticides on principle, and in it Steiner expounded several ideas that became foundational for the environmental movement. He called for a holistic approach that honored interconnections binding plants and animals to the whole of nature; he emphasized dynamic processes rather than the static substances analyzed by agricultural chemists; he described each farm as a living organism; he called upon farmers to nurture rather than to exploit the soil; and he explained that diseases are the result of imbalances and not of specific agents that must be eliminated altogether.

These ideas represent a more challenging vision for ecological farming than is embodied in contemporary standards for organic certification, which explains why idealistic organic farmers continually turn to biodynamics in the hope of finding something "more." But—to the delight of some and the dismay of others—what they actually discover in the Agriculture Course is more, even, than what I have just outlined. For Steiner also taught that forces streaming from the moon, the planets, and the stars must be enlisted for the renewal of the soil, and he proposed alchemical and homeopathic methods for doing so. These two dimensions—what we might call the "biological" and the "cosmic" aspects of biodynamics—cannot readily be disentangled.

ECOLOGICAL THEMES
IN THE AGRICULTURE COURSE

Holism was the leitmotif of the course. Almost at the beginning Steiner affirmed that "the interests of Agriculture are bound up, in all directions, with the widest spheres of life." "In great Nature," he echoed in the seventh lecture, "everything, everything is connected." Each beetroot was "like a magnetic needle" that could be understood "only in relation to the whole earth." Against the Linnaean impulse to "pigeonhole" everything "into species and genera," Steiner pointed out that "in nature ... all things are in mutual interaction." Against the agricultural chemistry of Justus Liebig, who had laid almost exclusive stress on nitrogen, phosphorus, and potassium, Steiner counseled attention to the subtle influences of trace elements, both on soil health and human nutrition. In another turn that anticipated late twentieth-century ecology, Steiner warned farmers not to cut down forests "in the hope of increasing our crops." True "economy" required "insight" into the "mutual relationships" connecting cultivated and wild spaces. And from the beginning, Steiner made it clear that the holism he had in mind was cosmic and not merely biological. "We must extend our view to the whole Cosmos," he insisted, and "summon all the Universe into our counsels!"[24]

The same balancing of biological and cosmic dimensions persisted when Steiner argued that forces and processes are more important to agriculture than substances. When he introduced the topic of manuring, he observed, mundanely enough, that "the greater part of what man ... receives into himself is cast out again." Steiner reasoned that, since animals derive "dynamic forces" from the plants they eat, returning those forces to the plant in the form of manure is a way of helping it "receive into its body the influences which the soil contains"—an insight that fits nicely with current research on the complex environmental interactions that determine whether humans and other animals are able to extract appropriate nutrition from their food. But Steiner framed this in esoteric terms, describing manure's "nitrogen-carrying forces" as "astral" and its "oxygen-carrying forces" as "ethereal." He went on to suggest that in animals the "head-organization" derives its substance from the earth and its forces from the cosmos, while the metabolic system derives its substance from the cosmos and its forces from the earth.[25]

One of the most original aspects of the Agriculture Course is Steiner's claim that each farm is a living organism: "A farm is true to its essential nature ... if it is conceived as ... a self-contained individuality." Steiner conceded that in practice it might not be possible to eliminate external inputs altogether, but he insisted that these should be seen "as a remedy for a sick farm." The biological implication of this ideal was that each farm would need to include both crops and livestock—indeed, it would need to have just the right mix of cows, horses, and pigs to produce the manure needed by its mix of crops. When you "get rid of the animals and order the manure-content from Chile," he warned, you are "neglecting the fact that this is a perfect and self-contained cycle." The biodynamic farm would also integrate areas of forest and wetland. In the terms of the later environmental movement, such principles ensured that biodynamic farmers would neither deplete the accumulated fertility of their farms nor rely on exploitative "externalities" to maintain fertility. But, once again, Steiner framed this in esoteric terms: forests and fruit trees are needed, for example, because they put "astrality" into the air and thus catalyze the evolutionary process by which animals will gradually "develop the real Ego-forces."[26]

Steiner also affirmed that "the soil of the Earth is the foundation of all Agriculture," anticipating British organics pioneer Eve Balfour's decision to name her movement the Soil Association. Steiner viewed healthy soil as an end in itself, rather than a means to the production of healthy food. Though he admitted that "We cannot help ... *exploiting* the land," he urged that farmers restore the forces of the earth.[27]

In keeping with the theme of balancing polarities, Steiner stressed that plant and animal diseases stem from ecological imbalances and are best treated with gentle measures. "You do more harm by removing the harmful influences," he told one participant, "than by leaving them alone. Nowadays ... people are always wanting to 'disinfect' things.

Undoubtedly they go too far in this." Comparing agricultural pests to medicine and yeast, both of which are dangerous in large quantities but helpfully stimulating in small doses, Steiner connected this point to the basic principles of homeopathy.[28]

Another aspect of the Agriculture Course is Steiner's emphasis on the role of the farmer, both in building a relationship to the farm individuality and in participating in agricultural research. He berated universities for allowing people who don't know "what it means to grow mangolds, potatoes and corn" to teach courses in agricultural economics, and urged his hearers to be diligent observers of everything on their farms, as "No one can judge of Agriculture who does not derive his judgment from field and forest and the breeding of cattle." He even encouraged farmers to gain "a personal relationship to the manure"! He also invited them to share their observations with anthroposophical leaders, for "If our indications are to be of use to you, we must know exactly what the things are like, to which these indications refer." Steiner reminded the farmers that "When a man works at a thing himself, he gives something to it which it retains."[29]

Steiner balanced biological and cosmic elements evenly when he articulated general principles, but tilted toward the cosmic when he came to specifics. At no point did he explain how to construct a compost bin, how to measure the biological diversity of the soil, or how to use companion plants to ward off pests. Such omissions help explain why Albert Howard, who published a detailed description of what he called "Indore process" composting in 1931, often receives credit as the founder of organic agriculture.[30] (*Wikipedia*, for example, acknowledges Steiner's firstness but summarizes his system inaccurately and asserts that it was not based on "a good understanding of science."[31]) Instead, Steiner's specific recommendations had to do with the creation of homeopathic "preparations," which were in turn grounded in alchemical interpretations of the elements and of the organs of plants and animals.

Steiner's first lecture, for example, emphasized the connections and distinctions between plants and human beings. Human beings, he asserted, are relatively "emancipated" from the "outer Universe": our biological cycles, such as menstruation or fevers, may mirror rhythms found elsewhere in nature, but they are not rigidly bound to them. But plants are still "immersed in the general life of nature," which is why a holistic approach is necessary for those working with plants. Plants both reproduce themselves and serve as nourishment for humans and animals, Steiner explained, and these two functions have distinct cosmic significances. Plant reproduction depends on forces that come "from Moon, Venus, and Mercury, via the limestone nature" in the soil, while the production of food relies on Mars, Jupiter, Saturn, and silica.[32]

In the second lecture, Steiner described the organs making up the individuality of the farm. The surface of the earth, he explained, is like the human diaphragm, and the farm is like an upside-down human being, with its head beneath the surface and its intestines reaching toward the sun. "We ... are going about in the belly of the farm." The farm's intestinal organs, Steiner went on, draw their cosmic influences from the inner planets, while the outer planets were concerned with the head-like organs located within the soil. Thus, "the ABC for our judgment of plant-growth" involves a distinction between "what in the plant is cosmic, and what is terrestrial or earthly." By subtly treating the soil, farmers and gardeners can "densify the cosmic" so that it contributes primarily to the growth of roots and leaves, or "thin it out" so it brings more intense colors and flavors to the flowers and fruits.[33]

One implication of Steiner's account of cosmic influences on plant growth is that even substances that seem irrelevant, such as the inorganic and insoluble silica that constitutes most of the soil, may have important roles as "physical carriers" for the workings of spirit. He devoted the third lecture to an intricate story about the elements nitrogen, hydrogen, oxygen, carbon, and sulfur, suggesting that mainstream science had failed to see they were governed by a different set of laws when "living" inside plants, animals, or the soil than when they were isolated in mineral form. (A science that analyzes only elements separate from living systems, Steiner pointed out, "can only understand the corpse.") Carbon, he said, was the "bearer of all the creatively formative processes in Nature" and the "Philosopher's Stone" of medieval alchemy. But it needed the "moistening" gifts of sulfur in order to do its work. Steiner described oxygen as the "physical element which with the help of sulphur carries the influences of life out of the universal ether into the physical," and nitrogen as the bridge between "ethereal" (i.e., life-giving) oxygen and "spiritual" carbon; its role was to "guide the *life* into the *form*." As "mediator between the Spirit and the mere principle of life," nitrogen corresponded to the human soul and to the astral body—indeed, the reason plants can thrive without astral bodies is that they are surrounded by the nitrogen in the soil, which carries a "mysterious sensitiveness" and even a kind of consciousness. The role of hydrogen, finally, was to lead "all that is living in physical forms ... back again into the great Universe ... to be purified and cleansed ... in the universal All."[34]

Steiner's account of planetary forces and elemental substances prepared his hearers for the eight "preparations" he described in detail in lectures 4 and 5. By far the best known is "horn manure," also referred to by the arbitrary number 500. Because manure has been inside a living organism, Steiner explained, it is already permeated with astral (i.e., nitrogen-carrying) and ethereal (oxygen-carrying) forces, but these can be intensified by placing it inside a horn, which is designed to send "the currents inward with more than usual intensity." He told his hearers to fill a cow horn with manure and bury it about two feet deep in good soil for the winter months, when "the Earth is most inwardly alive." This would allow the astral and ethereal forces of the earth itself to quicken the forces in the manure. He then instructed them to dig out the horn in the spring, dilute it in water, and stir it in a rhythmic pattern for at least an hour, both to transfer the forces to the water and to establish "a personal relationship to the matter." This personal connection, he noted, "is extraordinarily beneficial—at any rate for one who likes to see Nature as a whole and not only as in the Baedeker guidebooks." The water could then be sprinkled over the fields at planting time. Steiner then described horn manure's counterpart: horn silica, made from ground silica buried in a cow horn over the summer months, and sprayed on young leaves to foster fruit and flower growth.[35]

In the subsequent lecture, Steiner offered briefer instructions about six more preparations to be applied to composting manure. One (now known as 502) was made by placing yarrow in the bladder of a stag, exposing it to sunlight all summer, then burying it for the winter. The next involved stuffing chamomile flowers into bovine intestines: Steiner called this "a charming Operation" akin to sausage making. The others used stinging nettle, oak bark, dandelion, and valerian, each chosen according to the "hidden alchemy in the organic process" and each vitalized in its own distinctive way. The remaining lectures featured similarly alchemical and homeopathic remedies for agricultural problems, such as burning weed seeds and scattering the ash on the fields in order to inhibit the moon forces that contribute to weed growth, or spraying diluted horsetail to inhibit mildew and blight.[36]

Steiner acknowledged that many of his hearers would find these details "utterly mad."[37] But commentators have observed that an "alchemical reasoning" underlies the entirety of the Agriculture Course. Alchemists, Dennis Klocek explains, assume that "our consciousness is the most potent force for change," and thus seek to link "personal consciousness" to the "rhythms and patterns in the natural world." Consequently, they must use categories—such as the classical elements of earth, water, fire, and air—that are imaginatively accessible to human consciousness. Since these elements embody a set of polarities—between wet and dry, hot and cold, gravity and levity, solidity and fluidity—alchemy lends itself to practices that balance and harmonize opposites, rather than those that draw a sharp line between good and evil.[38]

Why did Steiner offer an alchemical system as the antidote to the depletion of the soil and the looming dangers of chemical agriculture? Most of Steiner's opponents, and a few of his friends, have portrayed him as an antimodern cultural critic, who preferred traditional wisdom to modern science. This dichotomous portrait does not correspond to Steiner's self-understanding or to the actual practice of biodynamic farmers. Steiner regarded contemporary science as incomplete but *not* evil, and his references to folk wisdom were by no means entirely positive. When he defended his system against the charge of insanity, he did so with a decidedly modernist analogy, recalling that just a few years ago the Swiss newspapers regarded the building of mountain railways as "utterly mad." Anthroposophy, he insisted, did not wish to "return to the old instincts," but rather to offer a "deeper spiritual insight" that would serve functions that old instincts no longer could. Chemists may have failed to recognize the living sentience of nitrogen, oxygen, carbon, and sulfur, but Steiner was still comfortable calling these elements by their chemical names. "Spiritual Science," Steiner explained, "must not come in a turbulent and revolutionary spirit, interfering with all that our time has achieved." Instead, it should honor what is true and oppose only what is false in the scientific worldview, and then "try to supplement genuine modern achievement with that which can flow from our own, living conception of the Universe."[39]

Steiner's balanced approach is also evident in the way his concern for agriculture was related to other aspects of his teaching. Decades before he gave the Agriculture Course, Steiner advocated for a "Goethean science," in which personally engaged observation was valued as much as quantitative data gathering. When he urged farmers to cultivate their powers of observation, he was repeating the advice he had earlier proffered to Waldorf teachers, anthroposophical doctors, and laboratory researchers. In his basic manual of spiritual practice, *How to Know Higher Worlds*, Steiner proposed meditative exercises closely related to gardening, instructing meditants to reflect on a seed, with its capacity to sprout into a complex plant, and then on a mature plant, with its capacity to wither and decay but also to produce seeds that will become new plants. Through such exercises, Steiner explained, one could "become aware that something I cannot see lies hidden in what I can see.... If I let this thought live within me, and the appropriate feeling unites with it, then after a time new force will grow in my soul and become a new perception."[40]

Perhaps the most intriguing connection between biodynamics and the rest of Steiner's teaching involves Steiner's esoteric Christology, according to which Christ is an exalted spiritual personality, closely associated with the sun, who came to Earth at the pivotal moment in our planet's evolution. Steiner said nothing in the Agriculture Course about Christ, but years earlier—not long after an intense clairvoyant experience forced him to shed his youthful antipathy to Christianity—he taught that "The secret behind the Mystery of Golgotha is one of the deepest in world evolution." When Christ shed his blood, Steiner explained, "Something happened ... which an observer would have seen in the astral atmosphere.... Events became possible that had never before been possible." More specifically, the racial divisions dividing the human community began to dissolve as "the substance of Jesus Christ" entered each individual. Because of Golgotha, Steiner affirmed, "The Earth is Christ's body."[41] In its original context, this teaching had little to do with agriculture, the soil, or ecology. To say that Earth was Christ's body was simply to say that diverse people could now connect to one another by forging individual connections to the spiritual substance Christ had brought to Earth. But Steiner's words took on new meaning among biodynamic farmers, who came to see that the best way to connect to Christ was to work with the soil. Thus Steiner made possible a new unity between seemingly pagan agricultural traditions and Christianity.

Just as biodynamics is based on specific alchemical practices, then, anthroposophy as a whole exhibits a sort of meta-alchemy. It balances the polarities of experimental science and traditional wisdom, of paganism and Christianity, as well as the polarities of warmth and cold or levity and gravity. This is the key to anthroposophy's importance for ecology. Any environmental movement must find a balance between protesting the damage wrought by technology and learning what science has to teach about global warming or the interdependence of species. More broadly, environmentalism must look both forward and backward, building on the progress achieved by recent social movements while seeking wisdom from indigenous cultures, and working to

sustain ecosystems without forgetting that ecosystems themselves continually evolve. Many environmentalists might resist Steiner's call to
find a balance between the earthly and the cosmic. But one should not
reject this call without first contemplating all the ways Steiner's work
has shaped environmentalism.

Roots

Biodynamics and the Origins of Organic Agriculture

The seed of biodynamics was one of the last planted by Rudolf Steiner in his lifetime: he died nine months after delivering the Agricultural Course. But this seed put down roots that were deep and wide. By 1930, biodynamics was practiced on four continents; by 1940, it was part of a global movement known as "organic agriculture." Though biodynamics was the earliest and best-organized component of this movement, it was certainly not the exclusive cause for the emergence of organics. Just as the organic pioneers insisted that soil health could not be reduced to nitrogen, phosphorus, and potassium, but depended on innumerable intertwined factors, so too their movement drew strength from sources as varied as composting techniques, spiritual ideals, scientific insights, economic theories, and friendships among the farmers. Biodynamics contributed to the emerging ecosystem at every level.

Three distinct groups of people spread the biodynamic impulse. Initially, the good news of biodynamics was spread by committed students of anthroposophy, who strategically packaged their message to be accessible to the broader community of people concerned about healthy agriculture. I will refer to these individuals as "evangelists." Other people were well informed, but less committed to anthroposophy in its entirety. These people, whom I will call "translators," learned to express the core ideas of biodynamics in nonanthroposophical language, making those ideas available to people who might have been hostile to other aspects of anthroposophy. Finally, there were many "allies," whose path to the organic movement had nothing to do with anthroposophy, but who embraced the evangelists and translators as partners in a common cause. This chapter will highlight several individuals in each category. The organic movement was shaped by, among others, evangelist Ehrenfried Pfeiffer, translator Lord Northbourne, and allies Eve Balfour and J. I. Rodale. A generation later it bore new fruit in the antipesticide impulse initiated by evangelists Marjorie Spock and Polly Richards and ally Rachel Carson. Similar constellations of evangelists, translators, and allies continue to shape the environmental movement to this day.

THE FIRST EVANGELISTS

People who attended the Agriculture Course were the first evangelists of biodynamics. They faced a different situation from their colleagues in the Waldorf School movement: while Steiner had personally trained the original teachers and given hundreds of lectures on education, the eight lectures of the Agriculture Course constituted the bulk of his teaching on farming. Sixty of the 111 people who participated in the course joined together in the Agricultural Experimental Circle (Landwirtschaftlichen Versuchsrings), which took on the task of fleshing out Steiner's indications through their own experimentation and then discerning how to make Steiner's teaching more publicly available.[1]

Two specific instructions from Steiner shaped the circle's mission. First was his insistence that farmers play the leading role in researching and disseminating biodynamics. Count Keyserlingk, who was responsible for estates totaling 7500 hectares in Silesia, took a leading role, along with Rudolf von Koschützki (perhaps the first biodynamic farmer to become a priest in the Christian Community) and Ernst Stegemann, who managed a 175 hectare farm at Marienstein Cloister near Göttingen.[2] From these men, the leadership gradually passed to the much younger Erhard Bartsch.

Steiner's second noteworthy instruction was that anthroposophical researchers would not be able to develop a convincing alternative to materialist science unless they were versed in materialist methods. One of the first to apply this challenge to the Agriculture Course was Lili Kolisko, a hospital laboratory assistant who had met Rudolf Steiner in 1914. Kolisko hoped to strengthen the theoretical basis for homeopathy by identifying the effects of extremely small quantities of various substances, and when the Experimental Circle was created, she asked to be included as an honorary member. "Of course!" Steiner is said to have replied. "You will be expected to work!"[3] Steiner had told her that planetary forces worked on substances in the liquid state, and so she dissolved mineral salts in water, dipped paper in the solution, and studied the pictures that formed as a result.[4] This method, which she called capillary dynamolysis, was the first of several "picture-forming" methods that used qualitative (rather than merely quantitative) observation to discern etheric and other spiritual forces described by Steiner. Kolisko also began the work—eventually extended by Maria Thun—of tracking the effects of moon cycles on plant growth, by comparing plantings separated by just a few days. In her written works, Kolisko emphasized the spiritual dimensions of scientific research, promising that "if we learn to understand matter in its whole depth, then we shall see Spirit shine forth and scintillate from things apparently the most empty and meaningless."[5]

Another researcher was Ehrenfried Pfeiffer, who had completed his studies in chemistry at the University of Basel just before the Agriculture Course. Steiner had chosen his courses for him, explaining that "You have to become thoroughly acquainted with the modern sciences so you can disprove materialism with its own weapons." He instructed Pfeiffer to maintain a double entry notebook, listing phenomena with both their mainstream and spiritual scientific explanations. Pfeiffer established the Goetheanum's laboratory in collaboration with Günther

Wachsmuth, who led the Goetheanum's Natural Science Section from 1923 to 1963.[6] One of the laboratory's first fruits was another picture-forming method, "sensitive crystallization," which observed the ways living matter affects crystal formation in chemical salts. Pfeiffer and his collaborator Erika Sabarth reasoned that, although etheric forces might not be directly observable, there might be material substances sensitive enough to reveal their effects. Questioned about this possibility, Steiner had promised Pfeiffer that he would be "surprised" by the results, and Pfeiffer and Sabarth discovered that when they added plant or animal fluids to a copper chloride solution poured onto a glass slide, it crystallized in distinctive patterns: "a finely branched formation" for iris, a delicately rounded form for waterlily, a "prickly concentric arrangement" for agave. Since the differences were not quantifiable, the researchers trained their powers of observation to notice the qualitative differences. Subsequent experimentation suggested that etheric forces waxed and waned over the course of each day. While the blood of each animal species revealed a common pattern, each human individual had its own pattern. Pfeiffer took this as confirmation of Steiner's comments about the "group souls" of animals and of the idea that only in humans are the etheric and astral forces guided by an overarching "ego."[7]

Pfeiffer and Sabarth soon realized that sensitive crystallization could be applied to both biodynamic agriculture and anthroposophical medicine. Crops grown biodynamically, they found, showed more orderly patterns of crystallization than those grown with chemical fertilizers, and the addition of the biodynamic preparations themselves to slides resulted in more orderly crystallization.[8] This seemed to confirm a claim, subsequently made by many organic farmers, that the fruits of chemical agriculture are less fully alive than the organic alternative. In the medical context, Pfeiffer applied the crystallization method to cancer diagnosis, building a bridge to other traditions that hoped to free science from materialist presuppositions. A homeopathic medical school in Philadelphia gave Pfeiffer an honorary doctorate, presumably because his research validated the homeopathic premise that medicines can carry healing forces even when they are so diluted that not an atom of substance remains.[9] More ambitiously, Günther Wachsmuth linked Pfeiffer to Albert Einstein and Alfred North Whitehead, suggesting that all three were dissolving the boundaries between "organic life processes and mental functions" on the one hand and "self-determined, chemicophysical processes in so-called matter" on the other.[10]

Pfeiffer was not one to restrict his research to the laboratory. A few years after the Agriculture Course, he was invited to manage the 230-hectare Loverendale farm in the Netherlands, where he established a network of initiatives including a market garden, a mill and bakery, a distribution network to bring farm products to urban consumers, a periodical, and an educational center. He conducted experimental comparisons of fields managed biodynamically and conventionally, accumulating evidence that he would present to the world in the late 1930s. These experiences equipped him to be the foremost evangelist of biodynamics.[11]

Soon the Agricultural Experimental Circle was global in scope. It held regular conferences during the second half of the 1920s, advertising them in anthroposophical newsletters.[12] In 1925, the Goetheanum published the text of the Agriculture Course, making it available to circle members willing to sign a confidentiality agreement. Confidentiality reflected both the esoteric principle that Steiner's lectures could not be properly understood except by those grounded in anthroposophy, and Steiner's concern that the Agriculture Course would be ridiculed unless it was validated by the concrete results of practicing farmers. But it was not uncontroversial: Keyserlingk insisted upon the confidentiality policy over the objections of von Koschützki and others in the circle.[13] Using the collection of confidentiality agreements preserved at the Goetheanum, John Paull determined that the initial 432 copies were mailed to addresses in Britain, Canada, Denmark, France, Germany, the Netherlands, Poland, Spain, Switzerland, and the United States. A copy that went to the first biodynamic farm in England was translated by George Kaufmann in 1928, and by 1930, copies of this translation had been sent to Australia, New Zealand, and South Africa, as well as the United States and the United Kingdom.[14]

Three years after the Agriculture Course, the farmers were prepared to share their research results at the Goetheanum. Rudolf von Koschützki began his report by explaining that the intricacies of preparation-making required a three-year delay: "A plant needs a year for its development. Its transformation into soul-purifying growth-fostering vivifying substance takes at least another year; and a third year is required for the crops treated with this substance, to mature." He also noted the contrast between the farmers' field-based research and the spiritual research that Steiner had used to prepare the Agriculture Course: not "even one of the new teachings given by Rudolf Steiner to the agriculturalists could have been deduced without Spiritual Science." Only because the farmers had personally experienced the spiritual truth of anthroposophy were they willing to follow Steiner's agricultural indications. But now they could report on research of a different sort. Field tests confirmed Kolisko's laboratory study of highly diluted substances. The preparations brought about "astonishing changes" in plant growth, slowing their maturation process but ultimately strengthening them, so that the harvest was quantitatively equal to that of conventional agriculture. And food produced using Steiner's method was "tastier, more nourishing, and more digestible." It received superior ratings from bakers, and a test showed that vitamin-deprived rats would survive if given half a gram of "biologically manured wheat" but would die if fed conventional wheat.[15]

It also took three years for the name of Steiner's agricultural method to mature: beginning in 1927, Pfeiffer referred to it as "Dr. Steiner's biological-dynamic methods."[16] By this time, biodynamic farmers were contending not only against the abstract principles of conventional science but also against the aggressive marketing of chemical fertilizers. In 1928, Erhard Bartsch observed that "Everywhere we see the placards calling for the application of Nitrogen, Phosphorus and Potassium manures." He appreciated a graffiti artist who had scrawled, "Luke

14:34–35," in response, alluding to Jesus's question, "If the salt has lost its savor, wherewith shall it be seasoned?" Bartsch claimed that widespread use of artificial manures was causing a catastrophic decline in soil fertility, confirming the fears of an "old peasant," who had warned that "Artificial manures will make rich fathers and poor sons." Bartsch stressed that the biodynamic difference was that it added "forces" rather than "substances" to the soil: "We do not add Nitrogen, Phosphorus, Potash and Lime to the soil in material quantities, but by our several preparations the Nitrogen, Phosphorus and Potash *processes* in nature are kindled, and the plant is thus enabled to build up for itself, by a hidden alchemy, all the necessary factors of life."[17]

Reports from the research circle were welcomed by students of anthroposophy, who held a wide array of protoenvironmental viewpoints. In 1927, a "woman farmer with wide-open outlook" wrote to the Goetheanum newsletter to express her dismay at flood control methods used on the Mississippi and at the building of the Panama Canal. Comparing the free flow of water to "the circulation of the blood," she wrote that "It is vain presumption *arbitrarily* to erect these dams."[18] Alfred Usteri described cases of damage to forests and crops apparently caused by aluminum factories, speculating that the causes might be etheric rather than physical. Spiritual research, he hoped, could help build a movement to limit factories and prohibit "products which are either valueless or a real public nuisance: poisonous gases, grenades, explosives." Usteri praised Austrian and Tibetan peasants for destroying radio transmitters they thought might hurt their crops. Scientists may have laughed, but "It does not matter to the real World-process, what the scientists may think of the events which are impending."[19] Anthroposophical skepticism about materialist science thus created an opening for concern about unintended consequences of new technologies.

Alongside the research circle there was a more loosely organized group called the Association of Farmers (Gemeinschaft der Landwirte). It sought to "keep hold of the produce ... and not allow it to be swallowed up in the general market," thus allowing word to spread of its superior quality. By the beginning of 1927, the farmers had rented a mill, partnered with a whole grain baker in Hannover, and begun using the name "Demeter" as a common symbol—even before the term *biodynamic* had been coined.[20] Demand outstripped supply, so that by the year's end, they were actively seeking additional land.[21] In 1928, the group pioneered a form of organic certification by articulating quality control standards, and in 1932, a formal "Demeter-Wirtschaftsverbund" was founded.[22] Forty years later, proponents of organic certification in the United Kingdom could thus lift up Demeter as a well-established model for emulation.[23]

THE GLOBAL SPREAD OF BIODYNAMICS

Biodynamics spread quickly because anthroposophy itself was a global movement, with a cosmopolitan sensibility and adherents on multiple continents. During his lifetime, Steiner had lectured on Waldorf education in Germany, Switzerland, the Netherlands, Great Britain, and Norway; by 1930, Waldorf schools were present in all these countries plus Austria, Hungary, Portugal, and the United States.[24] National branches of the Anthroposophical Society existed in Belgium, Denmark, Germany, Finland, France, Great Britain, the Netherlands, Norway, Austria, Sweden, Switzerland, and the United States.[25]

In the United States, biodynamics put down roots in centers of anthroposophical striving, embedding it within ecosystems of cultural activity. The first person to make biodynamic preparations in the United States was Henry Hagens, who did so for his own garden and those of his neighbors in Princeton, New Jersey.[26] A more influential center of activity was the Threefold Community in Spring Valley, New York, where a cluster of female friends led the way. Threefold grew out of the work of journalist Ralph Courtney, who encountered anthroposophy while he was the Paris correspondent for the New York Herald Tribune. Inspired by Steiner's idea of a "Threefold Commonwealth" (which he interpreted as a libertarian alternative to big government), he returned home to spread the vision. He persuaded several young members of the Anthroposophical Society in New York City, among them an heiress and art student named Charlotte Parker, to establish a cooperative household "as a first step toward an association of producers and consumers." Soon they added a vegetarian restaurant, called the Threefold Restaurant, located near Carnegie Hall. (One early participant said that customers might be impressed by an "attentive waitress" and then see the same waitress performing in a concert with her "fingers ... still stained by the red beets that Charlotte insisted must be slipped out of their skins just before serving.")[27]

A restaurant required a food supply, and in 1926, Parker purchased a farm in the suburb of Spring Valley. Elise Stolting and Gladys Barnett traveled to Europe, where they studied at two of the estates managed by Keyserlingk. Upon their return in fall 1927, they purchased bees and a cow and established a compost pile. A more experienced farmer, Paul Stromenger, arrived later in 1928. In 1933, Threefold Farm hosted a summer conference that brought Pfeiffer to the United States for the first time. He also visited the Kansas City farm of Minerva Brooks, which brought Brooks's friend Melrose Pitman and Pitman's student Evelyn Speiden into the orbit of Threefold. Speiden made her own educational trip to Dornach that winter, where she learned to test the agricultural influences of moon phases by germinating forty wheat seeds each day and charting their growth over the next three weeks.[28]

The organization of a biodynamics movement in Great Britain was even more rapid than in the United States. The United Kingdom's Bio-Dynamic Association was organized in 1938. By 1939, it had III members, about half of them farmers or gardeners, and a biannual publication (begun in 1935) called the *News Sheet of the Bio-Dynamic Method of Agriculture.*[29]

Biodynamics also found fertile soil for its development in German-speaking lands. The early years of biodynamics coincided with the rise of Nazism in Germany, and this had complex implications. In the wake of World War I, Steiner had made enemies on both the left and right because his threefold social order did not fit into conventional political categories. Many anthroposophists blamed the followers of Adolf Hitler for the burning of the first Goetheanum and for a murder attempt on Steiner himself. Many Nazis regarded anthroposophy (along with Theosophy and Freemasonry) as a cosmopolitan and occult movement that was inimical to German nationalism; in one article from 1921, Hitler referred to Steiner as a friend of the Jews and to threefolding as "one of the many completely Jewish methods of destroying the people's normal state of mind."[30] Nazi harassment of Waldorf schools began in 1933, with most schools in Nazi-controlled territory shut down between 1936 and 1941. (The resulting emigration of teachers contributed to the spread of Waldorf education and other anthroposophical initiatives to the rest of the world.)[31] Anthroposophical work with the disabled was also suppressed, both because of Nazi hostility to persons with disabilities and because many key individuals (notably the later founders of the Camphill movement) were of Jewish heritage.

The Anthroposophical Society in Germany was dissolved in November 1935, but the movement responded to this attack in a servile manner: the executive board of the international society wrote a letter to Hitler protesting the decision on the grounds that the society "has neither stood in relationship to nor in contact with Freemason, Pacifist or Jewish circles"; that Rudolf Steiner was of pure Aryan heritage; and that anthroposophical initiatives abroad serve "as a valuable and active representative of German intellectual life."[32] Throughout the 1930s, the anthroposophical movement had allies within the Nazi power structure, most prominently Hitler's deputy Führer Rudolf Hess, who limited the effects of official government policy. After Hess's flight to England in May 1941, the Nazi regime suppressed "occult" groups more systematically, and even ardent collaborationists were subject to interrogation and arrest by the Gestapo.

In this complex situation, biodynamics received more favorable treatment than other anthroposophical initiatives. Nazi ideology was generally favorable to farming communities, on the grounds that peasants possessed virtues that were lacking in the urban proletariat. Several Nazi leaders actively sought alliances with the biodynamics movement, among them agriculture secretary Richard Walther Darré. The so-called Green Wing of the party held a "blood and soil" ideology that linked Aryan racial purity to the unique characteristics of the German soil. Biodynamic practices that treated each farm as a self-contained organism appealed to them. Though Steiner had taught that Christ had overcome all racial differences when his blood united with the soil of Golgotha, the shared assumption that blood and soil can be spiritually linked was enough to persuade some anthroposophists to cooperate with the Nazis. Erhard Bartsch, who edited the *Demeter* journal during the Nazi period, was an enthusiastic collaborator. A biodynamic garden was established at the Dachau concentration camp. Direct official support for biodynamics dwindled after 1941, but Heinrich Himmler continued to promote agricultural research using the biodynamic preparations.[33] By the war's end, the biodynamics movement was weakened by official hostility and tainted by its own collaborationism. Its largest farms, moreover, were in Soviet-dominated territory. The German movement was thus forced to start almost entirely anew.

The development of biodynamics was also shaped by a power struggle, culminating in a 1935 schism, that raged in the Anthroposophical Society for a decade after Steiner's death. At the time of Steiner's death, leadership of the society had passed to the other five members of the executive council or *Vorstand*. (English speakers often use the German title.) These five held divergent views of their role. All agreed that they shared leadership of the society itself, but they disagreed about the leadership of the School of Spiritual Science, which was responsible for the continuation of Steiner's esoteric work, and specifically about the role of Vorstand member Ita Wegman. It is not clear what sort of authority Wegman claimed for herself, but three of the other Vorstand members—Marie Steiner, Albert Steffen, and Günther Wachsmuth—accused her of positioning herself, on the basis of karmic connections dating back to the time of Alexander the Great, as Steiner's esoteric successor. The fifth member, Elisabeth Vreede, supported Wegman, and in 1935 she and Wegman were expelled from the society, along with forty other individuals and the entire British and Dutch branches of the movement.[34] The schism paved the way for the society's collaboration with Nazism by removing many ethnically Jewish, non-German, and ideologically antifascist members. Ita Wegman in particular had repeatedly criticized anthroposophical accommodation of Nazism.[35]

The split could hardly have surprised observers who were familiar with the history of theosophy. Any emerging spiritual movement faces a crisis when its founder dies, as it must translate the founder's charismatic authority into a bureaucratic leadership structure. The challenge for anthroposophy was exacerbated by at least four factors. First, Steiner died at age 64, earlier than anyone had expected and just a few years after engineering a thorough overhaul of the society. Second, in keeping with his understanding of anthroposophy as an esoteric movement, Steiner had frequently given teachings to select groups of students and had encouraged all of his students to test his teachings against their own experience. If Wegman were indeed giving the sort of private teachings that her opponents claimed, this would have been consistent with Steiner's example, but it was also conceivable that she was claiming a degree of spiritual insight that she did not possess. Steiner's public teachings, in other words, did not help ordinary anthroposophists adjudicate between the two factions' competing claims. Third, Steiner's teachings, including his threefold theory of society, emphasized decentralized authority structures, such as the distinction between the society itself and its School of Spiritual Science. In the long run, decentralization helped anthroposophy by allowing individuals to exercise charismatic leadership without separating into independent societies. But in the short run, the lack of transparency about the boundaries between authority structures exacerbated the conflict. Finally, and perhaps most significantly, Steiner had died amid growing instability and conflict within and between the nations that were home to Anthroposophical Society members. The Vorstand members were German, Swiss, and Dutch; other prominent leaders were British, American, and in several cases were of Jewish ancestry. Their divergent views on Hitler's rise to power undoubtedly deepened their spiritual divisions.

People who wanted to expand biodynamics in an international context were thus forced to choose between the society and its alienated national branches. Ehrenfried Pfeiffer, who worked extensively in the Netherlands and Great Britain, might logically have sided with those two national societies, as did Lili Kolisko. But he had an unbreakable, chivalric loyalty to Marie Steiner. This created more complexity for the Dutch and British individuals who learned about biodynamics from Pfeiffer: had they been inspired to join their local branch of anthroposophy, doing so would have put them in conflict with their mentor. Many wound up standing aloof from anthroposophical organizations. Though the act of exclusion was formally rescinded on Easter of 1948, the Dutch society was not fully reintegrated until 1960 and the British not until 1963. The work of reconciliation continues even today.

PFEIFFER'S *BIO-DYNAMIC FARMING AND GARDENING*

Despite the challenges, the researches of the Agricultural Experimental Circle proceeded steadily, and by 1938, the results were ready to be shared. Ehrenfried Pfeiffer published *Bio-Dynamic Farming and Gardening* simultaneously in German, English, Dutch, French, and Italian.[36] This text was the defining handbook of biodynamics for a generation. During the formative years of the organics movement, it was available to the general public, while Steiner's Agriculture Course was accessible only to anthroposophists who had agreed to keep it secret. Pfeiffer's book echoed the content of the Agriculture Course, but its emphases were markedly different.

Like Steiner, Pfeiffer stressed the holistic context of agriculture. His preface declared that "every human being should be interested in the fertility of the soil," and he linked agriculture to "all that has been achieved by the human spirit." "The farmer," Pfeiffer affirmed, "has not only to deal with his soil and with *his* seed; he is connected with an encompassing life process in his wider surroundings." Pfeiffer echoed Steiner's emphasis on the integration of plants and animals in agriculture, affirming flatly that "a farm without cattle ... represents a biological onesidedness and is contrary to nature." He devoted an entire chapter to the holistic care of forests and urged gardeners to apply "the basic laws of the forest" by maintaining "constant ground cover and encouraging the mutualistic interaction of organisms.[37]

Like Steiner, Pfeiffer used the concept of "organism" to express his holistic ideal. His description of the soil as a "living organism" may have inspired other organics pioneers to speak of the "living soil." But Pfeiffer also applied the concept of "organism" to the farm, to agriculture, and to the entire earth. These entities did not merely contain living matter: their constituent parts "unite[d] to form a higher unity." Ultimately, Pfeiffer stressed, "the ways and means for the regeneration of the farm can be found only in a comprehensive view of the earth as an *'organism'* as a living *entity*."[38] This view, which was not fully taken up by other organics pioneers, anticipated the Gaia hypothesis advanced by James Lovelock decades later.

Pfeiffer also echoed Steiner's emphasis on the individuality of the farmer. He acknowledged that biodynamic farming is more labor-intensive and dependent on one or more people becoming "individually responsible" for it. Expressing sympathy for Depression-era homesteading experiments, Pfeiffer suggested that these would succeed only if the participants engaged in inner development: "The right basis has been created only when the homesteader has an inner relationship to his work, that is, when he learns to survey and comprehend the sum total of the life processes of an agricultural organism. He will then also love it as one can only love something that is alive."[39]

Though Pfeiffer believed that an agriculture with all these characteristics was in sharp tension with modern tendencies, he positioned himself midway between the wisdom of the peasantry and contemporary scientific research. He declared flatly that the "instinct" guiding traditional peasants "has been lost," while "the methods of so-called 'scientific agriculture'" have sown "uncertainty" and "led to an impasse."[40] Far from eschewing experimental science altogether, Pfeiffer—following the instructions if not the example of Steiner—devoted much of his book to the results of his own experiments, including a controlled experiment in which the growth of roots soaked in tap water and in dilutions of each of the biodynamic preparations was carefully compared. Similar experiments focused on bacterial and earthworm health in treated and untreated soil.[41] At the same time, Pfeiffer worried that experiments testing "detailed minutiae" would cause the researcher to lose "contact with reality." Though he wasn't willing to forego minute experiments altogether, he insisted that "the ideal experimental basis is, indeed, the *practical farm* on which the results are checked and controlled over a period of years." Only this sort of experiment "takes into account the full and normal effects of nature, as opposed to an unbalanced, compressed nature."[42]

Pfeiffer returned to this ethos of a middle way in a final chapter that described "the agricultural crisis" as "a human spiritual Problem" necessitating "the *creation of a method of thought founded on the principle of an Organic Whole*." Faced with the loss of "traditional culture," and with increasing polarization "between Orient and Occident," it was up to Europe to create a "new culture" capable of "*perceive[ing] life and growth as an organic whole over the entire earth*." Pfeiffer cautioned that this was the work of generations, and that it could not begin without the inner transformation of farmers themselves. Their training in close observation would bring about a "slow, inner change" culminating in the development of "a real farmer" with "an ethical feeling of responsibility toward that organism, 'the living soil.'"[43]

These words express the continuity between Steiner's 1924 lectures and Pfeiffer's 1938 book. But Pfeiffer's book had a distinctive flavor that was consistent with the other foundational texts of organic agriculture, most of which were published just after Pfeiffer's volume. It was relentlessly practical, reflecting fourteen years of experience by hundreds of farmers. Pfeiffer included suggested crop rotations, manuring schedules, and instructions for the construction of manure and compost piles. He also engaged with a scientific and activist literature on soil fertility that had emerged in the 1930s. Pfeiffer's chapter on "The World Situation of Agriculture" featured the North American dust bowl and incipient desertification in China, highlighting traditional Asian practices of "*humus conservation* and *manual labor*" as the only means to "keep a land in its original state of fertility."[44] His bibliography included an early publication of Albert Howard and scientific articles from Germany, Britain, and the United States.

Perhaps because of Pfeiffer's engagement with soil scientists, his rhetoric alternated between Steiner's radical holism and a more restrained emphasis on the preservation of humus. Even the chapter on the "wider connections" of the farm included an italicized assertion that "*Good manuring is always the basis of all agriculture.*"[45] The chapter on the soil as a living organism was devoted exclusively to the biological science of humus. Pfeiffer called attention to the soil-building role of bacteria and earthworms without mentioning Steiner's assertion that diverse microorganisms are a symptom of a living soil but not its cause.[46] He avoided the word *cosmic,* except in contexts where it did not obviously imply a critique of materialist science. In one passage, for example, he affirmed that a "significant quantity" of "cosmic dust and meteorites ... reaches the earth throughout the year," bringing about "a continual change of substances ... between the earth and cosmic space."[47]

To be sure, Pfeiffer acknowledged the existence of the biodynamic preparations, calling them "an essential feature of bio-dynamic farming." But whereas Steiner had offered detailed instructions for *making* the preparations, Pfeiffer included only minimal guidelines about how to *use* them. He compared the role of the preparations to that of yeast in bread, suggesting that Steiner had developed "certain plant preparations which induce the right kind of fermentation." He acknowledged that they were formed by burying "medicinal herbs" in "close contact with certain parts of an animal organism," explaining that "through a kind of hormone influence the fermentation is guided in a definite direction." In presenting his experimental data on the preparations, he again invoked fermentation rather than alchemical principles, alluding to vitamins and hormones as examples of substances that work in small doses. He encouraged his readers to obtain the preparations from members of the Experimental Circle, claiming that secrecy was "observed in order to prevent these preparations from being commercialized."[48]

Organics pioneers who knew biodynamics through Pfeiffer but lacked access to the Agriculture Course were thus not confronted with Steiner's "cosmic" challenge in all its radicality. Still, the publication of Pfeiffer's book marked an important transition: a movement that had been growing in partial secrecy was now mature enough to be shared publicly. Simultaneously, individuals and groups with no connection to anthroposophy were developing their own organic ideas. When these people met one another between 1938 and 1940, a global movement sprang to life.

THE OTHER SOURCES OF ORGANIC AGRICULTURE

The earliest strand of nonanthroposophical organics emerged in the same cultural milieu as biodynamics. The German Lebensreform (life reform) movement urged urban dwellers to return to nature through such practices as vegetarianism, nudism, and self-sufficient life on the land. Its adherents admired Goethe and the Romantics; many had esoteric spiritual practices; many were committed to scientific research but held theories rejected by the mainstream; many promoted decentralized social theories that defied the usual categories of left and right. Beginning in 1922, Friedrich Glanz and Heinrich Krantz promoted conservation tillage and composting as techniques for maintaining soil fertility without the use of artificial fertilizers *or* animal manures. A more comprehensive system of "natural agriculture" was articulated by Ewald Könemann in his 1925 article on "Farming without Animals," and in a three-volume manual that was published beginning in 1931. Also in 1925,

Walter Rudolf founded the movement's main journal, *Bebauet die Erde.*
Two years later the Natural Farming and Back-to-the-Land Association
(Arbeitsgemeinschaft Natürlicher Landbau und Siedlung) was established. In 1928 and 1933, the journal published standards for natural production, and beginning in 1933 the trademark "Biologisches Werterzeug-
nis" was introduced for marketing these products, just slightly after the
rise of *Demeter.*[49]

An intriguing difference between the Lebensreform group and the
biodynamics movement was the former's attempt to remove animals
from agriculture. Though Steiner was a vegetarian who warned his students about the spiritual harm caused by meat consumption, he insisted
that livestock and wild animals were indispensable to the health of the
farm organism. Seen against the background of Lebensreform, biodynamics thus appears not as the most extreme version of organic agriculture, but as a balanced middle path. Steiner insisted on animal agriculture in part because he believed that animals were carriers of "astral"
forces that represented an evolutionary advance beyond the etheric
forces of plants. Similarly, the plants' etheric forces represent an evolutionary advance beyond the material level, and humanity's ego forces
represent an evolutionary advance beyond the astral level. For Steiner,
recognizing the qualitative distinctions among these levels made it easier to honor their ecological interconnections. The relationship between
biodynamics and natural agriculture thus anticipated the later contrast
between anthroposophy and deep ecologies that refused to distinguish
humans from other creatures. A related difference was the biodynamics
movement's refusal to join other organic pioneers in exploring the agricultural uses of human excrement: according to Steiner, this contains
ego forces that could undermine human individuality if used in food
production. More generally, a view of biodynamics as a middle way fits
with anthroposophy's emphasis on balancing polarities.

The next major strand of the organics movement was Albert
Howard's work on composting. An English scientist posted to research
stations in India, Howard recalled that his "real training in agricultural

research" began on a seventy-five acre farm in Pusa, India, where he was able to learn from experience. He noticed that his peasant neighbors had fewer problems with pests, even though they didn't use insecticides or fungicides, and he resolved to regard "them as my professors of agriculture." Over the next twenty-five years, he perfected what became known as the "Indore process" for producing high-quality humus through layered, carefully balanced composting of manure and plant wastes. Howard shared this process with the world in his 1931 book, *The Waste Products of Agriculture*; nine years later he published the more widely read *Agricultural Testament*.[50]

Howard's detailed composting instructions, which were followed by organic farmers for decades thereafter, have led many to regard him as *the* founder of organic agriculture. This view assumes that organic agriculture is a matter of technique: the Indore process was the most widely adopted organic technique, while the biodynamic preparations were embraced by a small minority of organic farmers. But if we see organic agriculture as a social movement that combined agricultural techniques with social, cultural, and spiritual values, Howard remains indispensable to the whole, but not uniquely so. Virtually every other major writer on organic agriculture displayed a wider range of interests than did Howard, though even he ranged beyond the technical details of composting.

Howard was also more independent of biodynamics than other organic founders. He began developing his ideas well before Steiner gave the Agriculture Course, though he did not publish them until afterward, and he seems not to have had ties to theosophy, anthroposophy, or other spiritual movements. When Howard became aware of biodynamics, he was unimpressed. "I remain unconvinced," he wrote in *An Agricultural Testament*, "that the disciples of Rudolf Steiner can offer any real explanation of natural laws."[51] His work thus offers intriguing clues about what the organics movement might have been like without biodynamics. But there may well have been no movement at all, for despite his brilliance at the level of agricultural technique, Howard was no movement builder.

Judging from Howard's *Agricultural Testament*, an organics movement without biodynamics would have stressed the centrality of humus to successful agriculture, but it would have stopped short of portraying entire farms, much less the entire planet, as a living organism. Howard insisted that humus was a biological rather than a chemical substance, and he argued that a soil that "is alive and teems with a vast range of micro-organisms" should not be treated as equivalent to "simple dead matter like a sack of sulphate of ammonia." Howard buttressed this argument with research on "mycorrhizal association," or the symbiotic relationship between plant roots and fungus in the soil. He would doubtless have been confounded by Steiner's claim that the presence of micro-organisms in compost is a symptom of its aliveness rather than its cause.[52]

Similarly, a Howard-centered movement would have called on farmers to follow "nature's method" by modeling their farms on wild ecosystems, but it would have justified this approach on instrumental rather than spiritual terms. Forests, Howard explained, practice "mixed farming," with many different varieties of plants and animals coexisting. They keep the ground covered in order to prevent erosion. They balance processes of growth and of decay, keeping the supply of water and minerals in constant circulation. "Both plants and animals are left to protect themselves against disease," with weaker specimens often succumbing. All of these principles could be summed up in a pragmatic dictum: in nature "there is no waste anywhere." Howard believed this dictum was generally observed in India and China, and generally violated by westerners who were tempted "to convert ... fertility into money." This was cause for a jeremiad: "Mother earth deprived of her manorial rights is in revolt; the land is going on strike; the fertility of the soil is declining," and soon, Howard warned, "the whole fabric of our civilization must collapse."[53]

Like Steiner and the subsequent organics pioneers, Howard also saw nutritional, political, and economic reasons to model agriculture on nature. But his claims in these areas were relatively limited. Though he cited the work of researchers who had linked fresh, whole foods to overall health, he described this link as simply "a very promising hypothesis for future work." Howard acknowledged that artificial ferti-lizers had proliferated in the wake of World War I because explosives factories needed a new market for their nitrogen-fixing technologies. He faulted agricultural economics, along with chemistry, for imposing quantitative methods that were inappropriate to living beings and for treating farms like factories. And he sketched a program for the move-ment, including a call for people who were "brought up on the land" to develop new methods of farm-based research.[54] This proposal paral-leled Steiner's vision for the Experimental Circle.

Indeed, despite Howard's lack of respect for Steiner's scientific abili-ties, his critique of mainstream scientific methods paralleled Steiner's. He blasted "the NPK mentality," adding that purely quantitative meth-ods are inadequate to the challenges of "biology, a domain where every-thing is alive and which is poles asunder from chemistry and physics." He deplored the fragmentation of academic science, preferring "a syn-thetic approach [that looks] at the wheel of life as one great subject." And he rejected the logic of the famed Rothamsted experiment, which claimed to have demonstrated the validity of artificial fertilizers by comparing small adjacent plots under different management systems. Hinting at a concept similar to that of the farm as organism, he explained that small plots simply cannot be managed "in the same way as a good farm is conducted" because crop rotations are impossible and "the essen-tial relation between livestock and the land is lost."[55] Once again, Howard touched on the biological but not the cosmic dimension of Steiner's argument: for Howard, the farm might be biologically inte-grated, but it had no personality.

Two examples illustrate the practical divergence between Howard's and Steiner's visions. Like Steiner, Howard advocated a total rethink-ing of agricultural pests. "Insects and fungi are not the real cause of plant diseases but only attack unsuitable varieties or crops imperfectly grown." On this basis, he rejected the use of "sprays" to control pests and the wasteful burning of diseased plants.[56] Undoubtedly, he did not have in mind the homeopathic spraying of biodynamic preparations or the pesticide "peppers" that Steiner produced by burning the bodies of rodents and insects. Since the latter were not described in Pfeiffer's book, Howard probably had no awareness of them. But if he had known of them, he would have seen them as an unnecessary extravagance. Similarly, and like almost every successive proponent of nonbiodynamic organics, Howard urged his readers to rethink their prejudices about human excrement. "The *night soil and urine* of the population," he lamented, "is at present almost completely lost to the land." He devoted an entire chapter to methods for incorporating excrement and garbage into agriculture.[57] Though Howard deplored the encroachment of economics into agriculture, his position on this issue was calculating when compared to Steiner's: no spiritual principle could interfere with Nature's admonition to avoid waste.

A MOVEMENT EMERGES

By the time Howard published *Agricultural Testament,* the emergence of a movement was well under way. Many farmers were already using the Indore method or the biodynamic preparations. Equally important, a series of global crises had made Howard's concern about the survival of civilization more plausible. The deepening global depression raised questions about the viability of industrial capitalism, allowing back-to-the-land ideologies to thrive alongside socialism and fascism. The Dust Bowl in the North American plains provided frightening confirmation of earlier warnings about the depletion of topsoil. And Europe's slide toward war raised questions about whether the United Kingdom and other industrialized nations should rely on foreign imports to feed their people. Worries about health and nutrition easily sprouted up in this troubled milieu.

Viscount Lymington encapsulated the anxieties in *Famine in England,* published in 1938. Tapping into antiwar sensibilities and fascist sympathies, Lymington warned his British compatriots that war with Spain,

Italy, or Germany could mean starvation for a nation dependent on food imports, and he cautioned that the resulting vulnerability could lead to a communist takeover, "a yellow race war or a Jehad in the renascent Islam of to-day." Alternately criticizing Britain's arrogant policies in India and the "scum of subhuman population" brought into English cities by immigration, Lymington proposed a "healthy agriculture" as the antidote to every problem. It would begin with the realization that "the soil is not a factory that can work three eight-house shifts in the day at peak production," but "a living thing that will only respond to the way it is served."[58] This conviction was shaped by familiarity with Pfeiffer's and Howard's approaches to agriculture: Lymington had visited Loverendale annually beginning in 1935, and on one occasion he brought Howard with him. He was also making plans (ultimately abortive) for a three-way experimental study of Indore, biodynamic, and conventional fertilizing methods.[59]

Lymington's book offers vivid evidence for the affinity between the organic mindset and fascism. But Lymington's most racist and nationalist themes don't appear in books by other organics pioneers, even including Lymington's agricultural collaborators. Those others cannot easily be placed on the political left or right. Yet they cannot fairly be described as apolitical, since they recognized that political and economic structures could either help or hurt their movement. Their views might best be called agrarian or distributist. They were wary of both corporations and governments and were skeptical of Marx's dogma that the industrial proletariat, rather than the rural peasantry, held the key to humanity's future. Most were idealists, in the sense that they had faith in the efficacy of individual action motivated by ideals. This put them at odds with doctrinaire socialists who trusted only in structural change to improve the world. From the perspective of some socialists, idealism itself was objectively right wing. This classification wasn't always unfair: many idealists were people of privilege for whom idealism could be a cover for self-interest. Some also expressed their antipathy to capitalist finance in anti-Semitic terms. Nevertheless, when we understand organics as an idealistic and decentralized third-way alternative to capitalism and socialism, we can grasp the continuity between its early days and the seemingly leftist environmentalism of the 1970s. It also becomes easier to see why anthroposophy found a comfortable home in this milieu.

In the United States, the network of agrarian idealists involved in organics included people with roots in socialism, orthodox Christianity, and esoteric spirituality. The leading promoters of back-to-the-land ideals were Helen and Scott Nearing—she a former theosophist who had once dated Jiddu Krishnamurti and he an economist who had strayed from communism to agrarianism.[60] Ralph Borsodi, whose School of Life near New York City taught many back-to-the-landers what they needed to know, was influenced by individualist anarchists. Inspired by Catholic social teaching's alternative to capitalism and communism, both the radical Catholic Worker Movement and the more mainstream Catholic Rural Life Conference made agrarian settlements part of their programs on the grounds that "there is no unemployment on the land"—a claim that Ehrenfried Pfeiffer quickly learned to echo.[61]

In Great Britain, the network was equally complex and has been described by historian Philip Conford. The "heart of the organic movement," he suggests, was the *New English Weekly*, a journal founded in 1932 to defend rural England against industrialization and the ideology of free trade. It traced its lineage to the work of William Morris and to Guild Socialism and Social Credit—brands of socialism that had rejected trade unionism, party building, and Marxist revolution in favor of a quasi-medieval network of workers' guilds. The *New English Weekly*'s genealogy also included significant spiritual teachers. The founders' mentor, Dmitri Mitronovic, taught a cosmic Christianity in which "Universal Humanity" was a single, developing organism. Mitronovic was one of the few people not directly affiliated with anthroposophy to promote discussion of Steiner's threefold social theory in the English-speaking world. *New English Weekly* founder A. R. Orage was active in both the Fabian and Theosophical Societies early in the century, then devoted himself full time to "the Work" of spiritual teacher George Gurdjieff. The *New English Weekly* was his return to the political arena after years of Gurdjieffian immersion.[62]

NORTHBOURNE THE TRANSLATOR

Once the social and spiritual dimensions of the organic network are taken into account, Howard's *Agricultural Testament* begins to look less interesting than another 1940 volume by an Englishman, Lord Northbourne's *Look to the Land*. Northbourne coined the term *organic agriculture,* and this neologism is best understood as a translation of biodynamic ideals that Northbourne had learned from Ehrenfried Pfeiffer. Northbourne was by no means fully committed to anthroposophy, yet his role as a translator of anthroposophical ideals gave his work a broader scope than Howard's and allowed a full-fledged movement to crystallize. *Look to the Land*'s range of concerns was dazzling: Northbourne sounded virtually all the major themes found in Howard's book; discussed both nutrition and soil fertility at length; *and* incorporated extensive discussion of economics, politics, and spirituality. "The farm must be organic in more senses than one," Northbourne wrote in the passage that coined the term, and he consistently invited his readers to expand the range of interconnections that might be relevant to agriculture.[63]

Historian John Paull has unearthed the connections between Northbourne and anthroposophy. Northbourne *may* have been present when Rudolf Steiner spoke at Oxford in 1922 (during Northbourne's student years), and he certainly was familiar with *Bio-Dynamic Farming and Gardening* when it appeared in 1938. During that same year, Northbourne published an article on world economy in a British anthroposophical journal. He met Pfeiffer in 1938, traveled to see him at the Goetheanum in January 1939, and brought him to his estate in Kent for the Betteshanger Summer School and "Conference on Bio-Dynamic Farming" in July 1939. In organizing this conference, Northbourne worked closely with Viscount Lymington, and he also invited the nutritional reformer

Scott Williamson, who practiced biodynamics at his Pioneer Health Centre in Peckham. Albert Howard was deliberately excluded: Northbourne and Lymington agreed that he was no admirer of biodynamics. The summer school attracted forty students, who participated in the lectures, farm visits, and preparation-making demonstrations, with two hundred people present for the closing celebration. "For nine days," Northbourne recalled, "the possibility of war was scarcely alluded to; things more real and more constructive absorbed attention."[64]

Biodynamics could not prevent World War II, which broke out a few months later. In that context, Northbourne made the choice to leave explicit references to Steiner and biodynamics behind. Like Pfeiffer and Steiner, Northbourne was convinced that biology could not be reduced to chemistry and was equally convinced that biology was incomplete without spirituality: the spiritual, economic, and biological sicknesses of modernity were "almost certainly only different aspects of one phenomenon."[65] Still, he eschewed *biodynamics* as the umbrella term for the agriculture he supported, using *organics* instead, and he barely mentioned the preparations or other practices specific to biodynamics.

Northbourne's articulation of agricultural principles and practices ran parallel to the presentations of both Howard and Pfeiffer. He distinguished the organic from the artificial approach to agriculture, referring to artificial fertilizers and pesticides as "poisonous." Northbourne described the soil as "a living entity, not ... a dead medium," leaving ambiguous whether it was alive in itself or only by virtue of its containing organisms. He endorsed mixed farming as the only "real farming," explaining that "Fertility depends ... on the mutual reactions and interdependence of crops and livestock." His insistence on "faithfully returning to the soil ... everything that has come from it" was more than a principle of frugality; it was a way of siding with life in its cosmic struggle against lifelessness. "Everything that has had life can have life again, and in regaining life it can draw into the sphere of life some fragment of that which has been hitherto lifeless." Even burning, rather than composting, one's old trousers was "a sort of murder."

(Northbourne added an aside, the logic of which paralleled Steiner's objection to the use of human excrement: "But be careful of newspapers. There are few things so contaminating as printers' ink. There is probably a moral somewhere in that fact.")[66]

Like Steiner, Northbourne called for a holistic science that would avoid the reductions of chemistry, and he repeatedly hinted at realities transcending even biology. "Agricultural methods must be tested on the quality of the product," he wrote, "and that is a very subtle matter involving something more than appearance and taste, and more than chemical composition as revealed by analysis. That 'something' may be described as 'effectiveness as a vehicle of life.'" That phrase sounds like a definition of Steiner's life forces, and Northbourne's proposed research method had much the same goal as anthroposophical picture-forming methods. Northbourne also wrote that "The nature of living things is that they are not mere machines.... They are something more. That something more does not respond to mechanical or statistical treatment. It responds only to that for which we have no other word but love."[67]

More than Howard, Northbourne harvested the diverse strands of research and analysis that were coming together in the organics movement. He devoted one large section to the worldwide loss of topsoil. "Probably more soil has been lost since 1914," Northbourne concluded, "than in the whole previous history of the world." An equally extensive review of research on nutrition offered an ecological theory of health, according to which "the health of man and the health of his land are not two distinct matters."[68] Northbourne believed that "international debt and soil erosion [were] twin brother and sister" and that the existing economic system was rigged to the disadvantage of rural areas. Drawing on Social Credit, Guild Socialism, and Steiner's threefolding, his response bypassed the right-left political dichotomy. Northbourne worried that most political debates were too superficial, insofar as they failed to touch on "health of mind and body." When he turned to the question of labor, he echoed Steiner's concern that wage labor is inherently dehumanizing, but he attributed the idea to Guild Socialist

S. G. Hobson. Northbourne envisioned a decentralized society in which most people would live in cooperative communities, modeled on farms that "to be healthy, must be not too big, yet must be diversified so as to be as far as possible biologically self-contained."[69]

As this quote suggests, Northbourne's economic theory was informed by Steiner's notion of the farm as a living organism, which he extended, Steiner-like, to other entities. "The higher the degree of biological self-sufficiency achieved by a farm, a district, or a nation," Northbourne asserted, "the more alive, the more vigorous, and the more creative it will be." Though Northbourne stopped short of ascribing spiritual individuality to these organisms, he insisted that each "would have their own nature, to be studied as such."[70] On this point and elsewhere, Northbourne restricted himself to biological holism when discussing topics that Steiner regarded in cosmic terms. But Northbourne also identified spirituality as an integral part of the ecological whole. Against materialist and mechanistic science, he asserted that "The things of the spirit are more real than material things." Because "farming is concerned primarily with life," it belonged "on the side of religion, poetry, and the arts rather than on the side of business." When Northbourne called explicitly for a "'back to the land' movement," he did so primarily on spiritual grounds: "The spiritual value of contact with reality, of feeling oneself part of nature, like all the most valuable things, is not statistically measurable, but is no less real for that."[71]

Northbourne thus presents a puzzle. Despite being a holistic thinker, who regarded spirituality as integral to organic agriculture, and despite having received training in biodynamics from Ehrenfried Pfeiffer, Northbourne scarcely mentioned biodynamics in *Look to the Land*. The only explicit reference to biodynamics places it alongside Howard's Indore process as one of the two best-known organic composting methods. Without explaining the difference, Northbourne affirmed that biodynamics had been "highly developed in the course of some fifteen years' work on the Continent, and its effectiveness may be said to be proved."[72]

Other passages in *Look to the Land* might be interpreted as translations of ideas Northbourne found in Steiner. Northbourne insisted that while *vitality* may be an unscientific term, "Most practicing farmers and gardeners will know what is meant by it." This use of vitality could have many sources, but it is close to Steiner's etheric forces. Against economic rationalization and ever-increasing speed, Northbourne insisted that "life is a rhythmical process" and "'the music of the spheres' . . . is reflected in the life-processes of all creatures." The allusion to the "music of the spheres" is interesting given that Pfeiffer claimed literally to have heard it, but Northbourne gave no further hint that distant planets might shape biological rhythms. Northbourne echoed Steiner's insistence that land and labor belong to the political rather than to the economic sphere when he affirmed that "Land is not comparable with any other factor in economics." And Northbourne echoed Steiner's comments about the personal role of the farmer when he wrote that "A right relationship to the land brings with it right human relationships."[73]

Yet if one's attitude to human excrement is a reliable index of one's relationship to biodynamics, Northbourne was only half a practitioner. His first reference to this vexed topic seemingly rejected Steiner's position: "Sewage can easily and profitably be converted into a valuable organic fertilizer." But when he returned to the topic a hundred pages later, he groped for a compromise. "It is very unlikely that either the best method of preparation or the best way of using such material has yet been evolved," he wrote, adding that while the reluctance to use it directly for human food crops might be "mere prejudice," it might also be "soundly based, quite apart from any questions of the conveyance of infection." Presumably he was aware of but only half-convinced of the biodynamic position, and he finally suggested that human excrement be used only for pasture and feed crops.[74]

Northbourne's ambivalence may have had multiple causes. Since he was writing in Great Britain in 1940, it would not have been prudent for him to emphasize his German sources. The schism within the Anthroposophical Society would have made it difficult for him to have identified fully with anthroposophy even had he wished to do so. His primary contact with biodynamics, Ehrenfried Pfeiffer, was a staunch partisan of Marie Steiner, while the entire British branch had been expelled along with Ita Wegman. But Northbourne's position may have reflected the fact that he was heading toward a distinct, albeit-related, spiritual path. Soon after publishing *Look to the Land,* he came to know Marco Pallis, a student of Tibetan Buddhism, who was, with René Guenon and Frithjof Schuon, an advocate of the religious approach known as "perennialism" or "traditionalism." Northbourne soon began writing and translating perennialist books.

Like the theosophy from which anthroposophy had emerged, perennialism eschewed materialist approaches to reality and posited a common spiritual core underlying all religions. It repudiated the theosophical strategy of creating a new spiritual society, urging adherents instead to work from within the classical faith traditions. Moreover, whereas both theosophy and anthroposophy presented themselves as progressive, evolutionary movements that offered a spirituality for the modern world, perennialism posited a sharp choice between (in Northbourne's words) "progressive" and "traditional" worldviews. The former sought to liberate individual egos from environmental constraints, while the latter tried "to escape from the limitations of the *ego* as such."[75] Transcendence of ego, according to Northbourne, requires the hierarchical constraint of religions founded on divine revelation.

This spiritual perspective fit nicely with Northbourne's preference for agrarian lifeways. But his exposition of perennialism makes clear that he was either unconvinced by central aspects of anthroposophy, or else was never exposed to them despite his friendship with Pfeiffer. For Northbourne, there was an absolute distinction between the "traditional" reliance on revelation and the "progressive" reliance on observation. Our "inmost being," he claimed, could never be observed. Religion and science could be reconciled only when "the hierarchical superiority of the religious approach is recognized."[76] But observation of one's inmost being was the foundation upon which Steiner sought to build up a spiritual science not dependent on revelation! Anthroposophy sought to occupy a middle ground between Northbourne's polarities, affirming both science and religion, both progress and tradition. Ironically, Steiner's spiritual science led him to make claims that from the perspective of mainstream science were far more discomfiting than anything Northbourne wrote.

The anthroposophical counterpoint to Northbourne's antimodernism is evident in Ehrenfried Pfeiffer's lead editorial in the first issue of *Bio-Dynamics*, published a year after *Look to the Land*. After praising the Catholic Rural Life movement, Pfeiffer warned that "as long as the spiritual treasures of mankind are split up into creeds and as long as disharmony reigns between faith and science, we must move between extremes and be subject to uncertainties." While Northbourne thought the antidote was the subordination of science to religion, Pfeiffer was sure it was the balancing of culture, politics, and economics in Steiner's threefold commonwealth.[77]

The spiritual differences between Northbourne and anthroposophy underscore the fact that anthroposophy's emphasis on balancing polarities placed it in the middle of debates within the emerging organics movement. Practitioners of biodynamics worked alongside two different sets of allies. On the one hand were secularizing activists like Howard, who feared the cosmic dimension of biodynamics would undermine the work of promoting biological holism. On the other hand were spiritual antimodernists, whose views were superficially similar to those of anthroposophy but could be—depending on the case— more socially conservative, more monotheistic (and thus uninterested in astrological or alchemical practices), or more biocentric and antihumanist. All of these characterizations fit Lord Northbourne, who was perhaps the first environmentalist to absorb insights from anthroposophy without fully embracing it. More than the other organics pioneers, he anticipated the biocentric, "Gaian" worldview that would become widespread in the 1970s, especially among environmentalists who were connected to but not identified with anthroposophy. Northbourne concluded his book with a call for human humility and identification with nature. "If we are to succeed in the great task before us we must adopt a humbler attitude toward the elementary things of life than that which is implied in our frequent boasting about our so-called 'Conquest of Nature.'" Humans "cannot separate ourselves from nature if we would," yet our attempts to do so inflict suffering on "the whole of nature, which includes ourselves as well as the soil."[78]

TWO ALLIES: EVE BALFOUR AND J.I. RODALE

In the end, neither Lord Northbourne nor Albert Howard nor Ehrenfried Pfeiffer could pull the diverse strands of the organic impulse into a coherent movement. In Great Britain, that role fell to the indefatigable Lady Eve Balfour, who organized the Soil Association; in the United States, it went to the entrepreneurial J.I. Rodale, who built a publishing empire around *Organic Gardening* magazine. Both preferred Howard's system to biodynamics, though both also included Pfeiffer in their activities and though Balfour endorsed the broadly spiritual approach to agriculture exemplified by Northbourne.

In *The Living Soil* (1943), Lady Balfour synthesized the work of earlier organics promoters into a multifaceted vision, including sections on soil erosion, on the nutritional benefits of whole grain diets, on mycorrhizal associations, on composting techniques, on the interdependence of diverse species, and on the fruits of research. At the center of her program was a holistic view of health. Rejecting the traditional medical emphasis on disease, she invited her readers to contemplate the possibility that "the health of man, beast, plant and soil" might be "one indivisible whole." The "determining factor" for human health, she argued, was food, and the determining factor for the health of food was the soil. Indeed, she had switched to a whole food diet after reading Howard and other organicists in 1938 and was immediately liberated from several chronic health complaints.[79]

Balfour's holistic sensibility led her to critique the "fragmentation" of mainstream science in terms that often echoed Steiner's. Like Steiner, she was especially troubled by scientific dismissal of the "intuitive" wisdom of the "true peasant." But she did not cite either Steiner or Goethe in favor of intuition, choosing instead a quote from psychologist R.C. Oldfield.[80] Likewise, though she hinted that agriculture had a spiritual dimension, she gave no indication that she valued Steiner's spiritual guidance. "The chief need in the world to-day," she wrote, is "a spiritual and moral revival." Such a revival would recognize that "a better world is not like a manufactured article" but is "a living organism, and a pretty turbulent one at that." In a formulation similar to Steiner's Fundamental Social Law, she wrote that "Capitalism and socialism could go hand in hand if employers always put the interest of the workers before their own, and if the workers always put the needs of their firm before their own comfort." Balfour quoted Lord Godfrey Elton's book, *St. George or the Dragon,* as the source of this idea, making it likely that she was not thinking of Steiner, but simply expressing the sentiments of the community of spiritually minded reformers to which both she and Steiner belonged.[81]

The only direct mention of Steiner in *The Living Soil* occurs in a section on compost, in which she mentions some of Pfeiffer's research findings and adds a footnote indicating that Steiner's approach to compost "is more complicated than the Indore method. It involves injecting and spraying the heaps with certain organic extracts, as well as the inclusion in the heaps of certain weeds possessing specially valuable properties." This passage implies that Balfour thought of biodynamics as a composting method rather than as a comprehensively spiritual approach to agriculture. The characterization of it as a sort of herbal medicine rather than an alchemical or homeopathic practice makes clear that she was familiar with Pfeiffer's book but not with the Agriculture Course itself. She flagged her preference for Howard by describing his approach in detail and calling it "the most adaptable ... and the most foolproof" of the methods. Like most nonbiodynamic promoters of organics, she endorsed the use of human manure and deplored the waste of millions of pounds of nitrogen, potassium, and phosphorus by urban sewage systems.[82]

Nevertheless, Balfour liked Pfeiffer well enough that she contributed an introduction to a new edition of his book. She used the occasion to champion "ecology—the science of the study of the Whole." She also revealed that she had caught a bit of Steiner's cosmic vision. "After reading this book," she mused, "I was left wondering whether even [the study of the farm organism] is not too fragmentary an outlook.... Having started with the idea of a single living entity as our unit, we begin to catch glimpses of a vision—already a reality to the author—that the 'Whole' which we have set out to study is nothing smaller or less formidable than the entire universe!" Balfour echoed Steiner's understanding of the middle path between ancient wisdom and experimental science, faulting the latter for trying to be "not an interpreter of ancient wisdom, but a substitute for it." She praised Pfeiffer for incorporating the beliefs and observations of "our forebears" into his research method.[83] Three decades later, in a public address reflecting on the history of the movement, she placed Pfeiffer alongside Howard and William Albrecht as the three "research pioneers" in the "agricultural field," adding that she did not want "to discount the influence of one of the most important, who was even earlier, namely Rudolf Steiner."[84]

Eve Balfour's American counterpart, J.I. Rodale (1898–1971) was the other great organizer of the global organics movement. The child of a Jewish grocer, who grew up on the Lower East Side of New York City, Rodale lacked Balfour's patrician background and spiritual idealism, preferring to make the case for organic agriculture on bluntly pragmatic grounds. While Balfour established the Soil Association as a membership-based charity, Rodale created a profitable business named after himself. Anchored by the Rodale Organic Gardening Experimental Farm in Emmaus, Pennsylvania, Rodale, Inc., was primarily a publishing enterprise. In 1942, Rodale launched *Organic Farming and Gardening* magazine, and in 1945 he published his first book, with the telling title *Pay Dirt: Farming and Gardening with Composts*. Rodale shared Balfour's preoccupation with *health* as the primary motive for organic practice, and his health magazine *Prevention* eventually outstripped *Organic*

Gardening's circulation to become the flagship of the Rodale enterprise. The first issue of *Organic Farming and Gardening* paired "the Bio-Dynamic system and the Indore method" as the parallel starting points for organic practice. Rodale flagged his preference for the latter by noting that he had "read several times over Sir Albert Howard's book entitled 'An agricultural testament.'"[85] But Rodale mentioned Pfeiffer's book immediately after Howard's, and he published both authors from the very beginning. (The only other author, apart from Rodale himself, to appear in the inaugural issue was Charles Darwin.) Pfeiffer remained a regular contributor for years, though his personal relationship with Rodale became increasingly prickly.

Pfeiffer's inaugural contribution to *Organic Farming and Gardening* revealed both the terms on which biodynamics could be included within Rodale's movement and Pfeiffer's willingness to abide by those terms. Apparently a repurposed promotional pamphlet, it launched directly into the practice of biodynamics, without presenting the holistic philosophy found in Pfeiffer's book, much less the esoteric spirituality of Steiner. Biodynamics, Pfeiffer wrote, had "three fundamental steps." The first was the composting of manure and plant waste, facilitated by "the insertion into the piles at the time of setting up of certain pre-rotted plant materials in drug form which stimulate bacterial activity in the pile." (This is a reference to Steiner's preparations 502 through 508.) The second was the use of "two sprays," made from "specially rotted cow manure" and "powdered quartz," intended to aid "root development" and "the plant's assimilative capacity," respectively. (These are preparations 500 and 501.) Pfeiffer's third "fundamental step," which was not granted such prominent billing in either the Agriculture Course or Pfeiffer's book, was "healthy soil-conserving crop successions," adapted to local conditions. The result of these three steps, Pfeiffer claimed, was "a tremendous stimulation, in an organic, healthy way, of the micro-organisms in the soil, the earth worms and soil-bacteria." He then devoted more than half the article to the technique of building a compost pile. Curiously, he did not invoke the concept of the farm organism at all.[86]

BUILDING UP BIODYNAMICS

As Pfeiffer's contributions to *Organic Farming and Gardening* make clear, practitioners of biodynamics after 1938 understood themselves as committed allies of Rodale and Balfour within the larger movement. Yet they devoted most of their energies to fostering biodynamic initiatives. The war years were a time of significant institutionalization for biodynamics, especially in the English-speaking world, where a steady flow of war exiles from Germany and Austria enriched the movement. In the United States, the first national conference, featuring Pfeiffer as keynoter, dedicated to biodynamics took place at Threefold Farm in 1937. A year later, the Biodynamic Farming and Gardening Association (today known simply as the Biodynamic Association) was organized in New York City—eight years prior to the British Soil Association. O.F. Gardner, who raised oranges in Florida, was chosen as president. Vice President Roger Hale was organizing a short-lived Waldorf school in Maine, and his son Drake was a student at Ita Wegman's Sonnenhof in Arlesheim, an early anthroposophical school for persons with developmental disabilities. (Hale also had a connection to the traditional farming lore that Steiner only half-admired: in 1939 his brother-in-law purchased *The Old Farmer's Almanac,* which he passed on to Hale's son Judson in 1970.) Annual conferences continued to be hosted at Spring Valley until the center of activity shifted to Kimberton, Pennsylvania (about thirty-five miles southwest of Rodale's center in Emmaus), where philanthropists H. Alarik Myrin and Mabel Pew Myrin established a Waldorf school and an 830-acre experimental farm with dairy and beef herds. They persuaded Pfeiffer to relocate to Kimberton and also recruited Evelyn Speiden, a participant in the Threefold Farm conferences, who had just been selected as secretary-treasurer of the association.[87]

The Myrins were unlikely environmentalists. Mabel was the daughter of Sun Oil Company founder Joseph Newton Pew Sr. Her brothers blended their business activities with conservative politics and philanthropy. They staunchly opposed the New Deal and were once described as the "outstanding American Fascists." The Pew Charitable Trusts, organized in 1948, initially supported fundamentalist Presbyterianism and free market economics. The Pew brothers' small-government views were shared by Ralph Courtney at Threefold Farm and by several of the English proponents of organic agriculture. Alarik Myrin, a Swedish aristocrat, who married Mabel, shared them as well. But his philosophical interests and distaste for remunerative work clashed with the family culture, and the Pews sent him and Mabel to Argentina to manage a ranch. After their return, they established themselves at Kimberton and gave the final decades of their lives to anthroposophically oriented philanthropy.[88]

That legacy continues today through the work of several initiatives located on or near the Myrin estate: the Kimberton Waldorf School, several Camphill communities, the Seven Stars biodynamic dairy, and the Kimberton Community Supported Agriculture farm. Unfortunately, the Kimberton Farms Biodynamic Agricultural School was short lived: by 1944, Ehrenfried Pfeiffer, who griped that "biodynamics is not a rich man's hobby," broke ties with Myrin and relocated to a smaller farm in Chester, New York. But his four years in Kimberton were a time of bridge-building. Just a short drive away, Rodale was a frequent visitor to the Kimberton farm. Pfeiffer established a deeper and more enduring connection to a more spiritually inclined ally: Dr. R. Swinburne Clymer, leader of the Fraternitas Rosae Crucis at Quakertown. Though Steiner sometimes described anthroposophy as a modern incarnation of the Rosicrucian spirit, Clymer's group was independent of anthroposophy, tracing its lineage to the nineteenth-century teachings of Paschal Beverly Randolph and to Pennsylvania's long heritage of radical pietist occultism. As a result of Pfeiffer's influence, a small biodynamic garden became, and remains, part of Clymer's osteopathic clinic in Quakertown.[89]

Pfeiffer's task in Kimberton was to build up a community of American farmers by offering training courses in biodynamics. The first course lasted two weeks and the second six, with the latter attracting sixty-six fledgling farmers from eighteen states. Among the students was Richard Gregg, a Harvard-educated idealist, who had studied with

Gandhi in India and published the first American book on Gandhian nonviolence; his presence was perhaps a first clue that the ideological center of the organics movement might shift from the antigovernment right to the pacifist left.[90] Gregg, who would eventually marry Evelyn Speiden, was assigned the task of writing a report on the course, and his account suggests that participants received a more wide-ranging exposure to biodynamics and anthroposophy than could be found in Pfeiffer's book. Lecture topics included farm economics and bookkeeping, the construction of compost heaps, research findings, "the history of farming from the most primitive times," "most interesting and useful facts which a farmer should know about the stars," various aspects of plant ecology, animal husbandry, meteorology, and beekeeping. The mix of theoretical lectures and practical demonstrations, Gregg wrote, "gave one a strong desire to go out and apply the new knowledge." Gregg then joined a cohort of twenty-five students who were learning from Pfeiffer on a year-round basis. Most of the others were of college age and had no previous farming experience. Like the biodynamic farm apprentices of subsequent generations, they milked cows, built compost piles, established hedgerows, worked out crop rotations suitable for local conditions, and made the biodynamic preparations. They also learned the habits of farm-specific research that are a hallmark of biodynamic practice. In keeping with anthroposophical culture, they devoted a significant amount of time and energy to seasonal festivals, performing nativity plays in full costume each Christmas.[91]

Pfeiffer also launched the *Bio-Dynamics* journal, which is still in publication today. Strongly dominated by Pfeiffer's own voice throughout its early history, this journal was more forthcoming about anthroposophical spirituality than Pfeiffer's writings for Rodale, but it was still designed to be accessible to anyone interested in organic agriculture. The cover story of the first issue was entitled "Prosperity—Security—The Future," and it addressed the same questions of (anticipated) postwar reconstruction that preoccupied Balfour and Northbourne. Contrasting sustainable agriculture with both the war economy and the prewar "prosperity" achieved through rapid economic growth, Pfeiffer suggested that a mature humankind would soon embrace a balanced "self-maintenance" as the best way to achieve full employment and permanently fertile soil. He also named his allies: Secretary of Agriculture Henry Wallace, who had recently announced a policy intended to discourage monocultures (and who had been a devotee of Russian theosophist Nicholas Roerich); geographer Oliver Edwin Baker, who urged a return to rural society; and Catholic activists Luigi Ligutti and John C. Rawe, whose National Catholic Rural Life Conference was relocating unemployed miners to farming villages.[92]

In the second issue of *Bio-Dynamics,* Pfeiffer introduced the movement by affirming that biodynamics "looks upon the soil as upon a living organism"—a choice of phrase that left open the possibility that the soil was only metaphorically alive. As in the piece for Rodale, Pfeiffer stressed composting, crop rotation, and biodynamic preparations as the best tools for maintaining soil life. He concluded with a literature list that featured mostly biodynamic sources alongside books by Northbourne, Lymington, Ligutti, and Rawe—with Albert Howard conspicuous in his absence.[93] Other articles flagged Pfeiffer's interest in building bridges to mainstream science. In one piece, Pfeiffer and two coauthors drew on recent research on growth hormones and vitamins, suggesting that the biodynamic preparations were also "bio-catalysts" capable of stimulating plant growth even in extremely small quantities. They hinted at Steiner's notion of etheric forces by noting that while a material catalyst like boric acid had a specific concentration at which it was most effective, the preparations (according to their tests) were equally effective at any concentration, "show[ing] clearly that we have to deal with a dynamic effect because it is independent of the number of molecules present."[94] Similarly, a piece titled "Cosmic Rhythms," written by J. Schultz, hinted at the cosmic dimension of biodynamics by identifying a litany of natural phenomena governed by rhythmic cycles—primarily those of the day, month, and year, but with the "eleven-year sun-spot period and the various planet periods" also included.[95]

Very gradually, the journal became more forthcoming about the esoteric details of biodynamics. A 1943 editorial titled "The Bio-Dynamic Sprays" acknowledged that 500 is made from cow manure "transformed through half a year's fermentation," and 501 is "pulverized" and put "through a weathering process for many months," but it did not mention the use of a cow's horn to channel cosmic forces. The article assumed that farmers did not need to know exactly how to produce the preparations because they would purchase them from the association, but it gave instructions for diluting and spraying.[96] Articles that offered more details couched them in scientific rather than in alchemical or spiritual terms, referring to such ingredients as "dandelion, yarrow, oak, chamomile, nettle, and valerian" as sources of "bio-catalytic hormones."[97] The journal featured many articles devoted to research findings, and these more frequently involved conventional field tests than the picture-forming methods unique to anthroposophy.

Articles in the journal also sought to extend the interconnected context for agriculture. In "The Weed Problem," Virginia Moore praised weeds as "rich storehouses of the very minerals which our tame, civilization-serving plants require." As Shakespeare's tragedies demonstrated, she wrote, "evil must not be ejected but transformed into good."[98] William James McCauley's piece on "Why the Farmer's 'Pay' is Low" was an early attempt to connect biodynamics to Steiner's teachings on economics, proposing "that income must be based on a man's needs and the needs of his family, and not on the basis of his ability to produce economic values." After this rather utopian suggestion (echoed in contemporary proposals for a universal basic income, which is favored by many students of anthroposophy), McCauley noted that low pay is balanced by other compensations, above all "a feeling of freedom and independence that comes from the very fact that one is NOT fully immersed in the economic organism" and "the reverence that fills the soul of one who joins his hands in loving partnership with the good Earth."[99]

The war years were very difficult for biodynamics in Germany and Central Europe. Pfeiffer's research center at Loverendale was destroyed when Germany invaded the Netherlands; it was actually flooded by sea water for more than a year.[100] After the Nazis turned against biodynamics in 1941, the large farms that had once existed in Silesia were shut down. Many of these were in territory that eventually fell under Soviet domination—either in East Germany or in the reconstituted Poland—where there was no possibility of starting fresh.

In the United States as well, the final years of the war saw a disruption in activities of the Bio-Dynamic Association, in part because of Pfeiffer's relocation and his subsequent bout with tuberculosis. Regular conferences resumed at Threefold Farm in 1946.[101] Threefold expanded its hosting capacity by building a large auditorium and a biodynamics laboratory for Ehrenfried Pfeiffer. In 1952, Alice and Fred Heckel, among Pfeiffer's earliest students, took over the editorship of *Bio-Dynamics,* signaling that movement leadership was passing to a new generation. New farms clustered near Spring Valley and across the country: Walter Stuber's Golden Acres in Pennsylvania, Ludwig Piening's 280 acres in New York, and the Zinniker Farm in Wisconsin, now the oldest continuously operated biodynamic farm in the United States. As these names suggest, the biodynamic community in the United States may have become more German in the postwar years, as the traumas of war sent refugees westward.[102] But native-born Americans also found their way to the movement, among them Josephine Porter, a single mother from Pennsylvania, who had gained a reputation as the "milk lady" of the Poconos by providing families with fresh milk whether or not they could pay. As secretary-treasurer of the Biodynamic Association beginning in 1956, Porter anchored the movement as it entered into greater cooperation with the broader environmental movement of the 1960s.[103]

FROM ORGANICS TO ENVIRONMENTALISM

Though both biodynamics and mainstream organics were "ecological" in the sense that they took a holistic view of the farm organism and emphasized the interconnections among organisms, none of the people

I have mentioned thus far would have described themselves as participants in an "environmental" movement. Such a movement, with its own
network of interconnected parts, achieved self-awareness in the late
1960s, when the organics movement flowed together with such previously separate impulses as population control and wilderness preservation. In the 1940s and 1950s, as in the 1920s and 1930s, the theme of human
health loomed larger for organics proponents than the well-being of the
planet as a whole. When mass movement environmentalism emerged in
the late 1960s, longstanding practitioners of biodynamics experienced it
not as the fruit of their own efforts but as an external movement that
challenged them to develop aspects of Steiner's teaching that had long
lain dormant. Still, the ecological potential of Steiner's teaching was
not limited to the biodynamics movement, and the development of that
potential began soon after the Second World War.

During the postwar Baby Boom, for example, students of Steiner
joined the conversation about whether the planet could sustain a rapidly growing human population. In 1949, Ehrenfried Pfeiffer acknowledged that at current rates of productivity there was not enough land in
cultivation to support the existing human population, much less a
vastly increased one. But he warned against using chemicals to increase
yields, pointing instead to Swiss and Indian farmers, who were achieving high yields through intensive conservation methods. The real
obstacle, for Pfeiffer, was capitalist economics. Small farmers, pressured to achieve industrial rates of productivity, were bankrupted; and
when they moved to cities, their own land lost fertility because of
neglect while fertile suburban land was removed from agricultural production altogether. "Instead of asking ourselves whether there are too
many people in the world," Pfeiffer concluded, "we are really forced to
ask: Are there not too many people massed in some spots and not
enough left in others?"[104]

A decade later, Waldorf educator René Querido presented an apoca-
lyptic scenario of ecological devastation to a British anthroposophical
conference. "Man's survival on the Earth is threatened in a variety of

ways.... Will large portions of the Earth become uninhabitable and vast numbers of people be exterminated owing to the rapidly spreading dangers of uncontrolled radioactivity? Or shall we witness in the near future the terrible devastation caused by natural catastrophes accompanied by the death and suffering of hundreds of thousands of men, women and children?" Drawing especially on the work of Fairfield Osborn, who published *Our Plundered Planet* in 1948, Querido echoed Osborn's call for a "change of heart." But while Osborn emphasized the need for population control, Querido suggested that by recognizing "the necessity of co-operating with nature" humans could cease to be plunderers and become healers of the earth. He also folded in the standard anthroposophical critique of materialist science: If we view the earth as "a conglomeration of dead matter whirling in space ... nothing will be achieved." Querido's alternative was unabashedly cosmic: while the shedding of Abel's blood had "robbed [the Earth] of her virginity," he wrote, the shedding of Christ's blood had begun the process of transforming the earth into a sun. "But the redemption of the Earth cannot take place without the active participation of man."[105]

In 1965, the Anthroposophical Society in America expanded its newsletter into the *Journal for Anthroposophy*.[106] The second issue featured a piece on "The Dignity of the Earth" by Hermann Poppelbaum, a longstanding member of the Anthroposophical Society's executive council, who had recently succeeded Günther Wachsmuth as head of the Goetheanum's Natural Science section. He began with an arresting assertion: "The rise of modern science has been linked with a degradation of the earth." This sounds like the rhetoric of deep ecology. But the "degradation" Poppelbaum had in mind was not pollution or species extinction but rather the symbolic demotion of planet Earth. Copernicus had turned the center of the universe into "a speck of dust," Darwin had discredited "man's spiritual origin," and Freud had finished the work of converting humans into animals. This sounds like the antimodernist rhetoric of Lord Northbourne and other perennialists. Yet, following Steiner, Poppelbaum recontextualized Copernicus, Darwin, and Freud. The humiliation of humanity and the earth was also an "exalting of man's power to understand," and as such it was a test given by the "the spirit of the new age": could humanity love truth so much that we would accept our own dethronement? Passing that test, Poppelbaum suggested, opened humanity to recognizing the true basis of human dignity, which is not our physical centrality but our "striving after knowledge." This striving after knowledge would in turn reveal the "twin-secret" linking humanity to the earth: "The full image of *Man* thus arrived at could not fail to include a restored picture of the *Earth.*" Poppelbaum concluded that modern humanity is challenged to recognize that the earth's greatness, like that of humanity, depends not on its physical stature but on its capacity for ongoing development.[107]

In a sense, Poppelbaum's article might as easily have been written in 1925 as in 1965. It contains few ideas that cannot also be found in Steiner's writings, and its repeated assertion that humans are qualitatively different from animals would offend both scientifically minded environmentalists and nature-worshipping Gaians. But these assertions rest alongside evocative phrases suggesting the inseparability of humans and earth: "earth-conscious mentality," "humbleness towards the earth," "the *implantation of the Christ impulse into the spirit nature of the earth* acts as a seed which guarantees the regeneration of this unique place in the cosmos." In 1965 such phrases signaled anthroposophical alignment with a new movement that stemmed, in part, from the work of two biodynamic gardeners (one of them featured in the same issue of the *Journal for Anthroposophy*), who had launched a campaign against chemical pesticides a few years earlier.

EVANGELISTS AND ALLIES AGAINST DDT: SPOCK, RICHARDS, AND CARSON

Marjorie Spock (1904–2008) was a stalwart of anthroposophical activity in the United States throughout her long life. The sister of famed "baby doctor" Benjamin Spock, she found anthroposophy through the arts. As a teenager, Spock attended the Shakespearean camp founded by anthroposophist Katherine Everts, where she was enchanted by stories of Dornach. She delayed college in order to visit Dornach and managed to be present for both the burning of the first Goetheanum and the Christmas Conference, at which Steiner reconstituted the Anthroposophical Society. After completing a training in eurythmy at Stuttgart, Spock taught at the Rudolf Steiner School in New York City, at the short-lived Mainewoods School founded by Roger and Marion Hale, and at the Garden City Waldorf School. She met Polly Richards at a Waldorf conference, and the two women shared a household for much of the rest of Richards's life. Polly was as physically frail as Marjorie was robust, and together they treasured biodynamics as a means to keep Polly healthy. They were outraged when their home and garden in Long Island were included in a government program that sprayed massive amounts of DDT to control gypsy moths.[108]

In 1957, Spock and Richards launched a series of lawsuits to stop the spraying. Over the next three years, their case drew the support of former Audubon Society president Richard Murphy (also a gardener on Long Island, and thus a coappellant), the British Soil Association (which made a financial contribution), and the *Bio-Dynamics* journal (which devoted a full issue to the topic in January 1958). The case was thoroughly covered in the *New York Times* and made its way to the Supreme Court, where its original dismissal was confirmed. Spock and Richards collected thousands of pages of expert testimony for their lawsuit, and beginning in February 1958 they shared this information with environmental author Rachel Carson, who wrote them at least fifty-seven letters over the course of the trial. They also put Carson into contact with Ehrenfried Pfeiffer, who was one of the many expert witnesses participating in the trial. Carson used their evidence as the scientific foundation for *Silent Spring,* her brilliantly written 1962 account of the threat DDT posed to birds and, by extension, to all of the earth's species.[109] The DDT issue was continuously covered in the American *Bio-Dynamics* journal. In Great Britain, anthroposophist John Davy, who was the science correspondent for the *Observer,* published excerpts from *Silent Spring* in that paper, thus inspiring a publisher to release the entire book. Davy would later serve as vice principal of Emerson College (an anthroposophical training center) and general secretary of the Anthroposophical Society's British branch.[110]

Silent Spring is regarded as the founding text of contemporary environmentalism. It was written at a time when organic agriculture had faded from public view, but its effect was to give organics a new relevance by linking it not only to human health but also to the health of natural systems as a whole. This allowed organics to flow together with wilderness preservation, concern about species extinction, and campaigns against pollution. It also flowed together with the mostly leftist social movements of the 1960s, as Marjorie Spock suggested in a 1971 essay that bemoaned the consequences of imperialism in North America: "Indians were crowded into worthless reservations, Blacks denied recognition as a human species. The vast resources of the continent were exploited, nature polluted and laid waste."[111]

Yet few environmentalists in 1970 would have said that their movement had flowered from the seeds planted by Rudolf Steiner in 1924. In part this was because the anthroposophical leadership of the time did not fully share Spock and Richard's commitment to bridge-building. Charlotte Parker, of Threefold Farm, was the only anthroposophist who contributed financially to their case. Though Spock and Richards were convinced that "anthroposophists ought always to be in the forefront" of the "fight for the welfare of an earth threatened from all sides with ultimate destruction," the response at the time was "cold and really negative."[112] On the other side, Carson did not acknowledge her reliance on Spock and Richards, or indeed on *any* exponents of organic agriculture, in the pages of *Silent Spring,* and she did not live long enough to write the follow-up study on "wise soil management as the only adequate control of insects" that Marjorie Spock hoped for.[113] Agricultural historian John Paull, who has thoroughly documented this story, suggests that the most likely reason for this was Carson's activist strategy: during the trial, ties to the organics movement were accepted by judges as reasons to discredit an expert's testimony. Earlier books on DDT that were written by organic activists had failed to gain public attention. Thus, Carson chose to let her facts speak for themselves, without acknowledging the social movement and network that had given her access to those facts.[114] This had a serendipitous result: beginning in the 1970s, students of Steiner engaged with the environmental movement, not as something that they had created or should control, but as a new reality to be observed and learned from. Both anthroposophy and environmentalism were transformed as a result.

Branches

Anthroposophical Initiatives
and the Growing Environmental Movement

The ideals cherished by Rachel Carson, Marjorie Spock, and Ehren-fried Pfeiffer sprouted into a vibrant and visible global movement around 1970. On April 22 of that year, twenty million Americans participated in the first "Earth Day," which Senator Gaylord Nelson had designed as a "national teach-in on the environment." Building on the successes of the civil rights, antiwar, feminist, Chicano, and gay liberation movements—all of which had captured the limelight a few years earlier—Nelson and his allies pushed the Clean Air, Clean Water, and Endangered Species Acts through Congress.[1] Many significant activist organizations emerged within the next decade. In the United States, Greenpeace was founded in 1972, the Institute for Social Ecology in 1974, and Earth First! in 1979; in Germany, the Green Party emerged in 1980. Within the new environmentalism, sustainable agriculture played a central role alongside concerns about urban pollution, mass extinction, and rapid population growth. Rachel Carson had effectively shown that widespread pesticide use was equally threatening to wildlife and to healthy agriculture, and this insight led thousands of hippies and back-to-the-landers to establish organic farms. From his Kentucky farm, poet Wendell Berry eloquently expressed an agrarian version of environmentalism beginning in the 1970s, while the British economist

E. F. Schumacher made the case for local economies in *Small Is Beautiful*. Both men collaborated with anthroposophical organizations and drew on currents of alternative spirituality; both also insisted that the environmental crisis was at heart a spiritual crisis. Anthroposophy and biodynamics had much to offer environmentalists, who sensed that the solution to this crisis lay in a renewal of agricultural practice.[2]

THE EVOLVING ANTHROPOSOPHY OF THE 1970S

Anthroposophy was as central to 1970s environmentalism as biodynamics had been to the organic movement of the 1930s and 1940s. But after 1970, tracing linear "roots" of ecological ideas is difficult, simply because so many traditions were interacting freely and publicly. In the 1940s, Eve Balfour knew most of the leading figures in organic agriculture personally. When she combined ideas from Rudolf Steiner and Albert Howard in her own synthesis, she was aware that Steiner and Howard had themselves arrived at their seminal ideas through independent processes. For Balfour's counterparts in 1970, by contrast, ecological ideas were simply "in the air." In the terms of Rudolf Steiner's own ecology, the seeds planted a half century earlier were now tall trees with intertwined branches, and as such they were filling the air with spiritual forces that were freely available to younger plants and animals. It was an age that was inclined not to look back to its roots but simply to breathe the fresh air of the future.

The expansion of environmentalism coincided with a transformation of the anthroposophical movement. It had always held its "self-reinforcing" and "self-dispersing" tendencies in creative balance, but after 1970 the emphasis shifted toward the latter. Anthroposophical initiatives—farms, schools, intentional communities—began to supplant the society as the public face of anthroposophy. Before 1970, these initiatives were usually initiated by members of the society (or of one of the excluded national branches). Typically, these initiators had themselves come to anthroposophy on a spiritual search, and they shared the movement's commitment to textual study and meditative practice. Though many society members were involved in initiatives, others were not—and some were actively skeptical of practical anthroposophy. Midcentury anthroposophy, in other words, was barely distinct from other offshoots of theosophy, such as Alice Bailey's Arcane School or Nicholas and Helena Roerich's Agni Yoga movement.

Students of anthroposophy who planted initiatives in the early years often brought missionary zeal to the task, resulting in a dispersed network that covered five continents. In many cases, they also brought an exilic sensibility: many founders of initiatives outside Central Europe were themselves natives of Central Europe, who had fled Nazism or communism. Their counterparts in postwar West Germany were scarred by the years of Nazi oppression and (in some cases) shameful memories of their own collusion with Nazism. These factors intensified the inward-looking tendencies characteristic of any fledgling spiritual movement, and thus the growth of anthroposophical initiatives was limited by the number of committed students of anthroposophy prepared to lead them.

In the 1970s, the flow of initiatives was reversed. Anthroposophical initiatives began to be created by people who were primarily or exclusively interested in anthroposophy's fruits. Some people who came in search of educational, agricultural, and communal alternatives had little interest in esoteric spirituality. Parents demanded that new Waldorf schools be created, whether or not there were sufficient numbers of trained teachers. Young hippies dropped in on Camphill communities and stayed because they liked the people who lived there. Initially, many of the people who were attracted to anthroposophy's fruits became spiritual practitioners and full members of the society: after 1970, society membership continued to grow at the steady pace it had maintained since the Second World War, rising from thirty thousand to a plateau of slightly more than fifty thousand at the end of the century.[3] But this growth was dwarfed by that of the Waldorf School movement, which doubled between 1956 and 1975 and then grew fivefold between 1975 and 1992. From 1975 onward, twenty-five new Waldorf schools were created each year, compared to just two per year previously. The explosive growth in biodynamic farming came later, with a hundred new farms added per year during the first decade of the twenty-first century. The geographical pattern of growth also shifted. While the early initiatives were widely scattered, those founded after 1970 spread through local networks of influence. Before 1970, for example, the Camphill movement planted communities in England, Ireland, Germany, South Africa, and the United States, but within Scotland it did not venture beyond its Aberdeen base of operations until the 1970s, when it started six new communities.

When anthroposophists describe the transformation of the 1970s, they typically refer vaguely to the social upheaval of the 1960s. Suddenly thousands of people were searching for what anthroposophy had to offer! But it is important to delineate the story more precisely. The tide of new participants crested in the 1970s, not the 1960s. To fully understand this influx, it is necessary to distinguish the leftist social movements of the 1960s from the New Age spirituality of the 1970s. These were not unrelated, but they had distinct implications for anthroposophy.

One puzzle that confronts any historian of anthroposophy or environmentalism is that both movements seemed to change their political character during the 1960s. Before 1960, they were frequently allied with fascist, agrarian, or libertarian forms of conservatism; after 1970, environmentalists were routinely grouped with feminists, pacifists, civil rights activists, and socialists. Waldorf schools catered primarily to families that shared these "progressive" values. To explain the transition, it is necessary but not sufficient to point out that neither anthroposophy nor environmentalism was wholly "of the right" before 1960, and neither was wholly "of the left" after 1970. Both are better understood as "third ways" not reducible to conventional political binaries. Yet it is nevertheless the case that before 1960 they readily built alliances on the right, while after 1970 virtually all of their alliances were on the left.

One reason is that the left itself experienced a profound change during the 1960s. Previously, it had been dominated by Communist and Socialist parties and by labor unions, all of which emphasized economics and held a broadly materialist view of reality. Since anthroposophists and environmentalists alike refused to subsume nature or spirit to economics, and since they held spiritual and "life" forces to be as real as physical matter, they struggled to relate to the left. But during the 1960s, the anticolonial, civil rights, and student movements expanded the range of leftist concerns, bringing a new ethos of spiritual idealism. In the United States, this was well-expressed in the 1962 Port Huron Statement, which explicitly defended "idealism" and lifted up an idealistic view of humanity as "infinitely precious and possessed of unfulfilled capacities for reason, freedom, and love."[4] Students of anthroposophy could readily embrace such language. Even if they did not notice the Port Huron Statement at the time it was issued, they readily connected with young people formed by its vision. (Two decades later, a corresponding development on the right solidified the transition: Margaret Thatcher and Ronald Reagan wedded global conservatism to free market economics, which was in its own way as dogmatically materialist as Marxism. This displaced the forms of conservatism—agrarianism, fascism, and libertarianism—with which anthroposophy and environmentalism had once been allied.)

Though the New Left had engendered a youthful idealism that resonated with anthroposophy and environmentalism, it had also given rise—by the end of the 1960s—to sharp conflicts among activists, to militant styles of activism, to new (especially Maoist) dogmatisms, and to burnout among people whose ideals had not been realized. Many people who turned to environmentalism or to anthroposophy were disillusioned New Leftists, who had concluded that inner transformation was a necessary precursor to social change. The same disillusionment led people to Buddhist meditation centers, yoga studios, psychedelic experimentation, Goddess workshops, and hippy communes—and more than a few people passed through such practices en route to anthroposophy. (People whom I have interviewed have mentioned western Buddhism, Transcendental Meditation, psychedelics, Taoism, the Course in Miracles, the Gurdjieff Work, and other spiritualities.) These seekers rarely abandoned the leftist principles of economic, racial, and gender equality, but they spent less time directly pursuing such goals. On the other hand, they retained environmentalist practices, such as eating healthy food, that reinforced an ethos of inner work and personal transformation.

Put differently, the context for the parallel evolution of anthroposophy and environmentalism after 1970 is what is often called the "New Age" movement—a broad proliferation of spiritual and therapeutic practices. The New Age was a "self-dispersing" movement par excellence: participants almost never affiliated exclusively with a single teacher or organization but cobbled together worldviews and lifestyles from an enormous menu. Scholar Wouter Hanegraaff, using Colin Campbell's terminology, has suggested that "the New Age is synonymous with the cultic milieu having become conscious of itself as constituting a more or less unified 'movement.'" As such, it differed from anthroposophy, with its balance of self-dispersing and self-reinforcing aspects. Hanegraaff pointedly excludes anthroposophy from the New Age, on the ground that it "is a clearly demarcated organisation" that emerged earlier and whose members generally disavow the New Age label. But he acknowledges that outsiders often associate the two, and that this may indicate "affinities" or a genealogical connection.[5]

I would go further: anthroposophy and the New Age were connected genealogically and symbiotically. Several New Age founders were directly influenced by Steiner, and the two movements developed a mutually reinforcing way of interacting. The New Age provided anthroposophical initiatives with a broader constituency of potential participants. Anthroposophy provided New Agers (including those who did not become anthroposophists) with resources that are only available in self-reinforcing movements. It offered a rich set of spiritual practices: meditative techniques, cosmological speculations, festivals, liturgies, books to study, and more. It affirmed the insight that many New Agers had recently reached: that inner transformation was of more ultimate value than outer change. And it also helped seekers keep faith with the social ideals of the Sixties by providing a practical alternative to the hyperindividualization of meditative spirituality. While meditation (and yoga and psychedelics) focused relentlessly on the self, Waldorf education invited people to teach children and biodynamic agriculture invited them to heal the land. Such practices made it possible for people to turn from "outer" to "inner" without trading social responsibility for narcissistic self-absorption. Not coincidentally, Steiner himself had turned to education and agriculture after it became clear that the world was not ready to embrace his vision of political and economic reform.

This outcome was not preordained. Anthroposophy might have created an equally rich set of symbioses in the 1920s were it not for specific choices made by Rudolf Steiner. In the tumultuous 1920s, both anarchists and Roman Catholics in Germany promoted decentralized alternatives to capitalism and socialism that were structurally similar to Steiner's threefold commonwealth.[6] But Steiner refused to pursue alliances with them. He was, perhaps, too bruised by the hostility of Marxists and fascists, and by the complex tensions within his society. Perhaps he rightly sensed that a newborn spiritual society could not afford to dissipate its energies by supporting other people's initiatives—and so he reestablished the Anthroposophical Society on terms that privileged self-reinforcement over self-dispersion. In the 1970s, many of his students made a different choice: they welcomed hippies and radicals into their initiatives, cooperated with Buddhists and Catholics in expanding organic agriculture, and launched environmental impulses that are now independent of anthroposophy. In so doing, they contributed immeasurably to the thriving of the environmental movement as a whole, and perhaps to the reinvigoration of anthroposophy—though members of the Anthroposophical Society still debate whether their movement has swung too far in the direction of self-dispersion.

In this chapter, I will explore the process by which anthroposophy allowed its branches to mingle freely in the forest of environmentalism, focusing on the work of a new generation of anthroposophical "evangelists" and of a corresponding cluster of creative "translators." The evangelists were part of a new generation of leaders in the Anthroposophical Society. With the 1963 death of longtime leader Albert Steffen and some of his counterparts in the excluded branches, anthroposophical leadership shifted to people who either had never met Rudolf Steiner or had encountered him only at the end of his life. These leaders, most of whom forged careers within Waldorf schools or other initiatives, cherished anthroposophy's practicality and were eager to make anthroposophical practices accessible to others. They were less preoccupied by Steiner's warnings about the balance between the society and the initiatives. Among these leaders were Francis Edmunds in the United Kingdom, Henry Barnes in the United States, and Herbert Koepf, who succeeded Ehrenfried Pfeiffer as the leading expositor of biodynamics.

Simultaneously, people on the fringes of the Society translated anthroposophical ideas into the idioms of the New Left, the New Age movement, and environmental activism. Especially interesting in this group were New Age teacher George Trevelyan, gardener Alan Chadwick, and artist Joseph Beuys. The coordinated influence of translators and evangelists made anthroposophical environmentalism available to the seekers of the Baby Boom generation—both those who became students of anthroposophy and those who embraced Buddhist, pagan, Gandhian, and New Age spiritualities. Baby Boomers, in turn, shifted the ethos of the anthroposophical movement so far toward self-dispersal that, by the turn of the twenty-first century, some Anthroposophical Society leaders began acting like translators (that is, expressing core anthroposophical ideas without explicit reference to Steiner), while allies (that is, people with little knowledge of anthroposophy) took on leadership roles within some anthroposophical initiatives.

ANTHROPOSOPHY'S NEW EVANGELISTS:
BARFIELD, EDMUNDS, BARNES, AND KOEPF

The shifting character of anthroposophical leadership can be encapsulated in a contrast between two British exponents of Steiner's ideas, Owen Barfield (1898–1997) and Francis Edmunds (1902–89). They were allies in the work of maintaining anthroposophy in Great Britain while the British society was alienated from the international leadership in Dornach. They shared a commitment to making anthroposophy more accessible, and they pursued distinct strategies for achieving this goal. While Barfield focused on Steiner's ideas, Edmunds built his bridge out of anthroposophical practices.

Owen Barfield is best known today for his participation in the "Inklings," the literary circle that also included fantasy writers C.S. Lewis and J.R.R. Tolkien. Barfield's connection to anthroposophy began when he attended one of Steiner's final lectures in 1924. He cemented his academic reputation a few years later with *Poetic Diction,* a study of the poet's meaning-making powers that bore subtle marks of Steiner's influence. Subsequent books couched Steiner's ideas in terms designed to appeal to twentieth century idealists, who were uncomfortable with the materialism and consumerism of postwar culture. In *Worlds Apart,* he imagined a dialogue among scientists, scholars, and students, along with one Waldorf teacher, on the presuppositions informing their worldviews. The implicit message was clear: new *thinking* was needed to address twentieth-century dilemmas of the twentieth century, and Steiner had much to offer.[7]

Barfield lived his final years in Forest Row, a suburban community that became England's densest center of anthroposophical activity through the efforts of Francis Edmunds. The child of a Russian Jewish family that immigrated to England when he was two years old, Edmunds embraced Quakerism as a young man and found anthroposophy shortly after Steiner's death. He embarked on a career as a Waldorf teacher at London's Michael Hall, which had been founded in 1925. In the face of the schism that divided anthroposophy, he organized a British network of Waldorf schools and a training program for their teachers. While these activities might mark him as a consummate insider, Edmonds was equally devoted to outreach. During World War II, he lectured to soldiers stationed near his school, and this experience led him to dream of something more permanent and inclusive. In 1962 he founded Emerson College as an adult education center. The curriculum featured a "foundation year" focused on basic anthroposophical themes, followed by specialized training in education, agriculture, or the arts. Significantly, he named his school not for Steiner or anyone affiliated with anthroposophy but after transcendentalist Ralph Waldo Emerson. The goal was to provide practical life paths to anyone inspired by Emerson's emphasis on the primacy of the spirit, and the time was ripe: over the next decade, Emerson helped countless seekers connect their inchoate aspirations to practical careers within the anthroposophical movement.[8]

Edmunds's practical vision was shared by Henry Barnes (1912–2008), who led the Anthroposophical Society in America from 1974 to 1991. Like Edmunds, Barnes was a Waldorf teacher. He was himself a product of progressive education, having attended the John Dewey–inspired Lincoln School in New York. In 1932 Barnes's Lincoln classmate and Harvard roommate Peter Stockton committed suicide, prompting Stockton's mother to turn to Steiner's writings in the hope of a spiritual connection with her lost son. She brought Barnes to the first Threefold Farm conference in 1933, and soon he and his brother Edward—whose adolescent troubles reminded Henry of Peter Stockton's—traveled to Stuttgart so that Edward could enter the Waldorf high school and Henry could begin teacher training. Both hoped that Waldorf schooling would be a spiritually deeper version of Deweyan education—touching what Barnes called "the very foundations of human life"—and both found it to be so.

In Germany, Barnes met two sisters, Christy and Arvia MacKaye, fellow Americans, whose path to anthroposophy had also been shaped by the experiences of an emotionally troubled brother. The MacKaye family had roots in the theater, alternative spirituality, and the conservationist movement. Their father, Percy MacKaye, was a playwright whose first "civic masque," *Sanctuary,* highlighted the plight of birds whose feathers were used in hats. Percy's brother Benton, a forester, devoted his life to the creation of the Appalachian Trail. Through their father, Christy and Arvia met such luminaries as Rabindranath Tagore, Kahlil Gibran, and Isadora Duncan. After a family friend introduced Arvia to the writings of Rudolf Steiner, she visited Dornach just in time to participate in the re-forming of the Anthroposophical Society at the Christmas Conference of 1923. During a second stay in Dornach, Arvia was joined by her sister Christy, who pursued training in speech with Marie Steiner; by her brother Robin, who entered an anthroposophical sanatorium in southern Germany; and eventually by their parents. When Barnes married Christy, he thus gained a connection to the American conservationist tradition.[9]

Henry Barnes's marriage to Christy MacKaye also provided him with a distinctive perspective on the schism within the Anthroposophical Society. Since Henry was an admirer of Ita Wegman and Christy was a student of Marie Steiner, he learned from the "challenge of trying to understand and to reconcile two apparently irreconcilable points of view in a truly human way." He also got to know Francis Edmunds while teaching in England. Leaving Dornach on the eve of the Second World War, Barnes returned to the United States to begin a thirty-five year career on the faculty of the Rudolf Steiner School in New York City.[10]

Edmunds's biography also intersected with that of Herbert Koepf (1914–2007), who succeeded Ehrenfried Pfeiffer as the leading international promulgator of biodynamics. Koepf began his career as a farmer, obtained a doctorate in soil science, succeeded Pfeiffer as head of the Threefold Farm laboratory, taught at Hohenheim Agricultural College near Stuttgart, and then was recruited by Edmunds to teach biodynamics at Emerson College, where he served from 1970 to 1990. He became head of the agriculture section of the Goetheanum in 1972, retaining that role until 1988. Koepf was thus ideally positioned to interpret bio-dynamics in both the German- and English-speaking worlds. His vision for the movement is evident in his 1976 pamphlet, "What Is Bio-Dynamic Agriculture?" and in his subsequent book, *The Biodynamic Farm,* texts that superseded Pfeiffer's writings as introductory materials for new practitioners of biodynamics.[11]

Koepf's pamphlet—which, like Pfeiffer's book, was published simultaneously in English and in German—followed Pfeiffer by situating biodynamics within the broader organics movement and downplaying the aspects that distinguished it from other organic methods. Like Pfeiffer, he endorsed an experimental ethos while criticizing reductionist science. Yet he also softened the protective shell surrounding the alchemical core of biodynamics. The holistic vocabulary of environmentalism gave Koepf room to hint that his readers' worldview might need to become still more holistic.

Koepf opened by urging farmers to emulate the "many-sidedness and well-nigh closed cycles" characteristic of wilderness ecosystems. This approach, he asserted, could be reconciled with "intensification and high yields" through the use of nitrogen-fixing and humus-building plants, composting, and management oriented to the ideal of the "farm as organism." Unlike Pfeiffer, Koepf then offered an explicit description of anthroposophy as a whole, freely using such terms as *etheric body*. A purely sense-based science, he asserted, was a "science of dead nature." But people can train ourselves to observe the "indwelling principle of life" in the "innumerable metamorphoses of the archetypal motif spread out before us in many species." Alluding to Steiner's spiritual exercises, Koepf announced that "anthroposophy offers training methods open to everyone" that can awake the capacity to perceive not only the etheric body but also "human and animal soul life" (his paraphrase of the astral body) and "the spiritual individuality that is active in every human being."[12]

Turning to the content of the Agriculture Course, Koepf then said that Steiner's methods could help the farmer see how plants were "connected with their environment in the widest sense." While mainstream science separated "living processes" into "separate mechanisms," biodynamic methods kept "each single measure related to life's overarching wholeness." Koepf described the preparations in terms that hinted at but did not expose the alchemical content of the Agriculture Course. He used the names "horn manure" and "horn silica," albeit without explaining how these substances are made, and acknowledged that they were applied in homeopathic doses. Koepf mentioned mainstream research on the "manifold influences of trace elements" in support of the preparations, and similarly presented the work of Maria Thun as continuous with new discoveries about biological rhythms. (Thun's work, conducted in the 1950s and 1960s, identified intricate connections between the phases of the moon and the zodiac and the distinct development rhythms of roots, leaves, flowers, and fruits, thus allowing for the development of a detailed planting calendar.[13])

Koepf concluded his pamphlet by contrasting the farm organism ideal with a conventional agriculture characterized by "specialization, considerable dependence on purchased supplies, and a minimal work force." At the same time, he indicated that "self-containment is certainly not a rigid dogma; that would only alienate the farmer from life." He urged farmers to attend to local conditions, both social and ecological. He even admitted that "Rudolf Steiner's advice was actually intended for definite situations," and that farmers in tropical climates especially would need to seek new ways of applying Steiner's core insights.[14]

Another leader who supported a softening of the protective shell was Biodynamic Association secretary-treasurer Josephine Porter. At a 1976 conference, one participant criticized the "secrecy surrounding the making of the biodynamic preparations," prompting Porter to respond that there was no secret and that she would gladly offer a course on preparation making at her own farm that fall. Among those who accepted this challenge was Hugh Courtney, who discovered that preparation making could not be separated from other activities that make up "the totality of a farm organism." Courtney devoted his own life to Porter's vision of a center for research, teaching, and the creation of the preparations. The resulting Josephine Porter Institute, established in 1992, produces most of the preparations that are sold in the United States today, while training those who wish to make them themselves.[15]

THREE TRANSLATORS:
TREVELYAN, CHADWICK, AND BEUYS

Koepf and Porter could afford to be more open about the spiritual content of biodynamics because, during the 1970s, the environmental movement was suffused with New Age spirituality. One New Age progenitor had drunk deeply from the well of Steiner's teaching. Sir George Trevelyan (1906–96), a spiritually seeking nobleman like Lord Northbourne, recapitulated Northbourne's career as a translator of anthroposophy, who was influenced by Steiner but chose not to identify himself publicly with the Anthroposophical Society. This role followed stints as a practitioner of the "Alexander Technique," a posture-based healing practice that seeks to "make the change by non-doing,"[16] and as an outdoor educator at a school led by the same man who founded Outward Bound. Trevelyan embraced the vocation of teaching after his politically leftist father gave away the family estate. He trained riflemen during the Second World War, then led Attingham College, an adult education program catering especially to recently returned servicemen. As Trevelyan's interests became increasingly spiritual, Attingham became a seedbed of the New Age.

Trevelyan encountered Steiner's teachings one year after his father relinquished the estate and two years after Lord Northbourne published *Look to the Land*. His sister, who was interested in spirituality, invited him to attend a lecture by a leading anthroposophist; he agreed because *he* was interested in agriculture. "My whole soul inwardly shouted affirmation," he wrote years later, "The lecture ... in 1942 lifted me clear of agnosticism and released the spiritual vision."[17] Trevelyan credited Steiner with teaching him about the primacy of the spirit, about the threefold nature of human beings, about reincarnation, and about the Cosmic Christ, and he never concealed this debt. At the same time, he never presented himself as a teacher of anthroposophy, and reveled in his capacity to present Steiner's ideas without mentioning Steiner—even when speaking "to the most 'ordinary' audience in a village hall."[18] At the height of his fame in the 1970s, he quoted Teilhard de Chardin more frequently than Steiner. But he continually translated Steiner's ideas into the emerging idiom of the New Age. Trevelyan took Steiner's idea of the earth as a living organism and—without renouncing Steiner's teaching that humanity is central to earth evolution—shifted the accent from *Anthropos* to *Gaia*. "Planet Earth," Trevelyan wrote in 1977, "is truly alive, a sentient creature with her own breathing, bloodstream, glands and consciousness. We human beings are integrally part of this organism ... [and] points of consciousness for the Earth Being."[19]

Trevelyan does not seem to have used the term *Gaia* to express this idea until after James Lovelock had articulated the "Gaia hypothesis," which holds that the earth is a single, self-regulating system but not necessarily a bearer of soul or spirit. But Trevelyan may be a more important source than Lovelock for the "spiritual Gaianism" associated with such places as the Findhorn Community in Scotland. Findhorn, which counted Trevelyan as a friend from its beginning, is known for agricultural practices that involve communing with elemental beings, or "devas." Findhorn leaders described this as "a more direct spiritual way of obtaining the same results" as biodynamics. Trevelyan, for his part, assured Findhorn's leaders that Steiner himself had based biodynamics on knowledge of the elemental world.[20] Today, the Findhorn farm describes itself as "using organic and biodynamic farming methods."[21] Other Steiner-inspired elements, including a Waldorf school, are part of Findhorn's eclectic spirituality today.

Though George Trevelyan and his friends at Findhorn may have coined the term *New Age,* most of us associate that movement more with

California than with northern Scotland. Alan Chadwick (1909–80) was the link between biodynamics and the organic counterculture of 1970s California. Like Trevelyan, his roots were in the dispossessed English gentry. Chadwick retained an "aristocratic bearing" throughout his life, though his lifestyle was ascetic.[22] He also had an early connection to Rudolf Steiner—so much so that he told his garden apprentices that he was not Steiner's student but his "child." Some of them subsequently doubted Chadwick's claim to have spent a summer, at age fourteen, on a biodynamic farm, given their mentor's penchant for storytelling, yet Chadwick's relationship to anthroposophy was similar to that of many people raised within the anthroposophical movement.[23] He gave no evidence of having read Steiner and failed to abide by the distinctive tenets of biodynamics, yet he claimed a vital connection to Steiner and referred to his method as "biodynamic French intensive." Chadwick's charisma and confidence made him an important mentor to several important biodynamic practitioners of the Baby Boom generation, as well as a bridge between biodynamics and other spiritual traditions. Like Trevelyan and Northbourne, Chadwick was a translator who brought biodynamics to a broader audience even though his worldview was less balanced than Steiner's.

The process by which Chadwick became "the greatest horticulturist of the twentieth century" (in the words of E. F. Schumacher) is shrouded in mythology.[24] As a teenager, he apprenticed on a series of farms and learned the "double digging" technique that French gardeners used to produce a large amount of vegetables in a small space. A theatrical career took him to South Africa, where he shifted to full-time gardening in 1952. There he met Freya von Moltke, who provided another point of connection to Steiner: the von Moltke family had a long history of connection to alternative spiritualities, and Freya's husband was related to a prominent German general to whom Steiner had given spiritual advice. Von Moltke introduced Chadwick to Paul Lee, a religion professor, who was launching an organic garden on the University of California's new campus in Santa Cruz.

This university embodied the competing tendencies of the middle of the twentieth century. Founded in 1965 as part of a massive expansion of higher education, it drew countercultural scholars, among them psychoanalyst Norman O. Brown, alongside conventional chemists and biologists. For Paul Lee, it was the perfect setting for an archetypal conflict between "physicalists," who seek to reduce reality to its constituent parts, and "vitalists," who believe that "organic nature" follows a higher set of laws than physical matter.[25] Lee, who had studied existentialist theology with Paul Tillich at Harvard, and whose later career included running a restaurant and homeless shelter, as well as editing the *Psychedelic Review*, was squarely on the vitalist side, though he did not initially understand the motives that led him to launch a campus garden. As "flower power . . . waft[ed] down from the Haight-Ashbury on a cloud of smoke," he had an idyllic fantasy of watching flowers bloom while students worked. He remembered the creation of the garden as "one of the few experiences in my life in which . . . I have the feeling that I was guided."[26]

Like many people who allied themselves with biodynamics without embracing anthroposophy, Lee was more antimodernist than Steiner. He denied the existence of "Western culture" after Goethe, and while Steiner sought to balance the true spirit of the French Revolution with older impulses, Lee bemoaned the "rise and triumph of the revolutionary bourgeoisie." In the 1960s, he wrote, "we were unusually open to new ideas, and perhaps especially to ones that looked forward by looking backward."[27] Steve Kaffka, who was first Chadwick's student, then his adversary, and finally his successor as garden manager, similarly characterized Chadwick as "anti-science" and nostalgically attached to the medieval system of squires and peasants. Significantly, when Kaffka read Lord Northbourne's *Look to the Land* years later, he noticed an antimodernist spirit similar to Chadwick's.[28]

In 1967, there was no established method for running a university garden, but Chadwick undoubtedly would have ignored it had there been one. According to Paul Lee, the day after agreeing to supervise the garden Chadwick bought a spade and began digging alone. When Lee recruited students to help him, Chadwick took them as they arrived, teaching them gardening basics alongside diction, deportment, and drama. To teach them about pollination, he acted out "the nuptial flight of the queen bee"; for insight into medicinal herbs, he made them memorize the Friar's speech in *Romeo and Juliet*. Many of the students who began working in the garden were struggling academically, and under Chadwick's guidance they "learned to work for the first time in their lives"—though this work ethic did not necessarily translate to the classroom. Chadwick's cooking lessons provided a template for the trend known as "California cuisine," while his complaints about tasteless apples marketed as "Delicious" generated interest in heirloom varieties.[29]

Paul Lee wrote that "Chadwick mostly kept his mouth shut about Steiner, and used the French intensive system as a kind of screen or shield, as though to protect the biodynamic mysteries from profanation."[30] This implies that Chadwick, like Ehrenfried Pfeiffer, concealed the esoteric dimensions of biodynamics for fear of misunderstanding. More likely, Chadwick simply defined biodynamics in his own way. When asked if there were books about biodynamics, he ignored the many available books and replied, "Is there a book by which you could be a master painter? ... How could there be?" While Steiner insisted that biodynamics was a modern method that did not simply revive peasant wisdom, Chadwick declared that "There is nothing modern about this system." He never talked about the biodynamic preparations because he didn't use them. Steiner insisted on the essential role of domesticated animals in a healthy farm organism, while Chadwick declared that "Horticulture is the basis of agriculture." A devoted animal lover, he favored wild animals: when asked for tips on controlling garden pests, he rattled off a list of companion plantings but insisted that the main point was to provide an appealing environment for wildlife on the edges of the garden: "We want more deer. We want more birds. We want more insects, more butterflies. They've been eradicated. We want them back by the millions."[31] On one occasion, he stopped his car in order to escort a tarantula to safety by the side of the road.[32]

Yet Chadwick's lectures can sound more like Steiner than Pfeiffer's or Koepf's books, simply because he refused to downplay the cosmic dimension. The basis of biodynamics, Chadwick said, was "spiritual vision behind everything that you do." "Within horticulture," he insisted, "is the whole scene of man's marriage with all other living things in the world." To approach a garden, he asserted, was to "uplift" the true "image" of humanity. Just as Steiner counseled reverence as the first step on any spiritual journey, Chadwick urged young garden-ers to cultivate "reverence and obedience to the . . . laws of God." Steiner had personally taught him, Chadwick claimed, to "lean up against the different trees and to be resuscitated by them." Chadwick accurately cited Steiner's authority when he taught that "every part of the anatomy is connected with the planets" and that in past epochs people had eaten for the sake of "spiritual vision," as well as physical nutrition. Chadwick was fuzzy about how planetary influences affect gardens but was una-bashed in declaring their importance. When asked about elemental beings, he warned against "verbosity" but affirmed his belief in "gnomes, elves, undines, [and] nymphs." In an age that was beginning to sense magic might be the antidote to materialist science, Chadwick declared that garden plants held so much magic that "All the jewels in the world of all the maharajas put together are not the equivalent of the plants in one little back garden."[33]

Chadwick's relationship to anthroposophical leaders was tempestu-ous. Both Francis Edmunds and Herbert Koepf visited the Santa Cruz garden, the latter at the recommendation of the former. According to Steve Kaffka, Chadwick referred to his method as "biodynamic" only after Edmonds's visit.[34] But Chadwick walked out of Koepf's lecture at the garden. According to one intern, Chadwick may have perceived Koepf as a German anthoposophist with Nazi sympathies, or as an impractical academic "who couldn't sow a lettuce to save his life." But Steve Kaffka was inspired by Koepf's blend of anthroposophical com-mitment and academic rigor, sensing in him a unique capacity to "tolerat[e] cognitive dissonance."[35] Kaffka retained Koepf as a mentor and coauthor as he embarked on an academic career as a research agronomist and director of the University of California, Davis's Center for Integrated Farming Systems.[36]

As the first organic garden on a university campus, Chadwick's garden was influential. *Life* magazine featured it in a spread on the new campus. Two years after starting the garden, Lee took a summer canoe trip with Wisconsin Senator Gaylord Nelson, and he was thrilled to see Nelson announce plans for the first Earth Day on national television a few months later. When Lee started a restaurant using the garden's produce, he named it after his friend Stewart Brand's *Whole Earth Catalog*, and when the restaurant manager published a *Whole Earth Cookbook*, it sold over a million copies. It was one of the California counterculture's first cookbooks, but far from the last with a Chadwick connection.[37]

After five years, Chadwick was forced out, and the garden was handed over to his interns. Paul Lee remembered Chadwick's departure as a victory for the "physicalists" in the science departments, but Chadwick's irrational temper was also a factor. Still, his departure extended his influence on California cuisine. His second major garden was at the Green Gulch lay monastery established by the Zen Center of San Francisco. Chadwick had gotten to know the Zen monks at Tassajara a few years earlier and encouraged them to supplement their practice of bread baking with a monastic garden. Green Gulch was closer to the city, and this made it possible for the Zen Center, in conjunction with chef Deborah Madison, to establish the Greens Restaurant in San Francisco in 1979. Madison's mentor Alice Waters, who had founded Chez Panisse in 1971, began sourcing her produce at Green Gulch shortly after Chadwick's death.[38] Green Gulch was just a few miles south of a Gandhian ashram that modeled its own garden on the one in Santa Cruz. Members of that community published *Laurel's Kitchen* in 1976.[39]

Chadwick's relationships with Zen Buddhists were as tumultuous as those with university administrators. He "wailed at top volume" whenever the Zen students were called away from the garden to meditate, and according to a subsequent gardener he once strangled an intruding

blue jay and "hung the murdered bird at the entrance gate ... as a maca-
bre and ominous warning to all transgressors of the true Garden
Way."[40] After Green Gulch, Chadwick established gardens in Covelo
and Saratoga, California, and at the Paul Solomon Foundation in West
Virginia. Solomon was a New Age trance teacher inspired by Edgar
Cayce, and Paul Lee described his community as an ersatz version of
anthroposophy's Dornach headquarters, which hosted such teachers as
Buckminister Fuller and George Trevelyan. In December 1979, Chadwick returned to Green Gulch to die.[41]

Chadwick's interns continue his legacy today.[42] Sherry Wildfeuer,
who was already committed to anthroposophy when she arrived in Santa
Cruz, teaches biodynamics through her *Stella Natura* planting calendar.
Alan York guided the California vineyards that embraced biodynamic
methods. Stephen Decater followed Chadwick to Covelo in 1972 and
launched his own nearby biodynamic farm a few years later. Stephen and
his wife, Gloria, have worked together at Life Power Community Farm
since 1977; it is a fifty-acre, diversified farm that relies entirely on horse
and solar power.[43] Intern Michael Stusser was drawn more to Buddhist
spirituality than to biodynamics. After spending time in a Japanese monastery and training in Japanese landscape architecture, he returned to
California to launch the Osmosis Day Spa Sanctuary.[44] Closer to Santa
Cruz, Camp Joy Gardens has been managed by Chadwick apprentices
Beth and Jim Nelson since 1971; it combines family farming with education on gardening, food preservation, and sustainability.[45]

It is a long distance from Zen gardens to avant-garde performance
art, but another anthroposophical translator was one of the leading performance artists of the 1970s. Joseph Beuys (1921–86) was at once the
best-known anthroposophical artist of the late twentieth century and
the least typical. While most of the others used watercolors to explore
the spirituality of color, Beuys gained prominence in 1965 for "How to
Explain Pictures to a Dead Hare," in which he placed himself on
exhibit, holding a dead hare and talking to it about a group of drawings.
In subsequent years, Beuys embraced Germany's student movement,

cofounding the German Student Party in 1967. As a professor at the Kunstakademie Düsseldorf, he welcomed students into his courses even if they had not been admitted to the school—a practice that led to his dismissal in 1972. He also championed "an extended concept of art," according to which "Every human being is an artist creating new social forms." Drawing on Steiner's threefold theory of society, according to which the economic, political, and cultural spheres ought to be structurally independent, Beuys devoted himself to the revitalization of the cultural sphere. Arguing that private capital exercised excessive influence in the West, while the political state had too much power in the East, Beuys suggested that "The only way out is by starting from human creativity." He urged ordinary people to think of their social experiments as a form of sculpture, and this notion of "social sculpture" is still used by anthroposophically inspired activists in many contexts.[46]

Beuys's interpretation of threefolding resonated with the non-Marxist radicalism of the New Left. Whereas some earlier interpreters of Steiner's economics (notably Ralph Courtney in the United States) had stressed his critique of state-sponsored enterprises and aligned themselves with libertarianism, Beuys deployed stridently anticapitalist rhetoric. In a 1984 dialogue staged with mainstream and alternative economists, Beuys declared that the three principles "responsible for making the whole of society sick" were *"Wage dependency, private ownership of the means of production, and profit as the driving force."* The antidote was not a command economy but the reconfiguration of money as *"a regulator of rights for all creative processes."* Beuys's idea was that every person should be guaranteed enough income to lead a comfortable life, and that capital should be made available, through a democratic process, to any individual with a creative idea.[47]

There was a political movement ready to follow this path: the German Green Party, which was founded in 1980. Beuys was not the only prominent anthroposophist among the party's founders. Otto Schily, who was raised in an anthroposophical family, and who gained fame as the defense lawyer for members of the left-wing Red Army Faction, was both a party founder and one of the first Green members of Parliament, though he subsequently changed his affiliation to the Social Democrats. To this day, the Green Party enjoys strong support in those regions of Germany where the Anthroposophical Society is strongest.

THE BABY BOOMERS MEET ANTHROPOSOPHY

The expansion of anthroposophical initiatives in the 1970s was the work not only of open-minded evangelists and idiosyncratic translators but also of a new generation of idealists. Baby Boomers found their way to anthroposophy as part of a search for both spiritual and political alternatives. As a "result of the 1968 movement," explained one Baby Boomer, who is now a leader in the Anthroposophical Society, people of his generation became convinced that "The world can't just go on like it has traditionally. There should be new blood and new adventures coming around. That gave a huge new interest in something like anthroposophy."[48]

Initially, Baby Boomers were drawn to anthroposophy for the same reasons as previous generations. Some had had unusual spiritual experiences, or an intuitive sense that there was more to reality than the material world, and Steiner's writings offered a framework for explaining what they already experienced as true. This was the case for biodynamic gardener Sherry Wildfeuer, who spent time at Camphill Beaver Run and at Spring Valley before serving as a Chadwick apprentice. Raised in a Jewish community, whose faith she couldn't connect to her own experience, she was introduced to anthroposophy by a fellow student (also a future leader in biodynamics) during her first year of college. It changed her attitude to learning: "Before that I had been an A student and just giving it back as I knew what they wanted. Now I wanted to know what is true." Her professors did not seem to share her zeal for truth, so she moved on to Camphill. There she met her first biodynamic mentor, a seventy-eight-year-old woman who needed a helper to carry her basket "because she grew zucchinis like cudgels." Following the older gardener, the young helper realized that "she saw more than I was seeing"—and the desire to cultivate a deeper level of spiritual perception led her to a garden training at Spring Valley, to Santa Cruz, and finally to the Goetheanum, where she was charged with replicating Maria Thun's experiments with planting and cosmic cycles. These experiences equipped Wildfeuer to begin editing the *Stella Natura* calendar from her base at Camphill Village Kimberton Hills.[49]

Increasingly, anthroposophy appealed to Baby Boomers as a method for integrating spiritual and political ideals. Camphiller Michael Babitch told me that as a Wayne State student in the late 1960s, he had been a "flaming liberal" and an active leader in the movement against the Vietnam War. He attended an anthroposophical youth conference in 1970 because a high school friend was becoming more interested in anthroposophy, and he "was very impressed with who she had become since high school." The conference brought together hundreds of young people, as well as representatives of the recently reunited anthroposophical factions, who were just beginning to speak openly to one another. Unconsciously impressed by the spiritual work that was being accomplished, Babitch began "assiduously reading and studying" anthroposophy while he launched his social work career. He incorporated Steiner's ideas into his professional work whenever possible, finding it "a good discipline to have to translate jargon into other concepts." When he and his family finally made their way to an anthroposophical initiative, they committed themselves to building bridges between it and the larger society.[50]

Other Baby Boomers came to anthroposophy only after experimenting with other, less practical, spiritualities. John Bloom, who has participated in biodynamic agriculture and anthroposophical banking, told me that in the 1960s and 1970s his interests included Sufism and the teachings of Gurdjieff and Ouspensky. When he encountered Waldorf schools, he noticed a striking difference. The other traditions offered "tools for self-development, but they don't really help you be in the world." Steiner, on the other hand, offered not just ideas about education, but an entire curriculum. "From my perspective, it was very, very practical."[51]

Another biodynamic farmer told me that his childhood fascination with the paranormal led him to Transcendental Meditation. Because of his father's early death, John Peterson managed the family farm while in college, and he found the practice of farming to be meditative in a different sense. "I had a lot of row crops. I was on the tractor back and forth all day, long week after week, so it was kind of a meditative time when my mind would be free to ponder these things." These formative experiences remained with him when he encountered anthroposophy twenty years later. Steiner offered a link between meditation and farming, as well as "a very concrete, scientific context" that revealed the "capacity to develop our senses. So that we could actually see or experience behind the veil."[52]

Thousands of miles away, Swedish hippies started Mother Earth Farm in 1966 to demonstrate that the "industrialization of human society wasn't the only way." Convinced that healthy food should be free for everyone, they fed crowds of twenty thousand people at antinuclear demonstrations. They also drew broadly on "Oriental religion and philosophies." One of them, Lincoln Geiger, was the child of American artists, who had moved to a Swedish village. He was fascinated by folk traditions about gnomes, elves, and other elemental beings. When he encountered biodynamic ideas, as part of his search for appropriate farming techniques for Mother Earth, "A lot of bells or chimes inside me resonated with their philosophy, their spiritual ideas about reincarnation, about the elemental beings and the hierarchies." Since these chimes did not sound for his fellow communards, Geiger left Mother Earth in 1979 and joined the web of anthroposophical initiatives surrounding High Mowing Waldorf School in southern New Hampshire.[53]

By 1980, many Baby Boomers were coming to anthroposophy for reasons that might seem entirely practical. The director of one center for anthroposophical education told me that he helped found one Waldorf school in part because he hoped his children might be able to attend, and that he took his current job in order to be closer to a Waldorf high school that his son could attend.[54] Another Baby Boomer in a similar role told me that, although he had seen a copy of Steiner's *How to Know Higher Worlds* as a young adult (at a time when he was also reading such hippy favorites as Ram Dass and Steven and Ida Mae Gaskin), he did not investigate anthroposophy until 1984, when he was seeking a physician to attend the home birth of his first daughter. The doctor's intuitive attention earned his trust and convinced him to start teaching at the Waldorf school near the doctor's office. Both these leaders joke that their children led them to anthroposophy, though the latter shifted the credit one more generation, when he observed his granddaughter's zest for a close-to-nature lifestyle.[55]

Though people who first encountered anthroposophy as adults constitute the majority of participants, Baby Boomers raised in anthroposophical contexts have catalyzed the movement's transformation. Those born within the movement worry less about diverging from Steiner's explicit teachings because they carry an intuitive connection to Steiner's ideals. They tend to be impatient with impractical spiritual theories and with what they perceive to be sectarian tendencies. Veronika van Duin, a daughter of Camphill cofounder Barbara Lipsker, who has lived in Camphill communities her entire life, told me that she did not join the Anthroposophical Society until she was thirty-two because she didn't want to be part of a club. She has continued to push Camphill to break down the boundaries separating Camphill communities from the surrounding neighborhoods.[56]

Another bridge-builder told me that his commitment flows from his identity as a third-generation student of Rudolf Steiner. "There is something about going through multiple generations where you aren't so in love just with Rudolf Steiner's words. But you really are more wanting to say, how is it living in you as a person." For his grandparents, he explained, "Anthroposophy was study." When his father left a business career to work for an anthroposophical organization, his grandfather protested that "you can't make a living out of anthroposophy." Second-generation people like his father "really got into trying to implement a lot more practical things," while third-generation people like himself are "bridging those practical activities with others who are like-minded, and finding a language that goes beyond even anthroposophical jargon and really connects to a world awareness."[57]

These "born-inner" Baby Boomers exhibit a dynamic that Rudolf Steiner himself noticed in the early years of the movement. On one occasion, he told Ehnrefried Pfeiffer that "There were two types of people engaged in anthroposophical work: the older ones, who understood everything, but did nothing with it, and the younger ones, who understood only partially or not at all, but immediately put suggestions into practice."[58] If the impulse to move quickly to the practical sphere has been part of anthroposophy from the beginning, it has become the dominant feature since 1970.

NEW INITIATIVES FOR A NEW ERA

This practical ethos characterizes anthroposophical initiatives founded in 1970 and thereafter. The Hawthorne Valley Association is a conglomerate of initiatives that includes a Waldorf school, a four-hundred-acre biodynamic farm, a center for adult education and Waldorf teacher training, a publishing house, an art school, a theater, a research center on the threefold society, and another research center devoted to "farmscape ecology." Hawthorne Valley was launched in 1972 by Waldorf teachers and biodynamic farmers, who hoped anthroposophy could address the social and agricultural crises of the time.[59] In conversations that began in the mid-1960s, they noted that urban children were being alienated "from the living organism of the earth," and asked how many of their students "have a chance to come in touch more closely with field and garden?" They learned that some Waldorf schools in Germany had begun requiring students between the ages of 12 and 15 to spend four weeks each summer as "farm helpers" in a nearby rural area. A few schools maintained their own small farms.[60]

Founder Karl Ege, who'd been chosen by Rudolf Steiner to teach at the original Waldorf school nearly half a century earlier, articulated the vision in a 1965 essay on "An Evident Need of Our Times." The goal was to defend Steiner's original vision for "nurtur[ing] the human being *as a whole*" and to resist the broader culture's "one-sided" emphasis on "schooling for specialized scientific and more abstract intellectual studies." The "evident need" was for a farm-based school that would "kindl[e the student's] inner powers of feeling and of will through artistic activity and practical work with his hands." Such a school would give "the children a fuller, more direct relationship to life as a living whole."[61] At the time, Ege gave no indication that he saw people from beyond anthroposophy who shared this vision.

When the school opened seven years later, Ege expressed a new confidence that anthroposophical initiatives could "serve what is striving today to break through to the surface out of the depths of the process of historical evolution." Alluding to radical "cries ... for revolution," Ege insisted that the new school would not simply be "a repetition of the existing form of the usual Waldorf Schools" but would be a true community including "teachers, farmers, gardeners, artists, craftsmen and other workers, together with the pupils, of course." This aspiration was shaped in part by the Camphill movement of intentional communities, and Ege anticipated that coworker children from the new Camphill village in nearby Copake, New York, would be part of his student body. Expanding the biodynamic concept of the farm as a living organism, Ege promised that his farm school would be a true "organism of body, soul, and spirit," in which agricultural activities would provide a physical body and artistic activities would "complete the circulation." By planting "the seed of a living organism," Ege hoped to fulfill the "deep longing for true community" among young people in the 1970s.[62]

Hawthorne Valley, like Emerson College in England, became a place where community-seeking young adults could find mentors who had known Steiner personally. In 1950, Ege had married his longtime friend Arvia MacKaye, cementing a tie to Henry Barnes's bridge-building work as Anthroposophical Society general secretary. With Camphill Copake, Hawthorne Valley anchored a proliferating network of initiatives that stretched across the state line into Massachusetts's Berkshire Mountains; arguably, this area has become the most important region for anthroposophy in the United States. Two initiatives related to Hawthorne Valley illustrate its ethos.

The Nature Institute, which seeks to "view nature, science, and technology in context" by cultivating Goethean practice, was founded in 1998 by Hawthorne Valley teachers Craig and Henrike Holdrege. Its educational work focuses on empowering people (including Waldorf teachers and biodynamic apprentices) to conduct Goethean research by cultivating their individual powers of observation. Much of this work takes the form of week-long intensive courses in which participants spend much of their time immersed in ecosystems, observing and drawing natural phenomena but also observing their own "thought processes" and "how we form judgments about the world." Like most anthroposophical courses, they integrate artistic practices, underscoring the movement's reluctance to draw boundaries between science and art.[63]

The Nature Institute's leaders are active Goethean researchers. Craig Holdrege's short book *The Giraffe's Long Neck: From Evolutionary Fable to Whole Organism* offers a holistic revision of the standard Darwinian account of evolution. It is not helpful, Holdrege argues, to explain evolution by isolating causal mechanisms (such as the early giraffes' need to reach high-hanging leaves); a better approach explores the way an entire organism comes to embody a specific form. Holdrege's book *Thinking Like a Plant* similarly illustrates practical Goethean techniques, as it argues that plants can teach human beings how to live "rooted in the world."[64] Though Holdrege identifies as a scientist and not an activist, he has collaborated with the institute's senior researcher Stephen Talbott on critiques of agricultural biotechnology, including *Beyond Biotechnology: The Barren Promise of Genetic Engineering*, published in 2008 by the University of Kentucky Press. This work draws on conventional research at the same time that it portrays genetic engineering as a troubling fruit of an insufficiently holistic science. Attempts to develop a nutritionally enhanced "golden rice," for example, ignore the

cultural traditions that might lead hungry people to resist new foods—
and that have, in the past, achieved similar nutritional goals by cultivating rice alongside cultivated and wild greens, grains, and legumes.
"Golden rice," Holdrege and Talbott conclude, "can be seen in part as a
one-dimensional attempt to 'fix' a problem created by the Green Revolution.... But the fix offers no direct help to those who have been displaced by the revolution and who cannot buy the food they need."[65]
Arguments of this sort link the anthroposophical community to post-
colonial activists such as Vandana Shiva.

Down the road, Hawthorne Valley's Farmscape Ecology Program
"foster[s] informed, active compassion for the ecological and cultural
landscape of Columbia County, NY, through participatory research
and outreach."[66] It was created by botanist Claudia Knab-Vispo and
wildlife ecologist Conrad Vispo, who had done fieldwork in Venezuela
before moving closer to Conrad's family in Columbia County. Conrad
took a job in Hawthorne Valley Farm Store, where he caught the attention of association leaders, who realized he had more to offer than
stocking shelves. He and Claudia founded the program to fill a gap in
the academic practice of ecology: though much of the world's surface is
devoted to agriculture, ecologists are more likely to study wilderness
than farmland. Recognizing that humans are integral to farm ecosystems, Claudia and Conrad rounded out their team with social anthro-
pologist Anna Duhon. Together they explore a wide array of interconnections within a small region, with research methods ranging from
beetle counting to interviewing local residents about their "special
places." They are preparing a comprehensive "Ecological and Cultural
Field Guide to the Habitats of Columbia County, NY," which they
hope will inspire other ecologists to notice cultural and agricultural
elements. Other projects include a New Farmer Narrative Project,
focusing on the biographies of the young farmers getting started in the
area.[67]

There is an obvious affinity between the Farmscape Ecology Program and anthroposophy's emphasis on the human role within nature.

Yet none of the three researchers identify personally with anthroposophy, and they rarely read Steiner or Goethe. They are best described as
"allies," not "translators," and yet they are cherished members of the
staff of a prominent anthroposophical initiative. For them, the link is
personal: they have consistently felt affirmed by colleagues at Hawthorne Valley who *are* students of Steiner. The most important commo-
nality between their work and that of their colleagues, Conrad
explained, was an "experiential" emphasis on "what is in front of you."
They also appreciate Hawthorne Valley's holistic structure. They have
been allowed to constitute themselves as a "triumvirate," with no one
individual serving as director. Anna, who represents them on the central governing body of Hawthorne Valley, mentioned that she has
appreciated the open engagement with spirituality in planning meetings. "You can just talk at a level ... that is sharing a language of meaning and value that is extremely deep."[68]

As the Nature Institute and the Farmscape Ecology Program illustrate, the link between anthroposophy and environmentalism extends
beyond biodynamics. Another ecological topic that has interested students of Steiner in recent decades is water. Steiner's instructions regarding the biodynamic preparations emphasized stirring technique, and this
led his students to explore ways in which water might be a mediator of
the etheric and astral forces associated with living processes. In 1962,
Theodor Schwenk published *Sensitive Chaos,* a Goethean interpretation of
water that responded to the troubling fact that "Humanity has not only
lost touch with the spiritual nature of water, but is now in danger of losing its very physical substance."[69] Schwenk's Institute for Flow Sciences,
which gained the support of such environmental luminaries as Jacques
Cousteau, explored water's rhythmic patterns and its unique relationship
to living beings. "Water does not have the characteristics of the living,"
Schwenk declared, "but without water there is no life." He explained this
paradox in terms of water's self-renunciation: "by renouncing every life of
its own it becomes the primal substance for all life."[70]

Researchers at the institute strove to develop practical applications from this insight, and in 1970 John Wilkes introduced the "flow form," a beautiful, shell-like object that generates rhythmic patterns when placed in a stream. According to Wilkes, these patterns are both beautiful and purifying; one admirer told me that in a flow form the "elemental being of water becomes happy."[71] Flow forms are often integrated into garden irrigation systems or biological water purification systems, where they increase the aeration needed for biological processes to work. Their use is by no means restricted to specifically anthroposophical contexts: I have seen them in the garden at the Esalen Institute in California, an important center of the human potential movement, and at Tamera Ecovillage in Portugal, an intentional community with roots in psychoanalysis and free sexuality.

One American center for anthroposophical water work is the Water Research Institute in Blue Hill, Maine. Founder Jennifer Greene has roots in anthroposophy and American environmentalism: she attended a Waldorf school as a teenager, and her father was a Vermont politician who sponsored early conservation measures. She picked up her first copy of *Sensitive Chaos* ("still held together by duct tape") as a college student in 1965 and met Marjorie Spock three years later.[72] After studying with Schwenk, she introduced the flow form and the Drop Picture Method of testing water quality (a Goethean technique involving close observation) to the United States. She has also built bridges to mainstream environmentalism. In the wake of the passage of the Clean Water Act in 1972, she worked for municipalities developing water treatment plants, including the use of reed beds for biological purification. Her consistent message has been that it is not enough to deal with water problems, such as pollution; one must begin with a deeper consciousness of the "positive qualities" of water, especially its role as the "midwife of life." Since 1991, the Water Research Institute has conducted research and offered workshops to help Waldorf students, biodynamic apprentices, and others cultivate water consciousness.[73]

BUILDING BRIDGES TO A NEW CENTURY

While Schwenkian water research remains connected to the network of anthroposophical initiatives, other environmental organizations begun within that network have since moved into the broader world. A good example is *Orion,* a journal of environmental writing that works "to inform, inspire, and engage individuals and grassroots organizations in becoming a significant cultural force for healing nature and community."[74] *Orion* sprouted from the Myrin Institute, created in 1953 by the anthroposophical physician Franz Winkler, with financial support from Alarik and Mabel Pew Myrin, and with the enthusiastic backing of Sylvester Morey, who was then serving as general secretary of the American Anthroposophical Society.[75] The institute's founding mission was to seek "a genuine reconciliation of the modern scientific attitude with a spiritual world concept" and to "open the way for a philosophy of human freedom which is the safest protection against destructive ideologies and our only valid hope for lasting peace."[76] With such phrases as "philosophy of human freedom," this mission was clearly inspired by Steiner, but it did not mention him explicitly. In a letter explaining his decision to resign as general secretary and devote much of his time to the institute, Morey clarified why: "Its purpose is not so much to speak of Anthroposophy, but to remove the obstacles which litter the path which leads to it.... It wants to reach also those circles who are either unwilling or unable to accept certain peculiarities which characterize every occult society. To this end we must show that we understand the language of the world."[77]

The Myrin Institute thus hoped to institutionalize the translation work that Lord Northbourne had epitomized when he coined the term *organic* to express ideals he had learned from biodynamics. Its programming brought anthroposophical thinkers together with sympathetic outsiders. In the early years, the institute's *Proceedings* focused on educational topics (one issue centered on conservative intellectual Russell Kirk's proposal for university reform) and the dialogue between science and spirituality. In the early 1960s, successive *Proceedings* focused on American Indians (edited by Morey) and on "the racial question" (edited by Laurens van der Post, a white South African novelist and frequent ally of anthroposophy, who was critical of apartheid but inclined to romanticize African indigenous communities). In the 1970s, the institute turned its attention to environmental issues, publishing *The Secret of Peace and the Environmental Crisis* in 1971, followed by issues edited by Wendell Berry and Jacques Cousteau. In 1982, a new publication, *Orion Nature Quarterly*, was devoted to the exploration of the ways "man is linked inseparably to the earth and all other forms of life."[78]

Orion Nature Quarterly initially retained ties to anthroposophy, yet mostly published authors without such ties. The founding editor, George K. Russell, chaired the board of the Garden City Waldorf School; the editorial board included two sons of Anthroposophical Society treasurer Alfred Barten. The first issue opened with a speech by Laurens van der Post that moved subtly from the anthroposophical emphasis on the spiritual uniqueness of humanity to an ethic of reverence for all life forms. Western man, van der Post began, is "in search of a self … that honors both an external world and an internal one…. It is this element of becoming a more fully aware expression of all the life that has ever been … that gives man his dynamic and his greatest value." He then contrasted modern humanity with "the descendants of the first people of the world—the bushmen who still live in the natural surroundings of the desert," suggesting that "the man in the desert as I know him feels that wherever he goes he is known, wherever he goes he belongs." After recounting an indigenous folktale about a man who becomes one with a lion, van der Post exhorted his readers to reject "materialistic, industrialized life" and instead "live in partnership with nature." "In the beginning," he promised, "we were much nearer to the animals than we are now. A state of communion existed between us."[79] The articles that followed offered similar advice: one urged "restoration of nature" as the antidote to urban violence;[80] another featured the animal rights movement;[81] and the book reviews explored animal intelligence and mourned for "vanished species." The animal-loving, earth-centered tone continued in subsequent issues, which featured only a handful of identifiably anthroposophical authors.

Orion's approach to ecology gradually diverged from that of anthroposophy. While Steiner counseled his students to build bridges between modern science and ancient wisdom, *Orion* authors challenged modernity. And while Steiner offered a lofty view of humanity as qualitatively different from animals, they urged us to break down the boundaries between species. Once again, among the seemingly more "mainstream" environmentalists, the ones who were most willing to ally with anthroposophy actually held worldviews that were more radically antimodern or earth centered than those held by Steiner himself. But this was only a seeming paradox, since the balancing of polarities is an anthroposophical value. If anthroposophy, taken in itself, tends toward anthropocentrism, it is fitting for it to counterbalance that tendency by reaching out to critics of anthropocentrism.

Orion is not the only magazine occupying the middle space between anthroposophy and the larger culture of environmentalism. The *Utne Reader*, a digest of previously published articles on "personal growth and social change," has evolved in a direction opposite to that of *Orion*. It began in 1984 with little explicit connection to anthroposophy: founder Eric Utne was a spiritual seeker, who had trained in Chinese medicine and visited Findhorn before turning his attention to journalism. But Utne was also a Waldorf parent. When he discovered that he "needed to get out of the magazine" in order "to save my own soul," training as a Waldorf teacher was a logical next step. He characterized Waldorf education as a bridge between social activism (he noted the role of Waldorf teachers in the creation of the Green Party) and the "soul work" of education.[82] Three years later, *Utne* produced a special supplement, *An Emerging Culture*, to introduce its readership to Steiner-inspired initiatives.[83]

Lilipoh, founded in 1995 by Camphiller Claus Sproll, links anthroposophical initiatives to current conversations in American society. The title, a whimsical acronym for "life, liberty, and the pursuit of happiness," expresses its aspiration to connect Steiner's spiritual vision to American ideals. In keeping with Steiner's admonition to pay attention to spiritual impulses that are seeking to incarnate in the world, Claus Sproll has described *Lilipoh*'s work as "witnessing an emerging new consciousness," and among the signs of this consciousness he lists "the sharing economy ... the way we look at human sexuality beyond stereotypes based on gender ... the recognition that work and income have to be separated ... the willingness of different cultures and languages and religions to explore a greater understanding of each other ... viewing the earth's resources and climate as a basis for all human existence ... [and] a new culture of dying in which death is not seen as an end but a transition."[84] In most issues, about half of the articles focus on the work of specific anthroposophical initiatives and half apply anthroposophical principles to issues ranging from racism to vaccines to transgender identity. Within this mix, environmental issues stand out as first among equals. Nearly every issue has at least one article on biodynamics, and the pages are filled with advertisements for sustainable products and services.

The same can be said for the British *New View*, which was launched just one year after *Lilipoh*. The first issue described itself ecologically as "a flexible thought-form in plant fibre and pigment."[85] Though its mission was to "to sketch the broad range of anthroposophically inspired activities," it made clear that this could best be done in partnership: thus, the first issue announced a "Planet Tree Music Festival" held jointly with Greenpeace and Friends of the Earth as well as an "Earth Saver Account" offered by Friends of the Earth and the anthroposophical bank, Triodos.

One author who has appeared in most if not all of the journals just listed is the physicist Arthur Zajonc, who served as general secretary of the Anthroposophical Society in the United States from 1995 to 2002. In his academic work, Zajonc bridged mainstream physics to Goethe's phenomenological approach to light, and he has also been interested in the scientific foundations of meditative practice. During his term as general secretary, he conducted dialogues with the Dalai Lama on this theme, and since then he has worked with a series of spiritually eclectic but Buddhist-tinged organizations: the Fetzer Institute, the Center for Contemplative Mind in Society, and most recently the Mind and Life Institute. In many ways a translator like Trevelyan, Chadwick, and Beuys, Zajonc has received more direct support from the anthroposophical movement than they did, effectively abolishing the distinction between the "evangelist" and the "translator."

The same can be said for Ha Vinh Tho, a Zen teacher in the tradition of Thich Nhat Hanh and the founder of the Camphill-inspired Peaceful Bamboo Family in Vietnam. Ha Vinh got his Camphill start in Switzerland but gave the work a Buddhist flavor when he brought it back to Vietnam. After a stint with the Red Cross, Ha Vinh became the program development coordinator of Bhutan's Gross National Happiness Centre. This government-sponsored initiative is one of the best known attempts to replace the gross national product as a measure of national success. Rooted in the Buddhist philosophy of the Bhutanese royal family, its vision has affinities with Rudolf Steiner's vision of a threefold society. One fruit of this philosophy has been Bhutan's decision, announced in 2011, to work toward an entirely organic agricultural system.

Ha Vinh Tho's anthroposophically informed practice of Buddhism runs parallel to the work of Ibrahim Abouleish, who has built a biodynamic network called SEKEM in the Islamic context of his native Egypt. Abouleish first encountered anthroposophy while studying pharmacology in Austria, and after launching a career there he felt inspired to return home and devote himself to anthroposophically inspired development work. He told the woman who had introduced him to anthroposophy that "For my soul Austria was like a spiritual childhood garden. I hope that the souls of Egyptian people can be revitalized by a garden in the desert. After establishing a farm as a healthy physical basis for soul and spiritual development, I will set up further things, following the example of human development: a kindergarten, a school, a vocational school, a hospital and various cultural institutions."

Launched in 1977, SEKEM has realized this vision. Centered on its own biodynamic garden, it has helped hundreds of small farmers switch to organic production, and it partners with many of them in fair trade marketing. The SEKEM Development Foundation runs a network of Waldorf-inspired schools, ranging from a kindergarten to the Heliopolis University for Sustainable Development, launched in 2012.[86]

Early on, SEKEM faced criticism from a local journalist, who claimed participants were "sun-worshippers"—a charge that may have reflected the name SEKEM (an ancient Egyptian word for "vitality from the sun") or the anthroposophical view of the Christ being closely associated with the sun. Abouleish responded by inviting neighboring community leaders to visit SEKEM and explained biodynamics in Islamic terms: "I spoke about biodynamic farming, about the composting process and its preparations and described how the earth was enlivened through them. I explained how we wait for specific star constellations before planting and are thus inspired by Allah to act correctly. Then I led the discussion towards the arrogance of science, which states that it is only physical substances which allow the plants to grow, and not Allah." When a few listeners remained unconvinced, he turned to a close reading of the Quranic sura in which Muhammed receives instructions about the times of day for prayer. These times, he explained, corresponded to the phases of a plant's daily glucose cycle. "The Prophet Muhammed," he concluded, "recommended we think about Allah and turn to the supersensory at these five times throughout the day." These words muted the criticism, at least to the extent that SEKEM has survived several violent political transitions in Egypt.[87]

Ibrahim Abouleish shared the 2003 Right Livelihood Award, sometimes referred to as the "Alternative Nobel," with another activist committed to blending anthroposophy with social and ecological justice.[88] Filipino environmentalist Nicanor Perlas cut his political teeth as an opponent of President Ferdinand Marcos's nuclear power policies, and after Marcos's fall he founded the Centre for Alternative Development Initiatives. From this base, he influenced the Aquino government's decision to abandon nuclear power, ban many pesticides, and invest in the semiorganic agricultural system known as Integrated Pest Management. A fierce critic of economic globalization, Perlas linked Steiner's theory of social threefolding to the emerging emphasis on "civil society" as a counterbalance to government and corporate power. In 2009, he ran for the presidency of the Philippines—probably the first candidate in the developing world to make threefolding the centerpiece of his campaign.[89]

One of Perlas's allies in the struggle against elite globalization has been the Israeli politician's son Jesaiah Ben-Aharon, founder in 1982 of Kibbutz Harduf. The only kibbutz with a connection to anthroposophy, Harduf hosts an organic vegetarian restaurant, Israel's oldest Waldorf school (founded in 1989), an anthroposophical clinic, and schools for eurythmy and other artistic forms emphasized by anthroposophy. Of the kibbutz's 600 residents, 150 are people with special needs, reflecting the anthroposophical concern with disability issues. In 2003, Ben-Aharon published *America's Global Responsibility*, a work that connected threefolding to the antiglobalization movement that emerged during the 1999 meeting of the World Trade Organization in Seattle. Ben-Aharon's argument generally echoed the views of the Seattle activists, with a few significant twists: he warned that it is dangerous to rely on the state as a bulwark against corporate power, and he called for a rapprochement between "social activist streams" and "consciousness streams."[90] More recently, Ben-Aharon has promoted the concept of "The Event" to describe humanity's next evolutionary step, characterized by the rise of an ecological, nonreductive science and by a cooperative and decentralized economy.

Americans who are curious about connections between anthroposophy and environmentalism in the developing world might do well to attend events sponsored by the Presencing Institute at the Massachusetts Institute of Technology. Founded by management consultant Otto Scharmer, who grew up on a biodynamic farm in Germany, the institute describes itself as "an awareness-based action-research community that creates social technologies, builds capacities, and generates holding spaces for profound social renewal." Just as Ibrahim Abouleish translated anthroposophical ideals into the idiom of Islamic piety, and Nicanor Perlas translated them into that of civil society activism, so Scharmer has adapted Steiner's threefold picture of thinking, feeling, and willing into an organizational theory that he calls "Theory U." This approach "proposes that the quality of the results that we create in any kind of social system is a function of the quality of awareness, attention, or consciousness that the participants in the system operate from." The process of achieving this higher awareness follows a six-step, U-shaped curve that descends from mind to heart to will and back up again.[91]

In his public presentation of Theory U, Scharmer acknowledges but does not dwell on its roots in Steiner's writings.[92] But he elaborated in one essay: "One of the first things my father, one of the pioneers of biodynamic farming in Germany, taught me, was that the living quality of the soil is the most important thing in agriculture." As a result, Scharmer portrays social fields as "the *grounding condition,* the living soil from which grows that which *later on* becomes visible to the eye. And just as every good farmer focuses all his attention on sustaining and enhancing the quality of the soil, every good organizational leader focuses all her attention on sustaining and enhancing the quality of the social field that she is responsible for."[93]

The Presencing Institute is Scharmer's attempt to cultivate a social field by bringing people and organizations with anthroposophical roots into dialogue with other social entrepreneurs and activists. A conference held in 2014 opened with a lesson in "mindfulness practice" offered by Arthur Zajonc, then featured presentations by the Business Alliance for Local Living Economies, antiracist activist Phil Thompson, immigration activist Sofia Campos, progressive economist Juliet Schor, and Oregon first lady Cylvia Hayes, a proponent of alternatives to gross national product. Scharmer's associate Peter Senge offered a reflection connecting the Tao Te Ching to the work of Vandana Shiva, arguing that we should not seek to control nature but to be in relationship with its mysteries. During the small group sessions, participants worked through an exercise in "social structure" inspired by Beuys, with the goal of physically embodying the ideals of "conscious consumption" and "strengthening our sources of health."

BIODYNAMIC BRIDGE-BUILDING

The work of the Presencing Institute illumines the breadth of anthroposophical environmentalism today. Biodynamic practices continue to give depth to anthroposophical engagement with environmentalism, and few students of Steiner have been as committed to spiritual bridge-building as biodynamic leaders. The Biodynamic Association in the United States, for example, has made bridge-building to the mainstream organics movement, and especially to the youthful and dynamic permaculture impulse, its highest priority. Biodynamic conferences routinely feature speakers from other spiritual traditions and from indigenous communities, such as (at the 2016 conference) Native American actor and storyteller Larry Littlebird and Bronx-rooted urban farmer Karen Washington. They also host preconference forums at organic conferences, allowing attendees to get a taste of biodynamics, or else to immerse themselves fully in it but still have time to participate in other sessions. "For many years most of the focus of our work was about publishing books about biodynamics and the journal, and we had our own conference," noted codirector Thea Maria Carlson. But with the "recent uptick in people's interest in biodynamics," they have "developed much more of a focus on biodynamic education and community building."[94]

Serious biodynamic farmers know that they have to keep current with research on organic methods, because—as Camphill farmer Andreas Schad put it—"Biodynamics by itself is not really going to do anything unless you've got a firm footing in organic management. You have to be able to cultivate the soil to bring it to a peak of fertility.... and then you can start building fertility on top of that through spiritual means." For him, developing that foundation means reading magazines like *Acres* and attending sustainable agriculture conferences.[95] Another farmer, who said that the writings of Wendell Berry had initially drawn him to farming, suggested that one bridge between biodynamics and other organic approaches is the sheer practicality of farming. "I'm not a fundamentalist," he explained. "I believe in doing what works at many different levels. When it comes to farming practices, if I use a particular prep and I see results, however I measure them, then that for me works." Paying attention to such subtle factors as the happiness of the farmworkers is also "part of biodynamics" for him, and he is pleased when he meets other biodynamic farmers "who are open minded enough to say, hey, we don't know what biodynamics are necessarily," especially in regions like North America that are far removed from Steiner's Europe.[96]

At the time of this writing, the permaculture movement initiated by Bill Mollison in 1978 is the most dynamic form of organics, and biodynamics practitioners are eager to connect to it. One challenge is that Mollison, much like Howard and Balfour and Rodale before him, has embraced a posture of neutrality about worldviews. This can feel like rigid materialism to some students of Steiner. "Bill Mollison specifically said your philosophy is your problem," explained a biodynamic farmer who is active in permaculture and regenerative agriculture. "That was just a sneaky way of saying, it isn't my philosophy."[97] Yet Mollison's neutrality has made the permaculture movement an appealing arena for the pagans of Earth Activist Training (initiated by Wiccan teacher Starhawk), the New Agers of Findhorn, and people with roots in indigenous and neoshamanic spiritualities.

Probably no one has thought more about the differences between biodynamics and permaculture than Jan Bang, whose quip that "permaculture is clever but biodynamics is wise" is often quoted by biodynamic farmers. Bang is an intentional community activist, who cofounded the Israeli Permaculture Association while living on a kibbutz, then encountered anthroposophy and biodynamics when he moved to Camphill Solborg in his native Norway in 2000. The teachings of Steiner provided "the missing spiritual ingredient" that "enriched my Permaculture and added another dimension to it," inspiring him to team up with Craig

Gibsone of Findhorn to write *Permaculture: A Spiritual Approach*. The account of biodynamics included in that book makes for a revealing contrast with the introductory texts produced by Pfeiffer and Koepf. While Pfeiffer and Koepf downplayed biodynamic spirituality in order to make it accessible, Bang and Gibsone identified "communicating with the elemental beings of the plants and the soil," and "cultivating the soil and the plants together with the cosmic rhythms," as the movement's first two defining themes. (They followed up with the farm organism ideal, the self-development of the farmer, and the production of food that is nutritious for both body and soul.) Their emphasis on the cosmic dimension of biodynamics reflected the fact that, by the early twenty-first century, New Age spirituality had pervaded the organics movement. Overall, their book contains more New Age than specifically anthroposophical elements, but it does identify Goethean observation and Schwenkian work with water as important resources for permaculture.[98]

Biodynamics and permaculture usually occupy distinct ecological niches, with few permaculture practitioners actually earning a living from farming. "In the UK [permaculture] is just back gardens," observed one biodynamic farmer I met there.[99] But this difference creates the potential for the two to learn from each other. When I asked one American biodynamics leader about permaculture, she said that she had completed a permaculture design course after her time at a biodynamic farm, "and I think both of them have the value of bringing this bigger picture." She then told me about the work of Mark Shepard, a Wisconsin farmer with biodynamic roots, who is now a leading proponent of "farm scale permaculture" in the United States and Africa.[100]

The highest priority for the biodynamics movement today is mentoring and empowering young farmers. Increasing numbers of well-educated idealists with no family history of farming are drawn to organics, even as most family farmers (organic and conventional) are at or near retirement age, with no clear succession plan. In principle, it should be possible to transfer farmland from the latter to the former group; in practice, many aging farmers have no retirement assets apart from their land, while young farmers lack the financial assets and breadth of experience necessary to purchase and manage entire farms. Since the 1970s, the biodynamics movement has addressed this dilemma through apprenticeship and training programs. These programs originated in direct response to the expansion of environmentalism, which caused biodynamic farms to be overwhelmed with the numbers of young idealists eager to live and learn with them—some intending to become farmers themselves, others motivated simply by a "deep longing for a humanised science." One of the latter was Sue Coppard, a London secretary who wished to re-create her childhood experiences by spending a weekend on a farm. She had recently learned of the organics movement, and reasoned that organic farmers might welcome a short-term volunteer. As it happened, it was the biodynamic movement that was organized enough to help her realize her dream: at Emerson College, vice principal John Davy (Rachel Carson's British champion) befriended Coppard and pressured the college's farm managers to invite her and three friends for a weekend. These "Working Weekends on Organic Farms" gradually evolved into "Worldwide Opportunities on Organic Farms," a global network that immerses volunteers in farm life in over fifty countries.[101] For many future farmers, WWOOFing is the precursor to a formal apprenticeship.

Early in the 1970s, Swiss biodynamic farmers created a four-year apprenticeship program featuring deep immersion in four farms, as well as training at the Goetheanum. One participant described the curriculum:

> We became aware of the fact that agriculture, as the primary production, and the farm as an organism, related to the fabric of nature, are the best possible points of departure towards a social and cultural renewal.... Our age calls for groups of people who will build something new. The farmer needs knowledge that goes beyond agricultural knowledge. This is why we were also offered talks on education, curative education, arts, medicine, etc. Today we must also learn all that farmers in former times still knew ... [and also] find a possibility of understanding life out of the consciousness

of our time. Thus we learn something about the Goethean method, which is otherwise known only from books and is hardly taught in the universities. Daily exercises make it possible to draw a bit closer to an experience of the etheric forces.[102]

Around the same time, West Germany's Demeter-certified farms acquired government certification to offer apprenticeship programs, allowing them to offer their apprentices a formal credential after the completion of their studies. The anthroposophical initiatives centered on Jarna, Sweden, began offering training courses around this time, as did Emerson College in England. In the United States, Heinz Grotzke used the occasion of the fiftieth anniversary of Steiner's Agriculture Course to urge the Biodynamic Association to emulate the Waldorf movement, with its structures for teacher training, by creating a "recognized training school for farmers and gardeners."[103]

That call led Hawthorne Valley to launch its apprenticeship program in 1976, long before apprenticeship programs were common on other organic farms. Initially, it attracted mostly Europeans with prior connections to anthroposophy, among them the man who currently manages the Hawthorne Valley farm. By the 1980s, most interns were American; today, most are American women.[104] Cohorts of about five interns spend two years immersed in farm activities and classroom learning. A two-week intensive course (also open to the public) introduces the interns to biodynamic principles. Similar courses are available at Rudolf Steiner College in California and at the Pfeiffer Center in Spring Valley, New York. Another course, called Farm Beginnings, presents the business dimension of farming. That curriculum is modeled on one created by the Land Stewardship Project in Minnesota, a nonanthroposophical organization. At Hawthorne Valley, anthroposophical principles inform the teaching in subtle, nonprescriptive ways. "One of the major drawbacks to young farmers succeeding," explained the founder of the program, "is that they don't understand that their farms are businesses and they don't understand that there are actual developmental laws at work when you take a new initiative on that is a business. The same kind of developmental laws in the growth of a plant or a human being or a social organism."[105] Hawthorne Valley interns also study Goethean science at the Nature Institute and farm ecology at the Farmscape Ecology Program.

In 1994, Hawthorne Valley joined with neighboring farms (including Roxbury Farm, another large biodynamic farm) to establish the Collaborative Regional Alliance for Farmer Training (CRAFT) in the Hudson Valley/Berkshires/Pioneer Valley. CRAFT's cross farm partnerships allow interns to experience dimensions of farming, such as dairying, beekeeping, or the use of draft animals, that may not be present at their home farm. One consequence is that young farmers with no previous exposure to biodynamics, or even those who consciously decided not to work on biodynamic farms, are introduced to biodynamic techniques during visits to biodynamic farms. Participants in biodynamic internships may also discover practices that are agriculturally and spiritually more eclectic than pure biodynamics.

I saw the fruit of this eclecticism when I visited the farm at the Abode of the Message, a Sufi spiritual community near Hawthorne Valley. The farmers are former Hawthorne Valley interns who mingle biodynamics and Sufi alchemy, even though they are not spiritually committed to either anthroposophy or Sufism. The centerpiece of their farming practice is the use of draft horses, a practice that is not especially widespread in the biodynamics movement but is one that allows them to honor Steiner's teaching about the importance of animals to farming while refraining, in keeping with the Abode's vegetarian ethos, from meat or dairy production.[106]

Such experiences are by no means limited to Columbia County, New York. Another biodynamic farm, Angelic Organics in Illinois, helped establish the second CRAFT in the Upper Midwest; by 2015, the CRAFT website listed a total of seventeen regional alliances.[107] More broadly, the Biodynamic Association oversees the North American Biodynamic Apprenticeship program, which includes two years of structured on-farm training, along with classroom study, at fifty mentor farms. When they have completed all their requirements, the apprentices receive a certificate and participate in a formal graduation at the annual North American Biodynamic Conference.[108] The structure and coordination enhance the experience of apprentices at isolated farms; without such support, many farms would not be able to have apprentices at all, as government regulations require a strong educational component to any apprenticeship. The host farmers are keenly aware of the advantages of a two-year program over a single summer. Only by participating in two distinct growing seasons, and gradually taking on direct responsibility for part of the farm, can an aspiring farmer gain the depth that is intrinsic to biodynamics. Of course, one farmer told me, apprentices often make mistakes when they are given responsibility—but "I tell every apprentice, the only difference between me and you is I've made more mistakes.... That's what experience is."[109]

In 2010, the Biodynamic Association launched the Biodynamic Initiative for the Next Generation, which fosters a wider network of aspiring young farmers, along with environmental activists and educators. BING's email list has more than twenty-four hundred subscribers, and BING meetups focused on conversation about the future of agriculture have attracted up to seventy-five people.[110] The North American BING also collaborates with BING Nordic, which offers three-year farm internships in Norway, Denmark, Sweden, and Finland, and together they are in the process of initiating a truly global network of young people entering farming.[111]

Internship programs cannot fully address the economic challenges facing young farmers. Many former interns still lack the funding to purchase their own farms; in addition, some have an ideological commitment to smallness that makes them reluctant to take on the challenge of managing ordinary-sized family farms. When I asked leaders of apprenticeship programs to tell me about their former apprentices, most mentioned people who do not make their living from farming, such as a veterinary student and an English teacher who maintains a "little homestead" on the side. (The leaders at Hawthorne Valley, who gave me these examples, added that about half their interns are still in farming, though they did not know how many of those were in situations that would be economically sustainable over a lifetime.)[112]

Hawthorne Valley itself offers an alternative economic model for farming: it is a large farm that is not privately owned but is subsumed within a nonprofit corporation. As such, it is free from the economic challenges of succession. It honors the biodynamic principle of diversity without expecting any individual farmer to master the full spectrum of crops and livestock. "If you do it yourself," explained one farmer, "it is almost overwhelmingly difficult to have a diverse farm that is somewhat sustainable." As a consequence, he predicted, "The family farm ... is [not] going to carry the future. The future is carried by consciously collaborating individuals on one farm that is very diverse."[113] Other prominent biodynamic farms, including Temple-Wilton Community Farm in New Hampshire and Angelic Organics in Illinois, began under private ownership and are now transitioning to nonprofit or cooperative ownership, while still providing for the retirement needs of the founders.

Practitioners of biodynamics are active in the land trust movement, in which nonprofit organizations purchase the development rights to farmland, protecting farmers from inflated land costs. In 2000, students of anthroposophy established the Yggdrasil Land Foundation in order to protect the Filigreen Farm in Mendocino County, California, and the Krusen Grass Farm in East Troy, Wisconsin. Both are leased to biodynamic practitioners; in the case of Filigreen, Yggdrasil made it possible for the land to change farmers while remaining biodynamic. The trust has since expanded to include four farms, totaling 340 acres.[114]

Filigreen also includes a vineyard, making it a participant in the most rapidly expanding segment of the biodynamic movement. The story of biodynamic wine begins around 1981, when former investment banker Nicolas Joly converted his family vineyard in France to biodynamic production. Almost simultaneously, Frey Vineyards in California became the first organically certified vineyard in the United States; its embrace of biodynamics in 1996 cemented the reputation of biodynamics as the leading edge of organic wine. Twenty years later, Demeter certifies about 450 vineyards worldwide. The view of the farm as a self-contained organism appeals to winemakers, who want to ensure that their product retains a distinctive local flavor—even though it may require them to shift some land to livestock grazing. But the connection is somewhat paradoxical, as Steiner described alcohol as "Ahrimanic" and warned that its consumption is inimical to spiritual evolution. Anthroposophical leaders resolve the conflict by stressing the freedom intrinsic to anthroposophy and the value of mediating between Ahrimanic and Luciferic extremes: thus, production and consumption of wine may be part of a healthy balance for some people. The Goetheanum remains alcohol-free, yet it recently sponsored a conference on biodynamic wine at an offsite location, allowing participants to sample their wares.[115]

Even as biodynamic practitioners embrace a panoply of new economic strategies, many insist that the key to farming's future is as much spiritual as economic. After Hawthorne Valley's Steffen Schneider said that the future of agriculture was on cooperative community farms, Rachel Schneider added that the future of such communities depends on the practice of mindfulness. Farmers might recognize that "We can't do it ourselves, we have to do it together," she explained, "but they are so independent minded that without some kind of mindfulness training, what happens is that they come to blows with one another.... In order to build farms that are large enough to make an impact, we have to work collaboratively. In order to do that, we really need some inner practice."[116]

This insight, along with the example of Otto Scharmer's Presencing Institute, has led Hawthorne Valley to create the Institute for Mindful Agriculture. This institute, which was still emerging at the time of this writing, combines outreach to other spiritual traditions with an attempt to reinvigorate what the founders see as an underdeveloped aspect of Steiner's teaching, namely, his view of "the farmer as a meditant." The Schneiders envision a "new kind of agriculture" with three characteristics: the use of mindfulness practice by individual farmers, collective awareness of the "multifunctionality" of agriculture, and an evolutionary ethos that affirms that it is "not sufficient ... to base your entire agricultural practice on a mimicking of nature." This combination of themes is characteristically anthroposophical. The founders can articulate the second point in terms that seem antimodern, emphasizing that traditional "cultures were also based on their agriculture, and their religions and their festivals and their celebrations were all based on a knowledge of the land." On this basis, they seek "global collaboration" with Eastern traditions and with "the children of these ancient cultures [who] are still holding parts of the old wisdom." But this is balanced by an evolutionary view of the farm as an "organism" that is capable of evolving spiritually, "the same as a person." On this basis, they place themselves in creative tension with Gaian ecologies that downplay humanity, insisting that "we can't leave ourselves out of this picture."[117]

Nearly twenty years into the twenty-first century, anthroposophical initiatives continue to be associated with the radical fringe of environmentalism. But it would be more accurate to place them at its spiritual center. Students of Steiner have welcomed the rise of spiritual Gaianism and of animal liberation, while continuing to insist on humanity's unique role in the earth's future. They have partnered with back-to-the-land hippies and communitarians but have refused to turn their backs on modernity. They have taken sides in the raging battle over genetically modified organisms and related forms of biotechnology but have also deepened their commitment to scientific research. Perhaps most significantly, as organic agriculture and other environmental movements have migrated from the political right to the political left, most people rooted in anthroposophy still practice a social idealism that cannot be fairly characterized as either "left" or "right." Nowhere is this more evident than in the recent revitalization of Steiner's economic ideals. That piece of the story deserves a chapter of its own.

Flowers

New Economies for Environmentalism

The most important way anthroposophy reaches beyond organic agriculture to touch the environmental movement as a whole is through banking and finance. Rudolf Steiner's ideas about economics and what he called "social threefolding" inspired the world's earliest ethical and ecological banks. These banks in turn played midwife at the birth of social finance institutions rooted in other spiritual traditions. Today, a wide spectrum of environmental initiatives, both for-profit and nonprofit, receive grants, loans, and investments from the GLS Bank in Germany, the Triodos Bank in the Netherlands and Great Britain, RSF Social Finance in the United States, and half a dozen other institutions inspired by anthroposophy. These institutions' commitment to financial transparency makes it easy to see who has been affected by their work. RSF's website, for example, includes a complete list of current loan recipients. Among them are DC Central Kitchen, a training program for unemployed adults that describes itself as "America's leader in reducing hunger with recycled food"; gDiapers, a producer of fully compostable diapers; Malibu Compost, a recently launched business that is the first to market biodynamic compost in the United States; and a few land trusts. The list also includes a Hindu ashram, a Buddhist meditation center, and around two dozen Waldorf schools.[1] Especially since the financial crisis of 2008, anthroposophical finance has experienced dramatic growth. At the end of 2014, RSF held more than $175 million in assets, while Triodos boasted over 700,000 members and a balance sheet topping 7 billion euros. The oldest of the anthroposophical banks, GLS in Germany, is about half the size of Triodos, with over 3 billion euros on its balance sheet.[2]

Anthroposophical finance does not merely provide environmental initiatives with money; it also holds them together through a dense network of relationships. This is because Steiner's ideas about finance do not begin with an explicitly ecological vision but rather with the idea that work with money should always involve the cultivation of human associations—hence the frequent use of "associative economics" as an umbrella term for Steiner's economic insights.[3] The economic sphere, Steiner believed, is the one in which human beings are most deeply interdependent. Purchases, loans, and gifts represent three distinct and important ways of being connected to other people. Because anthroposophical bankers consciously seek to keep people connected through their work with money, their work can be seen as the flower of anthroposophical ecology: the organ through which anthroposophy exchanges its pollen with environmental activists of many political and spiritual stripes.

Anthroposophical finance is also like a flower in that it emerged relatively late in the history of anthroposophy. This is ironic, since it builds on ideas that Steiner expressed early in his career, well before he organized the first Waldorf school and inaugurated biodynamic farming. In a sense, the historical unfolding of anthroposophical initiatives recapitulated Steiner's career in reverse. Steiner focused on education and agriculture in his final years because his earlier, ambitious effort to transform Central European politics and economics had failed. He concluded that people needed a different sort of education and a healthier source of nutrition before they could reconstruct society as a whole. And so it was that, fifty years later, people who were connected to anthroposophical schools and farms began rereading Steiner's neglected writings on economics and envisioning a new network of initiatives.

THE ROOTS OF THREEFOLDING

To understand Steiner's views on economics, one must grapple with his broader vision for "social threefolding." Like much of anthroposophy, threefolding is simultaneously descriptive and normative. It offers a way of observing how society functions right now and a vision for how it could become more balanced and healthy. (This vision assumes that it is better to foster evolutionary trends in society than to impose radical alternatives.) In a nutshell, the theory holds that economics, politics, and culture represent three distinct social spheres, each with its own inner processes. In keeping with the logic of correspondence that governs Steiner's entire system (and most other esoteric spiritualities), the three social spheres correspond to Steiner's tripartite anthropology of body (economics), soul (politics, or the "rights sphere"), and spirit (the spiritual and cultural sphere, which includes arts and education). They also correspond to the human functions of willing, feeling, and thinking; to the metabolic, rhythmic, and nervous organ systems; and to the threefold slogan of revolutionary France. For Steiner, the economic sphere is to be governed by "fraternal" cooperation, the rights sphere by perfect "equality," and the cultural sphere by absolute individual "liberty." Steiner saw the spheres as interdependent: the cultural sphere, for example, relies on free gifts drawn from surpluses generated by the economic sphere, while the rights sphere is responsible for giving each individual access to land and capital. He believed that society was healthiest when each sphere was structurally autonomous, and he warned against both the socialist tendency to allow the state to dominate economic life and what he saw as an Anglo-Saxon inclination to give economics priority over the other two spheres.

Steiner began developing social threefolding in an essay entitled "Spiritual Science and the Social Question," published in 1905 and 1906.[4] This piece, composed in the social milieu of the Theosophical Society, was a response to the rising socialist and labor movements of the early twentieth century. As an association of idealists devoted to "a Universal

Brotherhood of Humanity," Theosophy attracted educated, middle- and upper-class individuals who often sympathized with socialism. (Annie Besant, the president of the Theosophical Society during Steiner's membership, had previously been a leader in Britain's Fabian Society.) Theosophists aspired to maintain an active commitment to social betterment, guided not by the materialist premises of Marxism but by their conviction that all reality flows from spiritual sources.

Steiner encountered theosophy at almost the same time as he began lecturing on history and philosophy to the adult education college sponsored by the socialists of Berlin. During those years, he developed a strong sympathy for the aspirations of the working class, coupled with a distrust of the materialist philosophy of socialist leaders, and he felt a parallel ambivalence about many theosophists. When he set out to defend theosophy against critics who said it had nothing to say about the "social question," he began by faulting theosophists themselves for lending credence to such criticisms. He then turned to a question that has bedeviled social idealists of all stripes: do "the causes of the good and bad in social life" lie "in men themselves" or "in the conditions under which men live"? Steiner chose the utopian socialist Robert Owen rather than Karl Marx as a representative of the latter position. Owen, Steiner conceded, "was "incontestably one of the noblest of social reformers," but his approach did not go deeply enough. Since social conditions are created by human acts, true reform could be achieved only by rooting out "egoism," which required the inner spiritual transformation offered by theosophy.[5]

As the basis of this transformation, Steiner proposed "a fundamental social law": "In a community of human beings working together, the well-being of the community will be the greater, the less the individual claims for himself the proceeds of the work he has himself done; i.e. the more of these proceeds he makes over to his fellow workers, and the more his own requirements are satisfied not out of his own work done, but out of work done by the others." Contemporary society, Steiner went on, has some institutions that are consistent with this law (otherwise it would "fall to pieces at once") and others that violate it. Chief among the latter was the practice of paying individuals wages for their labor. He proposed the abolition of the wage system and the creation of "conditions under which each will, of his own inner, private impulse, do the work of the community." This phrasing was deliberately vague: Steiner was wary of any violation of individual freedom and believed that there could be no solution "that shall hold good for all time." But he was convinced that spiritual practice could empower each individual to enact the Fundamental Social Law "within his own sphere of action."[6]

"Spiritual Science and the Social Question" thus offered an intriguing path to economic justice. encourage individuals to find alternatives to wage labor that allow them to enact their desire to work for the well being of society as a whole. This is the vision of today's impulse toward "social entrepreneurship." But in the first decades of the twentieth century, Steiner's total rejection of *both* the capitalist wage system *and* Marxist materialism limited his prospects for gaining allies. This limitation became more obvious as Steiner elaborated his vision in the context of the First World War and the subsequent social and economic crisis in the defeated nations. Steiner spent the war years in Dornach, Switzerland, where individuals of many nationalities worked harmoniously to build the first Goetheanum. At the same time, his lectures on the spiritual mission of the German people implied a level of sympathy for the Central Powers, and he gained notoriety as a spiritual advisor to German general Helmuth von Moltke. At the war's end, another highly placed student of anthroposophy, German diplomat Otto von Lerchenfeld, invited Steiner to share his spiritual insights on how the Central European nations might reconstruct themselves and achieve lasting peace.

Steiner fleshed out his social vision in "An Appeal to the German Nation and to the Civilized World," which was signed by such intellectuals as Hermann Hesse. In the "Appeal," Steiner described Germany's defeat as a spiritual crisis: it had entered the "larger world arena without an essential direction or goal to justify its existence," and other nations had responded by destroying it. The only antidote was to abandon institutions "imbued with old thought patterns and habits," to attend to current evolutionary trends, and to create new institutions "permeat[ed] ... with full consciousness."[7] Subsequent publications fleshed out the details of a threefold social order. These contained less explicitly esoteric material than Steiner's other writings, and for a time they were widely circulated and translated. Many sympathizers saw threefolding as a viable middle path between Anglo-American capitalism and Russian communism. But both fascists and communists considered Steiner a dangerous rival, and their attacks soon led Steiner to rethink his choice to enter the political arena.

As Steiner's political prospects faded, he and his followers turned their attention to economics. In an October 1919 lecture in Dornach, Steiner spoke of the need to provide a secure economic basis for the spiritual impulses he hoped would flow from the Goetheanum. In that context, he proposed the creation of "something like a bank with the goal of serving commercial and spiritual initiatives whose goals and practices are aligned with an anthroposophic worldview." Emil Molt, the Stuttgart cigarette manufacturer, who also sponsored the first Waldorf school, stood up and proposed the creation of economic enterprises whose profits would support the Goetheanum.[8] Despite some hesitation expressed by Steiner, other members of the Anthroposophical Society took up this suggestion, creating a German stock company called The Coming Day (Der Kommende Tag) in March 1920, followed by its Swiss counterpart, the Futurum, a few months later. These companies included interrelated medical, pharmaceutical, and agricultural businesses, including the business known today as Weleda. By cooperating across industries, they hoped to avoid the inefficiencies associated with capitalist competition—but this made the entire network vulnerable to weaknesses within one or two of its constituent parts. Postwar Germany, which soon succumbed to hyperinflation, was not an auspicious environment for such ventures! Steiner's ambivalence did not help either: though he invested heavily in the projects, he found that business meetings did not fit comfortably with his spiritual research. Within a few

years, both ventures had failed, and Steiner and his wealthiest supporters suffered great losses. Steiner then shifted his attention to the more
basic activities of education, agriculture, and medicine, while his benefactors relied on more conventional business models to support their
donations.⁹ When Steiner reorganized the Anthroposophical Society, he
accepted the presidency on the condition "that these financial experiments in connection with all manner of industries, which have brought
us such bitter experiences in the past few years, shall not be repeated."¹⁰

The Coming Day and the Futurum struggled, in part because of an
ambiguity in their fundamental purpose. Did they exist primarily to
support anthroposophy by ensuring that the economic resources of
Steiner's students would remain within the anthroposophical network?
Or did they exist for the sake of the larger world, as the first fruits of a
new and improved social order? Either purpose could have contributed
to the evolution of anthroposophy; after all, some organisms find their
ecological niche by conserving resources for their own use while others
thrive by maximizing exchange with other organisms. Either purpose
was in harmony with aspects of Steiner's teaching: in the Agriculture
Course, he had described the healthy farm as a self-contained organism
that recycles all its own waste products, while in his lectures on World
Economy he had celebrated the capacity of free trade and the division
of labor to foster global interdependence. But Steiner seems not to have
known which path was appropriate at that moment, and he gave con-
flicting guidance to his supporters. (A similar ambivalence challenges
anthroposophically inspired economic activity even today, with ongoing debates over the relative values of purity and "scaling up." For the
most part, though, today's more fully evolved movement has supported
enterprises that choose both paths.)

Anthroposophical economics entered a long abeyance period after
Steiner's death. The educational and biodynamic impulses developed
gradually, despite significant disruptions during the Nazi period and as
a result of the spread of communism in Eastern Europe, but Anthroposophical Society leaders and major donors alike hesitated to embark on

significant economic experiments. As early as 1928, one leader raised the question of whether Steiner's hesitation may have reflected conditions that had now passed but concluded that the time was still not ripe: "If we go in for economic undertakings, to-day too in most cases we shall have to reckon that we are giving good money away, only to lose good money which we might have used directly for our good cause."[11] Many shared the attitude of an earnest study group participant, who advised his stepson not to leave a business career for a job at Threefold Community, on the grounds that "You can't make a living out of anthroposophy."[12] (The stepson, Siegfried Finser, disregarded the advice and eventually became the primary founder of RSF Social Finance.)

THE REBIRTH OF ANTHROPOSOPHICAL ECONOMICS

Nevertheless, some subtle foundations were laid by members of the Anthroposophical Society, who combined business careers with an active interest in Steiner's social theories. One such individual was Herbert Witzenmann, a student of both Steiner and Karl Jaspers, whose hope for an academic career was dashed when the Nazis forced Jaspers out of his faculty position. Witzenmann worked instead in his family's mechanical engineering business, then joined the executive council of the Anthroposophical Society in 1963. He led the Goetheanum's youth and social science sections through the late 1960s. This combination of roles positioned him to mentor a new generation of individuals who hoped to combine anthroposophical striving with business careers.[13]

Among these mentees were Peter Schnell, cofounder of Software AG, Germany's second-largest vendor of software, and Götz Werner, founder of Drogerie Markt, a German retailer with nearly three thousand stores and fifty thousand employees. Schnell launched his business in 1969, while Werner started his in 1973, and the different styles of the two organizations perhaps suggests the rapidly expanding vision of anthroposophical economics around 1970. Software AG, at least judging from the way it presents itself publicly, is a conventional business that informs potential customers that "The digital revolution creates disruptive new business opportunities" on which they might "capitalize with a solution from Software AG."[14] Schnell has served anthroposophy in a conventional way, by creating a foundation that gives grants to anthroposophical organizations and other entities serving causes related to anthroposophy, such as the environment and care for the disabled. It has attempted to endow chairs in anthroposophical medicine at major universities, a strategy that has created controversy. Drogerie Markt, by contrast, has cultivated a reputation as an alternative business, one that seeks to empower employees with flat hierarchies and "leadership through dialogue." It has enacted associative economics by partnering with Alnatura, a chain of organic supermarkets that was also founded by students of Rudolf Steiner. Götz Werner, who has earned a billion euros for himself along the way, is at the forefront of one of the first attempts to bring threefolding principles into the political sphere since 1920. He is a leading advocate of a state-funded universal basic income of about a thousand euros a month—a policy that would honor Steiner's wariness of wages by freeing individuals to work for the common good rather than for the sake of wages.[15]

The world's oldest anthroposophical bank was founded in 1974, one year after Drogerie Markt.[16] But the Gemeinschaftsbank für Leihen und Schenken ("community bank for loans and gifts," now known officially as GLS Gemeinschaftsbank) traces its roots back to 1956, when attorney Ernst Barkhoff (1916–94) was recruited to the executive council of a new Waldorf school in Germany's Ruhr region. Barkhoff was attracted to Waldorf education in part because he had a special needs child; the Waldorf school was attracted to Barkhoff because it needed a lawyer. It soon became clear that Barkhoff's true gift was for creative, community-based financial strategies. His first innovation was the "loan community" (*Leihgemeinschaft*): by establishing a cooperative organization, parents of limited financial means could gain access to bank credit that would otherwise be inaccessible to them. Such measures allowed the school to become the largest Waldorf school in the world. Local supporters then organized a teacher's training center and a student house at Bochum University. Barkhoff then lent his financial expertise to a circle of biodynamic farmers, some of whom were inspired by the student activism of 1968. They hoped to create "multi-functional" farms that would be engaged in community building and curative education as well as food production.[17]

Barkhoff's desire to create permanent institutions for community financing of anthroposophical initiatives was initially opposed by the German Association of Waldorf Schools, but the intervention of a few key allies allowed Barkhoff and his colleagues to organize a charitable trust in 1961 and eventually a full-fledged bank in 1974. GLS was, and continues to be, organized as a cooperative, under the democratic control of its members. Its goal was to facilitate the free flow of money and ideas; indeed, from Steiner's perspective, both money and ideas are aspects of what is commonly called "capital." Barkhoff proved to be a tireless evangelist of creative economic thinking, traveling throughout Europe and in the United States to share the GLS story and encourage others to start similar ventures. Back home, he inspired GLS employees to pool their incomes in a common fund, from which they would be able to draw resources for other people, but not for themselves individually. The idea was to cultivate an awareness of the needs of one's coworkers. This practical implementation of Steiner's Fundamental Social Law mirrored practices already well developed in Camphill.[18]

Barkhoff always encouraged people to adapt GLS's ideals to their own circumstances, rather than directly imitating its structures. Each finance institution that emerged in its wake adopted some distinctive strategies. While GLS was organized as a cooperative, the Triodos Bank in the Netherlands (founded in 1980) adopted a "guardian ownership" model, according to which a charitable foundation safeguards its mission and ideals. As one cofounder explained it, "anthroposophy always works through people," and this model appealed to the founding circle, many of whom had been students of Dutch anthroposophist

Bernard Lievegoed. The founders also cherished transparency. They wanted their economic activities to serve the awakening of consciousness, and to this end they published lists of all Triodos borrowers, so that depositors would know, and thus consciously share karmic responsibility for, how their money was working in the world. The founders were also lucky that the United Nations published "Our Common Future," its landmark statement on sustainable development, in 1987, just a few years after the bank was founded. This statement functioned as a sort of official endorsement of the founders' conviction that "economy and ecology ... can go hand in hand" and that "it makes long-term economic sense to pursue environmentally sound policies." Early on, they articulated a threefold commitment to "profit, people, and planet," placing equal stress on financial viability, environmental sustainability, and the well being of employees and customers.[19]

The notion that "anthroposophy always works through people" was also evident in the founding of what began as the Rudolf Steiner Foundation and is now RSF Social Finance. As treasurer of the Anthroposophical Society in America, Siegfried Finser participated in Ernst Barkhoff's American lecture tour, and was inspired by Barkhoff's exuberant presentations and his own seemingly miraculous capacity to translate them. Around the same time, his son Mark had the disconcerting experience of seeing his employer abruptly eliminate health insurance benefits. "Accidental, unplanned occurrences" brought them together with another Barkhoff fan, a Waldorf teacher curious about economic initiatives and a participant in a study group on Steiner's World Economy lectures, who was frustrated that the other members of the group were unwilling to move from study to action. The Finsers sympathized with this frustration and galvanized a new circle of coworkers into action.[20]

Just as the founders of GLS were startled by the initial opposition of the Association of Waldorf Schools, so too the Finsers were taken aback by the unwillingness of the Anthroposophical Society's leadership to invest in their vision. From Siegfried's perspective, the moment was propitious: the society, which had never held a significant endowment, had just sold its New York City headquarters for a million dollars. Siegfried hoped that the full proceeds would be invested in anthroposophical initiatives and ideals, and he was horrified by the typical structure of charitable foundations, which invest their capital "who-knows-where and for what purpose in the economy in order to provide a trickle of benefit to society."[21] But other leaders took the opposite position: as Mark Finser put it, their view was that "you basically have your conventional stock portfolio for retirement and reserves, and you pretend you are as poor as a church mouse, and then you move into a place of service for anthroposophy, but to bring the two together was kind of shocking."[22] The Finsers were, however, able to take over a tiny anthroposophical foundation that had been established in 1934. Although what they had in mind was not exactly a foundation (hence the later name change to RSF Social Finance), this allowed them to avoid the expense of fresh incorporation. They honored the fund's original purpose by donating its balance of six thousand dollars to an anthroposophical cancer research clinic in Switzerland and began moving forward.[23]

At just that moment, a fire destroyed the Pine Hill Waldorf School in Wilton, New Hampshire. As RSF's founders understand it, this concrete human need called forth the network of relationships at the heart of finance. "This wonderful work did not begin with the acquisition of money but with the recognition of a need and by facilitating the movement of money in the service of life." Parents and other school supporters asked GLS for financial advice and were referred to Siegfried Finser. RSF staffers were enchanted by the commitment of the parents, who were willing to make legally binding pledges to pay the full building cost, and they promised the school a $500,000 loan, even though they did not yet have any capital. Because RSF was not a bank, it could not lend money directly to the individual parents, as was the practice at GLS. So it created its own distinctive form: the "pledge community," in which the commitments of many individuals serve as collateral on a loan to a nonprofit organization or social enterprise. To fund the loan, the Finsers turned to another relationship—their long-term friendship with biodynamic gardener Polly Richards, who offered $200,000 from a family trust as RSF's founding investment.[24]

Though each anthroposophical bank has a distinct structure, all share a commitment to changing consciousness, to building relationships, to honoring the distinct and limited role that finance plays in the overall social ecology, and to partnering with nonanthroposophical endeavors. RSF articulates its approach to changing consciousness by declaring that its mission is to "transform the way the world works with money"—a statement that is ubiquitous in RSF publicity and falls easily from the lips of its leaders. RSF raises consciousness by publishing a blog called "Reimagine Money," by systematically surveying investors and borrowers about the way they have been changed by their association with RSF, and by sponsoring day-long conversations in which individuals of diverse backgrounds are invited to share and learn from one another's "money biographies." These conversations have engendered some of the most significant explorations of race and class that I have seen in the anthroposophical movement. In one conversation, RSF's director of organizational culture John Bloom told me, a "fairly well-to-do white person" was preaching about the need to consume and spend less, when another participant pointed out that many immigrants come to the United States in search of a better life and that "to tell them they shouldn't buy a gas-guzzling car, for example, fails to understand their hopes and expectations of opportunity."[25]

Consciousness raising flows from the testimonies of staff people like Siegfried Finser, whose book on economics is filled with autobiographical anecdotes, and John Bloom, who told me that economics never fully made sense to him until he encountered Rudolf Steiner's idea that gifts are as foundational as loans and purchases to an economic system. "Human life starts in gift," he explained. "As a baby, as a little child, our material needs, which is what economics is about, are met by our relationship to our mother[s].... We then receive that gift, it gives us strength to grow. We build capacities ... and then become productive in the world. So without gift, nothing starts."[26] Similarly, the Triodos journal, "The Color of Money," uses color coding to distinguish Steiner's three types of money.

Changing consciousness flows directly into the work of building relationships. One of RSF's "spiritual guidelines" holds that "helping clients become conscious of their interdependence creates a framework for building community." Another is that "Collateral in land and material assets is inferior to collateral in people and their strength of commitment."[27] As Mark Finser explains it, what RSF offers is *social* finance, not primarily because it has a positive effect on society as a whole, but because it knits its immediate constituency into a face-to-face community. One transformative practice is the rate-setting meeting, in which borrowers and lenders meet and listen to one another's stories, after which they advise RSF how to set interest rates.[28] The theme of relationship building also has a karmic dimension, as John Bloom pointed out. To be "embedded in a sea of transactions" is also "to be embedded in a sea of relationships." Just as dollar bills are covered with fingerprints, so each transaction carries the "after image" of the other people involved, whether we are conscious of it or not. "If I don't have a relationship ... money doesn't move."[29]

To honor those relationships means refusing to reduce any human being to an economic function. RSF's principle that "there is a difference between taking initiative and financing it" means that financial institutions should remain within their proper sphere, even as they respond to the initiatives of people with creative ideas. This reflects Steiner's understanding of the interdependence of the three social spheres, according to which new initiatives—even for businesses—originate from the cultural rather than the economic sphere. Practically, it means that anthroposophical banks resist making profit an end in itself. Early on, RSF's founders rebuffed schemes that might have helped them speed the accumulation of capital, insisting that their "motive would remain, for all time, to render service to those human beings of any religious, scientific, or artistic persuasion who were initiators of activity that benefited the advance of the human spirit."[30]

As RSF's vice president of organizational culture, John Bloom has developed a complex assessment system for RSF's work, which seeks to "tease out of all our activities the transformative effect we are having on our whole system." This involves extensive surveying of borrowers and investors, focusing on how they have been changed by rate-setting meetings. "It isn't really the interest rate question that is so exciting for people, though that is important," Bloom notes. "It is when they connect the dots, see that their money makes something possible for another entrepreneur," and realize that even a small rate increase could prevent an emerging business from doing something truly creative that the interdependence becomes real. RSF's assessment plan also includes attention to "field building"—the impact that their activities have on the emerging field of social finance and on the banking sector as a whole.[31]

ANTHROPOSOPHICAL FINANCE
AS BRIDGE-BUILDER

Though all the finance institutions began by funding Waldorf schools and biodynamic farms, all have achieved remarkable success in building bridges to nonanthroposophical initiatives. In part this is because the values of consciousness, community, and transparency, though traceable to Rudolf Steiner's teachings, can readily be expressed in publicly accessible language and in practical action. In part it was because many of the founders were determined to break out of what they saw as anthroposophy's sectarian tendencies. "In keeping with the spirit of the times," wrote Siegfried Finser, "we were not interested in working solely with those organizations devoted to the world impulse of Rudolf Steiner."[32] Even though RSF's original mission statement identified it as "an instrument of the anthroposophical society," its founders understood this not as a "power source" for the society but as an expression of anthroposophy's commitment to serving the world. Mark Finser recalls pushing hard to expand the mission beyond anthroposophical initiatives because he believed that those initiatives themselves could not thrive unless interaction with the world prodded them to ongoing evolution.[33]

In keeping with this spirit, GLS initiated an "international bankers' conference" in the 1980s. This brought together anthroposophical banks and nonbank financial institutions such as RSF, so they could learn from one another's innovative practices. GLS, for example, helped RSF create a collective risk pool, in which borrowers agree to pay a slightly higher interest rate should the default of another borrower threaten RSF's capital reserves. Muhammad Yunus, founder of Bangladesh's Grameen Bank, was an early presenter at these gatherings, and his presence helped many of the other banks incorporate microfinance and sustainable development into their portfolios.[34]

The work of the bankers' conference continues today in at least three distinct networks. The International Association of Investors in the Social Economy (organized in 1989) is an inclusive body that includes nonprofits and academic organizations as well as banks. The Global Alliance for Banking on Values (2008) is restricted to full-scale banks with assets over $100 million, and has included many institutions from beyond the anthroposophical movement, such as Crédit Coopératif, a French credit union founded in the nineteenth century; Chicago's now defunct Shorebank, a community development bank focused on affordable housing for urban neighborhoods; Bangladesh's BRAC and other innovative economic projects in the global south; and banks organized directly by the Green Party, such as the United Kingdom's Ecology Building Society and Germany's Ökobank. Finally, the Global Impact Investment Network (initiated in 2009 by the Rockefeller Foundation, with support from Triodos and Shorebank) links social finance institutions to mainstream banks and foundations. These networks serve as the public, international face of ethical and ecological banking, demonstrating that banking that serves "the triple bottom line of people, planet, and profits (or prosperity)" is as viable in Bolivia as in Germany—and in Canada, Mongolia, Peru, and half a dozen other countries.[35]

The partnerships fostered since the 1980s took on a deeper dimension at the turn of the twenty-first century, when Germany's Ökobank fell on hard times as a result of mismanagement and was unable to cover loan losses of eighteen million marks. Founded in 1988, Ökobank had grown rapidly—perhaps too rapidly—to become Germany's largest alternative bank, and it turned to the smaller but older GLS for a rescue. A mutually agreeable consolidation was worked out in 2003, and the fusion of Ökobank's 24,000 members with GLS's 12,000 accelerated the process by which GLS expanded beyond its anthroposophical base. GLS CEO Thomas Jorberg's role in the merger positioned him to offer ever-more creative support to environmental initiatives in Germany. These include a partnership between the city of Schonau and homeowners with solar panels, which allows the entire city to function as a power company producing its own electricity for sale.[36] Also in recent years, an academic center known as the Institute for Social Banking has been established in GLS's hometown of Bochum, Germany.[37]

In addition to partnering with other alternative banks, the anthroposophical banks have been keen to influence mainstream banking. Early in Triodos's history, one leader realized that it was difficult for sustainable enterprises to compete economically with businesses that externalized their costs onto the environment. So he worked with the Dutch finance ministry to create a set of tax exemptions that would level the playing field. Once this legislation passed through parliament, he received commendations from conventional bankers, who recognized that the tax exemptions were stimulating important new ventures. These bankers urged Triodos to stay independent and alternative. "You are small and you can go in the harbor with a small boat," they told one Triodos leader. "We are much too big for that. So please stay independent and play this triggering role."[38] Similarly, RSF was one of the first financial institutions in the United States to introduce donor-advised funds.[39] RSF actively tracks instances when mainstream banks embrace its "open source" intellectual property as part of its assessment of its "field-building role."[40]

The growth of anthroposophical social finance has accelerated in the wake of the economic crisis of 2008. RSF, which has maintained a default rate of less than 2 percent because of its community-building practices, responded proactively to the crisis by phoning individual investors to ensure that they still felt confidence in the organization.[41] Because GLS and Triodos are full-fledged banks, they attracted depositors who had become disgusted with the speculative behavior of conventional banks. Some observers have suggested that it is only since 2008 that anthroposophical banks and other social finance institutions have had sufficient size to function as "constituent parts of a new culture of finance."[42]

Such growth raises challenging questions about the relationship between anthroposophical banking and anthroposophy itself. All the organizations discussed in this chapter strive to make their work fully accessible to people from outside the anthroposophical movement. When RSF selected a new CEO, they chose someone who was new to anthroposophy. Mark Finser and John Bloom told me that they were the only long-time students of Steiner employed by RSF (though such persons still constitute a majority on the board, and several staff attended Waldorf schools). Even long-term Triodos employees are at times challenged to explain what the "Tri" in their name refers to.[43] The banks' efforts to embrace diversity have partly compromised their founding commitment to transparency, insofar as outsiders cannot readily discern their deep roots in anthroposophy. Neither GLS nor Triodos nor RSF mentions Rudolf Steiner or anthroposophy on the first page of its website. In the case of RSF, a single click brings the viewer to an "about us" that offers a straightforward explanation, but Triodos omits Steiner and anthroposophy on both its mission and history pages.[44] More generally, Bloom explained, the challenge is to balance spiritual "depth" with a capacity to "be out in the world." It wouldn't work to tell people they must have an inner spiritual path in order to get a loan or make an investment, but it is necessary for staffers to be "vulnerable," "mindful" and "compassionate about who they are standing in front of" when meeting each borrower or investor. "That's not scalable in the normal sense of seeking efficiencies."[45]

One way to strike the balance is to stress the importance of "spirituality" and inner work in general. A large portion of Triodos's lending goes to religious organizations, and the publicly available list is remarkably diverse, including the Union des Centres Culturels Islamiques in Belgium, the Abundant Life Full Gospel Church and other Pentecostal congregations in the United Kingdom, the British Federation of Synagogues, New Age organizations such as Findhorn and EnlightenNext, and a host of Buddhist meditation centers and yoga studios throughout western Europe.[46] RSF has used "spirit matters" as its tagline, and "Inspired by the work of Rudolf Steiner" appears on many documents. Mark Finser mentioned that he sometimes used the "spirit matters" slogan as a screen in job interviews, by asking applicants what comes to mind when they hear the word *spirit.* "It didn't have to be some big spiritual thing," he added. "It could literally be a spirit of work. Or someone gave a story of taking used glasses to Bali." Such testimonies were enough to reassure Finser that the candidate would bring something distinctive to the karmic community of the RSF staff group. To cultivate the diverse spiritualities of its staff, RSF offers regular artistic activities for employees and as part of its staff and board meetings. Asking "people to draw and do clay and observe ... and try to draw each other" can be "pretty scary if you are in finance." Yet these activities are among the RSF innovations that have been embraced by more mainstream institutions.[47]

In the midst of their rapid growth and struggle to balance depth and breadth, practitioners of anthroposophical finance remain committed to the vision of inner, individual transformation articulated by Rudolf Steiner. Mark Finser opened our conversation by describing RSF's mission and noting that while "it sounds very lofty," in practice it "happens one person at a time, one individual at a time. We can't transform how the world works with money if human beings don't go through their own transformation."[48] This is an essential clue to anthroposophy's role in the ecology of environmentalism. Even as anthroposophy repeatedly

gives birth to ideas or organizations that downplay their anthroposophical ties as they scale up, many individual participants in the movement
keep their own focus on practices and relationships that do not scale.
This ensures that even the best new ideas cannot turn the ecological
movement into a monoculture.

Currently, it would be difficult to count the number of innovations in
ecological economics that have roots in anthroposophy and the potential
to scale up dramatically. Many students of Rudolf Steiner have been
active in creating organizations that break down the traditional barrier
between "for-profit" and "nonprofit" organizations. RSF, itself a nonprofit
that began by giving loans exclusively to nonprofits, now has a complex
organizational structure consisting of eight or nine distinct corporations,
allowing them to lend to diverse entities, with about a 50/50 split between
for-profits and nonprofits. At first "it wasn't a piece of cake" to understand
how for-profit businesses think, and how to finance them effectively. But
RSF has embraced the concept of social entrepreneurship to the point
that they encourage their nonprofit borrowers to think of themselves as
social entrepreneurs as well. "Do you have a mission to do something
positive in the world?" John Bloom asks borrowers. "Well, then you are a
social entrepreneur."[49]

One vehicle for social entrepreneurship that RSF has supported is
the Business Alliance for Local Living Economies, created by Philadelphia restauranteur Judy Wicks in 2001. At that time, Wicks had eighteen
years of experience running the White Dog Café, a restaurant devoted
to local, organic food, living wages for its employees, and partnership
with local schools and community organizations. Wicks realized the
importance of partnership with like-minded entrepreneurs when she
found a local supplier of organic pork, who didn't have a refrigerated
truck to bring his product to her restaurant. She loaned him the money
for the truck, then realized they could have a greater impact by making
that truck available to additional partners. This network grew into the
Sustainable Business Alliance of Greater Philadelphia, and Wicks
dreamed of making similar support structures available across the

nation. When she presented her vision for such an association at a gathering sponsored by the Social Venture Network, Mark Finser was one of those who immediately approached her with an offer of financial support. He also joined the advisory board, alongside "new economy" icon David Korten. Today, notes Finser, BALLE has thousands of member businesses. "In some ways," he adds, "Steiner's idea of economic associations is what BALLE is doing." The relationship between BALLE and RSF became even closer when Don Schaffer, BALLE's second executive director, was recruited as the first CEO of RSF from beyond the anthroposophical movement.[50]

RSF also played a role in the creation of an innovative organization dedicated to developing new organizational forms that blur the for-profit/not-for-profit distinction. Founded in 2006, B Lab was the brain child of a group of entrepreneurs, who had sold their enterprise to a larger business and seen its "heart and soul ripped out." Mark Finser heard them speak at a gathering of "angel investors" and thought, "Wow, this is like Steiner downloading some organic threefold ideas." Shortly thereafter, he was asked to join their founding board. They proposed the creation of a new category of "benefit corporations" that would be chartered to work for profit *and* for the benefit of society as a whole. This would prevent stockholders from forcing corporate boards to maximize shareholder value at all costs. B Lab has pursued its vision on two fronts, simultaneously developing model legislation for the formal incorporation of B Corps and creating a certification process (similar to fair trade or organic certification) that allows companies to demonstrate "rigorous standards of social and environmental performance, accountability, and transparency." In less than a decade, they have certified more than a thousand enterprises in thirty-two countries and passed legislation in many judicatories, including Delaware, a state previously associated with unaccountable corporate power because many enterprises have incorporated there owing to its low taxes and lax regulation.[51]

B corporations, local business alliances, and social enterprises all manifest Rudolf Steiner's insight that the world economy is *already* a dense network of cooperative relationships, and that it will be strength-ened if those relationships are recognized and all the players are given decision-making power. At the same time, none of these are the unique intellectual property of anthroposophy. In Steiner's time, similar ideas were promoted by anarchist theorists Theodor Hertzka, Silvio Gesell, and Gustav Landauer, the last of whom briefly held power in post–World War I Bavaria. Exponents of Roman Catholic social teaching advocated an economy managed by councils of workers and capitalists rather than by either the state or capital alone. Likewise, Judy Wicks and the B Lab founders formulated their essential ideas before connect-ing with Mark Finser or other students of Steiner. For their part, while leaders of anthroposophical initiatives are proud of the way they've supported elements of the new economy, they are generally less inter-ested in taking credit than in expressing gushing admiration for their partners. This admiration, with its concomitant capacity to build rela-tionships, is an anthroposophical contribution to a sustainable economy that marks a major difference between post-1970 anthroposophy and Rudolf Steiner's own practice. Even though such admiration is itself a manifestation of Steiner's dictum that one should look to what is already emerging in the world, Steiner himself was too preoccupied with the overt hostility of doctrinaire Marxists and fascists to see the creative things that were happening around him.

COMMUNITY SUPPORTED AGRICULTURE

One piece of the new economy that *is,* arguably, the intellectual prop-erty of anthroposophy is community supported agriculture (CSA). In this model, consumers partner with farmers, either by contributing a portion of the farm's overall budget after a collaborative process (the original model) or by paying a set fee for a weekly box of vegetables (now the more common practice, and the reason CSAs are called "box schemes" in Europe). In less than thirty years, the movement has grown to encompass more than six thousand farms in the United States, with a few individual farms boasting more than a thousand customers.[52] In Europe, four thousand CSA farms provide regular food shares to 400,000 people.[53] Relatively few of these farms are biodynamic or associated with anthroposophy, yet it was the anthroposophical banks and the biodynamic movement that introduced the CSA idea in the 1980s.

This story begins in the 1960s, when biodynamic farms in Europe experimented with new structures inspired by threefolding principles. One of the more challenging aspects of threefolding is that Rudolf Steiner understood the "economic" sphere to encompass the buying and selling of the *products* of human labor but *not* human labor itself or the land. These belong in the "rights" sphere, where equality is the guiding principle. All humans have a right to an income sufficient to support their basic needs, and society has a responsibility to connect land to farmers who will nurture its ecological integrity while producing food for their neighbors. It was not easy to achieve these ideals in the final third of the twentieth century, when the industrialization of Western agriculture was forcing small farmers into bankruptcy.

In Germany, one biodynamic farm, Niederried, responded by committing to training young people who were drawn to a life on the land in the late 1960s. To avoid "harmful tension between expenditures for wages and net gain for the owner," they adopted a system of "open bookkeeping," in which all coworkers had access to the farm's financial records, and each one had a personal allowance for farm-related purchases. Each year's net gains were then placed in a "social capital," fund from which each could draw—again, up to a certain maximum—for personal expenses. To round out the threefold structure, the farm community also set aside time for "communal and individual spiritual-cultural endeavors," including the course for apprentices.[54]

Just east of Hamburg in northern Germany, the ninety-hectare Buschberghof farm embraced a cooperative economic model in 1968, when it was converted from private ownership into a community land trust. The previous owners, who had established biodynamics in the 1950s, gave the land as a donation to the trust, which also received donations from other community supporters. It in turn rented the farm to several farm families, who agreed to farm biodynamically and avoid debt and the sale of land. They ran the farm at their own risk and on a basis of mutual cooperation rather than employment. One effect of the community trust model was to put into place the germ of a broader farm community, in the form of the trust's shareholders. This set the stage for Buschberghof's formal conversion to the CSA model in 1988. Well before that, they added another dimension of community building. In 1973, people with developmental disabilities were invited to join the farm community and to participate in all aspects of food production, under the supervision of the community land trust.[55]

Similarly, the Dottenfelderhof near Frankfurt is a thousand-year-old farm that was home to a monastic community for many centuries. After periods of both biodynamic and conventional management, it was reorganized in 1968 as a "business community" of five families, who worked the land cooperatively and shared the profits, without the need to pay anyone a wage. One reason they chose to organize as a community was that they believed the stirring of biodynamic preparations was a "common social task," and they calculated that at least three farmers were needed "to stir together at one time," in order to supply a farm of 450 acres.[56] They established a farm school, bringing significant numbers of fledgling farmers into their community. In 1981, they created an "agricultural community" open to consumers as well as farmers. Members of this community make an initial investment and pay annual dues, they meet regularly on the farm to stay connected to its annual cycle of operations, and they are entitled to a share of its proceeds. Today, more than a hundred people reside on the farm and participate in its activities.[57]

Dottenfelderhof's agricultural community was created in conjunction with GLS Bank, which was at the time actively promoting the idea of "borrowing communities" as a tool for ensuring the economic stability of biodynamic farms and Waldorf schools. As one enthusiast described the model at the time, a borrowing community of one hundred families could approach a bank jointly, requesting a loan of 250 pounds for each family. "Each member of the borrowing community is individually liable for the repayment of his own loan, together with interest. However, when the farming season is at an end and the wheat, say, has been harvested, all members are entitled to a share—either a share of the grain itself, or of the income when it is sold for breadmaking." By 1981, eleven German farms had adopted this system, and GLS's leaders held a seminar near Emerson College to explore ways to adapt it in the United Kingdom.[58]

One contributing stream not related to anthroposophy was a food cooperative in Geneva, founded by an admirer of the Chilean cooperative movement of the Allende years. This group of 180 families jointly managed a small farm and several urban garden plots, asking participants to pay a percentage of their annual income in advance of each growing season. They in turn provided the primary model for Topinambur Farm in Zürich, which was founded by a local organic produce vendor and a traveling American, Jan VanderTuin, with an interest in cooperatives. (VanderTuin also visited anthroposophically inspired farms in Basel and Liechtenstein.) They found an "ancient" Swiss garden that had never been farmed with chemicals, and linked it to an urban storefront, where shareholders could obtain local vegetables as well as products from a partner cooperative in Italy twice a week. In the Topinambur model, consumers paid their annual shares in advance and committed to covering cost overruns. Topinambur was able to expand rapidly by networking through a large student travel cooperative, and they quickly incorporated other innovations, such as a bicycle delivery service.[59]

Three of these streams came together in the mid-1980s to launch the CSA movement in the United States. Jan VanderTuin, eager to bring his Swiss insights home to America, relocated from Topinambur to Great Barrington, Massachusetts, where he began networking with local anthroposophists and cooperative-minded people to create an American CSA. Trauger Groh, after many years at Buschberghof, arrived in the towns of Temple and Wilton, New Hampshire. And the Biodynamic Association, after an organizational self-study, decided to invest in a "field director" committed to outreach, as well as an executive director. For the new role, they chose Clifford Kurz, who had gotten his own start with alternative farm economics at Dottenfelderhof.[60] At the time, the Biodynamic Association was headquartered in Kimberton, Pennsylvania, the site of Ehrenfried Pfeiffer's early work in the United States.

The CSA movement was thus born simultaneously in three leading centers of anthroposophical activity in the United States. This simultaneity and the subsequent spread of the CSA idea were both possible because of the dense network of relationships connecting biodynamic farms and other anthroposophical initiatives. Temple-Wilton Community Farm is located just steps away from the High Mowing high school, the fourth oldest Waldorf school in the United States (founded in 1942), and another short walk from Pine Hill elementary school, the school whose burning helped RSF get its start. VanderTuin's Indian Line Farm is about equidistant from Camphill Village USA (founded in 1960) and the Great Barrington Rudolf Steiner School (founded in 1971). And the Kimberton CSA is located on the Myrin estate, land now entirely devoted to anthroposophical initiatives. In these environments, it was easy to implement community agriculture, because there was already a community of idealistic, interconnected customers.

The anthroposophical subculture made it possible for the first CSAs to organize themselves on extremely idealistic terms. Indian Line Farm, which seems to have pioneered the practice of establishing a uniform price for a uniform "share" of vegetables, offered consumers refunds when they overestimated their costs. Brookfield Farm in Amherst, Massachusetts, created by former Camphillers Ian and Nikki Robb very shortly after Indian Line, offered its forty-five families a "pay-as-you-can" policy, though they did provide a recommended subscription rate. And Temple-Wilton Community Farm, organized by Trauger Groh in conjunction with a group of New Hampshire farmers and neighbors led by Lincoln Geiger, asked its sixty-two founding families to pledge a monthly contribution based on their ability to pay.[61] The farmers presented a detailed production budget, negotiating with the families to raise pledges if they were not sufficient to meet costs. Once vegetable production began, the produce was placed in a common storeroom (no boxes!), where families took as much or as little as they needed, regardless of the size of their pledges. The farm's founding document explicitly stated that, if members took an inappropriate share of the produce or otherwise exploited the system, "the others can have no claim against them" but should instead "jump in to help prevent an eventual loss." "Everything concerning the farm," the founders stressed, "originates from the constantly renewed free will of the participants." Obviously, this approach relied on a level of mutual trust that is easiest to achieve within a tight-knit social or spiritual network and cannot readily be scaled up. Temple-Wilton has never expanded to serve the Boston market (now served by many CSAs that are geographically much farther from Boston), and it remains small after twenty-eight years.[62] Temple-Wilton nevertheless stands as a beacon of idealism that challenges and inspires larger and more pragmatic farms.

Temple-Wilton's founding document included a section on "spiritual aims" that announced a commitment "to make the annual renewal of life on earth possible, in such a way that both the individual and humanity at large are free to discover their spiritual destination." It also affirmed a commitment to use farming as "a way of self-education" and a therapy for "those who suffer from damages created by civilization and from other handicaps that need special care."[63] This phrasing illumines much about anthroposophical culture after 1970. Neither Rudolf Steiner nor anthroposophy (nor even biodynamics) are explicitly mentioned; clearly, the founders wanted to make space for people of other spiritual paths. But anthroposophy is evident in the specific activities that it links together: surely few, outside of anthroposophical culture, would think to connect farming so emphatically with both education and persons with disabilities. The document thus presents anthroposophy as a network of initiatives, rather than as a set of spiritual teachings. It also bears some marks of the broader spiritual movement of the 1970s: Steiner himself probably wouldn't have placed "renewal of life on earth" ahead of the evolutionary development of humanity, and—given his penchant for such futuristic phrases as "The Coming Day"—surely wouldn't have indulged in such a sweeping reference to "damages created by civilization."

From its beginnings in 1986, the American CSA movement spread along the lines connecting the anthroposophical network. At the close of Temple-Wilton's first summer, Trauger Groh traveled to Kimberton, Pennsylvania, to advise the farmers responsible for land owned by the Kimberton Waldorf school (founded 1941). This was part of the Myrin estate that had been Ehrenfried Pfeiffer's first base of operations in the United States, and it was at the time host of the national office of the Biodynamic Association. Rod Shouldice, who was then leading the association, had learned of the CSA idea from Jan VanderTuin even before the commencement of Indian Line Farm. These connections made it possible for the Kimberton group to recruit as farm directors Kerry and Barbara Sullivan, who had coordinated the *Mother Earth News* demonstration garden in the 1970s, before receiving their biodynamic training at Emerson College in England.[64]

By the end of the 1980s, biodynamic CSAs were serving the largest metropolitan areas in the nation. The movement arrived in New York City with Roxbury Farm CSA in 1991. Its founding community of consumers heard about CSAs from a talk given by Rod Shouldice at New York City's Center for Anthroposophy in 1990; they then recruited farmer Jean-Paul Courtens, who had received formal training in biodynamics in Germany and worked at Hawthorne Valley and Camphill Village Minnesota before starting his own farm. Initially, he found it difficult to recruit New York City customers from beyond the anthroposophical milieu, but he received a big boost when a Roman Catholic group in Albany partnered with the farm. Today, Roxbury Farm brings vegetables and grass-fed meat to 1300 families from Albany to Manhattan, albeit without the benefit of formal biodynamic or organic certification—since they prefer to build trust through direct relationships with their customers.[65]

The first CSA to serve San Francisco, and also the first west of the Mississippi, was Live Power Community Farm. One of its founders, Steven Decater, was an Alan Chadwick apprentice, who had launched his own farm with his wife, Gloria, in 1977, eleven years before turning it into a CSA. John Bloom, who helped the Decaters organize the CSA, emphasized the idealism of Live Power, especially its understanding of itself as an alternative to market economics rather than as a clever marketing scheme. "The farmers are not going to market. They do not have a product to sell. The land is no longer a commodity. It has been protected and cannot be sold.... There really are no externalized costs. They use no fossil fuels on the farm. It is all farmed with animals.... The have solar panels.... It is 100% self-contained."[66]

By contrast, Angelic Organics (founded in 1990), the first CSA serving metropolitan Chicago, has marketed itself so successfully that it currently has twenty-five hundred customers. But one could hardly accuse founder John Peterson of lacking idealism. Raised on some of the land that he farms, John speaks about farms as though he might be a beneficiary of some of the natural clairvoyance that Rudolf Steiner ascribed to the European peasantry in the Agriculture Course. "I had a tremendous relationship to the farm as an individuality since a child," he told me. "These farms just always told stories to me." The farm buildings speak to John, telling him what to build next—and he is always "acquiescent," even when what they want is a disco ball. John's father died when he was a teenager, and he has had primary responsibility for the family land ever since, even when he was a student at Beloit College during the late 1960s. At that time, the farm was a communal arts center for his countercultural peers. He lost most of the land during the farm crisis of the 1980s. After spending time in Mexico, where he immersed himself in artistic activity and encountered homeopathic medicine, John returned to Illinois intending to resume farming on what land he had left.

John was primed to encounter both biodynamics and the then nascent CSA movement, and he did so, in so many small ways that he cannot fully reconstruct the process by which he embraced both impulses. He may have first heard about biodynamics at an organic agriculture conference, where he was seeking homeopathic models for agriculture. A farm intern who had worked for a failed attempt at a CSA "insisted" that he learn more about Steiner. Once he decided to give community supported agriculture a try, he discovered that Waldorf teachers and other students of Steiner were eager to establish a drop-off site and seek customers.[67]

John embraced the CSA model both as an economic strategy for saving his beloved land and as a vehicle for his community-building impulses. John's idealism flows on two parallel tracks. On the one hand, he is devoted to his customers and works hard to make the farm a beautiful and quirky place for them to gather and celebrate festivals. On the other hand, it is obvious that the farm itself is his first love. Though the Angelic Organics mission statement once began with the goal of "providing healthy, nourishing food for people," John revised it to start with the farm itself: "Angelic Organics is dedicated to creating and forwarding an economically viable, organic, Biodynamic farm that nurtures its soil, plants, animals, and community of workers, and enlivens the connection between people and the source of their food."[68] "If the farm is healthy and the farm is taken care of," John explains, "it is a very dynamic kind of force, a centralized force really. . . . It is like a child. . . . You raise the child in the most responsible way, you take care of the child, you nurture the child, you discern what the child needs, and then the child becomes a gift out of that child's initiative. . . . But you don't try to say the child is going to be a cash machine . . . or a food provider and that everything else comes second."[69]

This idealism has turned Angelic Organics into an incubator of new CSAs. Peterson regularly hears from other farmers who were inspired to begin farming or to adopt the CSA model, after seeing the biographical film, "The Real Dirt on Farmer John."[70] The Angelic Organics Learning

Center, now an equal partner with the farm itself, sponsors a farmer-training initiative, which has taught sustainable farming techniques and socially responsible marketing strategies to hundreds of beginning farmers over the past fifteen years. Of the one hundred CSAs currently serving the greater Chicago area, about one third are led by graduates of this program—though few have embraced biodynamic methods. Nearly one hundred farms participate in the Collaborative Regional Alliance for Farmer Training that Angelic Organics cofounded with a dozen other farms, building on the model established by Hawthorne Valley and Roxbury Farms.[71]

Farmer training is just one of five aspects of the learning center's work. They conduct on-farm experiential education workshops for roughly 2500 children and adults each year, including students from Waldorf, Montessori, and public schools. Their urban farm initiative has helped a group of public-housing teenagers in Rockford develop their own CSA and provide free food to elderly people, and it has helped Chicago Waldorf students partner with a group of survivors of torture in developing a neighborhood garden. In Chicago, the learning center is developing an urban farmer incubator in partnership with Englewood-based community organizations like Real Men Charities. The learning center's civic engagement initiative focuses on creating "civic spaces that allow people to come together," so that all stakeholders gain a genuine voice in shaping rural and urban agricultural policies. Currently more than thirteen hundred people participate in Advocates for Urban Agriculture, a coalition cofounded by the learning center. Five hundred have joined a backyard chicken alliance facilitated by the learning center. Finally, the learning center and the Angelic Organics farm are developing a "Farms Forever" initiative to protect the land base of Angelic Organics Association in perpetuity for organic/biodynamic agriculture, farming education, and land conservation. Through Farms Forever, the learning center will share strategies to ensure that organic and biodynamic CSAs and local food farms will endure after the retirement of farmers like John Peterson.[72]

It would be misleading to suggest that there is an ideological rift between a first generation of small, "pure" biodynamic CSAs and a rapidly growing network of farms that have "sold out." As the Angelic Organics Learning Center demonstrates, the biodynamic pioneers of the movement have invested much of their energy in helping it spread. It would be better to think of the two sorts of farms as evolutionary cousins that have evolved to fill different ecological niches—one that thrives through expansion, one that thrives by maintaining intense pockets of idealism and innovation. To illustrate this, it may help to return to Wilton, New Hampshire, and consider one of Temple-Wilton's neighboring farms.

In 1971, biodynamic farmer Samuel Kaymen created The Rural Education Center in partnership with the Waldorf schools in the Temple-Wilton area. The center taught the homesteading skills that the 1970s generation of back-to-the-land enthusiasts was suddenly demanding. A decade later, Kaymen and his family began making yogurt from the milk of a seven-cow herd of Jerseys. They recruited environmentalist Gary Hirshberg to serve as the CEO of the new venture, which they dubbed Stonyfield Farm. Previously affiliated with the nonprofit New Alchemy Institute (which, despite its name, was not associated with anthroposophy or esoteric spirituality), Hirshberg was eager to determine whether a for-profit enterprise might be more successful than a nonprofit in promoting ecological consciousness. Hirshberg boosted annual sales to more than $500,000 in his first three years, and almost $1.5 million after five years. After building Stonyfield into the preeminent brand of organic yogurt, Hirshberg negotiated its 2001 sale to the biggest name in conventional yogurt, Groupe Danone. Though this was a disappointment to some, he successfully incorporated many of Stonyfield's social ideals into the sale. It still donates 10 percent of its profits to environmental organizations and buys much of its milk from a farmer cooperative.[73]

It pleases me to think that the bees that pollinate vegetables and pasture crops at Temple-Wilton also visit Stonyfield Farm. As the environmental movement expands outward *and* deepens inward, it relies on both the intense idealism of small-scale visionaries and the pragmatic good sense of ambitious entrepreneurs. By renewing Rudolf Steiner's economic ideals almost a century after their first formulation, anthroposophical bankers and businesspeople have helped both sorts of flowers to bloom.

Fruit

The Broader Ecology of Camphill

The environmental commitments of anthroposophy are most evident in biodynamic agriculture and recently can be seen in the field of anthroposophical finance. Yet to fully understand the ecology of anthroposophy—the way its environmental impulses are embedded in a wider web of relationships—we must turn to the other anthroposophical initiatives. Rudolf Steiner's ecological vision bears its most significant fruit in the context of educational, medical, artistic, and community-building activities, for it is with those that sustainable practice becomes part of the fabric of human life as a whole. In this chapter, I will focus on the initiative I know best: the international network of Camphill communities, where people with and without developmental disabilities share daily life, labor in the fields and craft workshops together, and celebrate nature-based seasonal rituals.

THE BIRTH OF CAMPHILL

Founded in 1939, the Camphill movement is representative of a second generation of anthroposophical initiatives that have been shaped as much by the charismatic personality of founder Karl König as by the vision of Rudolf Steiner himself. Its roots can be traced to early stages of Steiner's biography, for one of his first jobs was as tutor to a young boy suffering from hydrocephalus, then understood as a debilitating developmental disorder. Steiner's success with the boy, who achieved a career as a medical doctor, prompted him to articulate a system of "curative education," intended to honor the human dignity of persons with developmental disabilities and help them express their individual gifts. Steiner's approach was characterized by close attention to the specific experiences of each individual, the use of physical and artistic therapies to balance the underlying polarities of human nature, and an insistence on providing each child with experiences appropriate to his or her biological age, regardless of apparent abilities. (Steiner thus anticipated the trend toward "mainstreaming" persons with special needs by more than half a century.) Anthroposophical curative education also presupposes an esoteric understanding of human nature, according to which the astral and etheric bodies must be nurtured alongside the physical. Since anthroposophy includes a belief in reincarnation, Steiner believed both that persons with disabilities possess an inner soul that transcends their disabilities (since they will incarnate in a series of bodies with different abilities) and that the disabilities themselves serve a karmic purpose, such as to help the individual achieve a higher level of spiritual development.[1] Building on Steiner's indications, anthroposophical doctors and teachers began creating homes and schools for persons with disabilities in the 1920s. As head of the Goetheanum's medical section and director of a curative home in Switzerland, Ita Wegman mentored others who wished to undertake this work in their home communities.

Karl König, who never met Steiner personally, was one of the young anthroposophical doctors who was mentored by Ita Wegman. A Viennese Jew with a strong attachment to his city's cosmopolitan and socialist traditions, he worked from 1928 to 1936 as the doctor for a curative school in Silesia that had been founded by the sisters Mathilde (Tilla) and Maria Maasberg. The Maasbergs had been raised in the Moravian Church and had discovered anthroposophy about the same time as

König; the marriage of Tilla and Karl thus allowed Moravian and Jewish elements to flow together into Camphill. The school was located on the Pilgramshain Estate of the aristocratic von Jeetze family, whose descendants are active in Camphill to this day. König also organized an anthroposophical youth group in Vienna, drawing together a cluster of friends, many of them Jews and medical students, who were devoted to anthroposophy but culturally out of step with the older generation of anthroposophists. They were, of course, much more out of step with the nascent Nazi regime, which forced the closure of Pilgramshain in 1936 and annexed Austria in 1938. Forced into exile, the members of König's youth group pledged to reunite abroad, and they did so in Scotland, where König was able to find local benefactors willing to finance a curative education school at a baronial estate called Camphill, located in the Dee River Valley between Aberdeen and the royal palace at Balmoral.[2]

From the beginning, König and his friends aspired to do more than run an anthroposophical curative education school. Having seen the destruction of their cherished Viennese home, they hoped to plant the seed of Central European cosmopolitanism in fresh soil and catalyze the emergence of a "new social order." Committed to all the dimensions of Steiner's anthroposophy, they incorporated biodynamic farming, Christian Community rituals, and the Waldorf curriculum (for both the children with disabilities and the children of the teachers) into their shared life. Much more than other midcentury anthroposophists (who were still reeling from the economic failure of The Coming Day), Camphillers sought to embody the principles of the threefold social order, and they did so in a manner that was colored by the communalism of Tilla König's natal Moravianism. While Steiner had criticized wage labor and urged individuals to find ways to work for the benefit of others, the Camphillers implemented a comprehensive system of "trust money," according to which "coworkers" received no individual salaries but simply trusted the community to meet their economic needs. This system engendered intense personal devotion and concentrated economic resources, allowing Camphill to grow rapidly in its first two decades, to expand to three continents, and to create "villages" for adults as well as schools for children. Worldwide, Camphill represents only about a third of anthroposophical curative education establishments, and curative education as a whole is smaller in scope than Waldorf schooling or biodynamic agriculture.

Camphill makes an interesting case study of anthroposophical ecology because it contains multiple dimensions of anthroposophy within a single organizational context. At a typical Camphill place, one can encounter individuals who see themselves primarily as curative educators, primarily as biodynamic farmers, primarily as artists, primarily as Christian Community priests, as well as many people who value Camphill because it allows them to shift their energies among multiple vocations. This diversity is especially apparent at the "villages" for adults (as opposed to the schools for children), which today comprise the majority of Camphill places. While schools focus intensively on pedagogical tasks, villages describe their work as "life sharing"—a holistic engagement in the activities of ordinary life. When Camphillers began creating villages, they understood themselves in relation to other agriculturally inclined "back-to-the-land" movements. At the opening of the Botton Village in 1956, König described village life as an antidote to "three great errors" of modern civilization, two of which had ecological overtones: the idea that humans rather than God are "master and heir to the earth and the universe" and the notion that the "survival of the fittest" is the primary determinant of human development. (The third error is the use of "measurable intelligence" to determine social standing.)[3] Virtually all villages make care for the land integral to their daily rhythms, and a few place biodynamic agriculture on a par with social therapy in defining their missions.[4]

Structurally, most Camphills are incorporated as charities or non-profits, with boards of directors responsible for ensuring that the community fulfills its charitable purpose, but this model has always been a poor fit. In practice, power at Camphill is dispersed among long- and short-term coworkers, persons with disabilities, employees (a rapidly growing segment of the movement), and board members. Camphill life provides opportunities for economic practice (growing food, making or purchasing clothing, providing housing), for activity in the political or "rights" sphere (usually through a decentralized system of consensus, in which various circles of participants make decisions about specific aspects of community life), and for cultural and spiritual activity. When a Camphill community takes on a specific environmental practice, such as installing solar panels or creating a community supported agriculture (CSA) garden, it must consciously place that practice within an established economic, political, and cultural ecosystem. This reality both slows Camphill's embrace of new environmental practices and imbues those practices with greater depth.

A THERAPEUTIC ECOLOGY

Camphillers consider biodynamic agriculture a powerful ally in therapeutic work with children and adults. As one Botton Village farmer explained in 1956, "Farming deals with organisms, with living soil, with plants, animals, and with men. At every single step, the overriding consideration must be whether the life processes of these organisms are helped and enhanced." Since the ultimate goal of therapy was empowerment, this farmer also stressed that "the Camphill Village Trust was established so that also those who are handicapped can take their place in the community and can participate in man's responsibility towards the earth."[5] Half a century later, and on the other side of the Atlantic, farmer Andreas Schad of Camphill Special School in Pennsylvania offered a similarly therapeutic interpretation of biodynamics. "If I am working with a child, I want to try to understand what is happening with that child and I want to try to use those understandings to better the life of that child. There's a certain intentionality with working with whatever subject you are working with, in terms of trying to be able to penetrate deeper into what is happening and make positive change to it. And since Camphills exist in places ... developing a relationship with the land and engaging in it through the seasons, through the years ... goes in line with that." Moreover, he went on, Camphill therapies acknowledge that "The substances that we take into ourselves, from the minutest quantities to big quantities ... have profound effects on how we develop and how we think and how we behave." Since Camphill Special School accepts students from kindergarten to age 21, he is keenly aware of the greater potential to make changes through nutrition if one starts earlier.[6]

A leader at a nearby Camphill village noted that Camphill residents experience much lower rates of obesity and diabetes than other developmentally disabled adults. "It is not because we are such great caregivers. It is because there is a whole environment here that people are a part of. They are walking. They are enjoying life, they actually have real tasks that they are doing, that have an effect that they can see." Her observation is confirmed by a study conducted by the physician who serves Botton Village: he found rates of obesity, psychological problems, and psychological medications among Botton villagers that were less than half the corresponding rates for adults with developmental disabilities elsewhere in Britain.[7]

Camphillers' care for one another shapes the way they treat the other creatures inhabiting their communities. On many Camphill farms, cows are allowed to retain their horns, calves are allowed to nurse before their mothers are milked, and all the animals are treated to a concert of carols on Christmas Eve. In 2001, Camphill Oaklands Park in England faced a more severe test of its commitment to its cows. Foot and mouth disease was detected on a neighboring farm, and in accord with British policy, they too were classified as infected. Effectively under house arrest, the Camphillers refused to cull their animals as their neighbors were doing, instead holding morning gatherings to pray for their animals and those of other farms. They advocated, ironically, that they should be allowed to vaccinate their animals and test them instead of culling them—an exception to their usual opposition to vaccines. On Good Friday, they learned that the cattle at another Camphill had been slaughtered, and two days after Easter they received word that government veterinarians were on the way to do the same to their animals. At that point, they built a barricade in their driveway and invited friends and the media to join their protest. After a month-long standoff, the government backed down and allowed them to test their animals. But still they grieved the killing of three million animals elsewhere, only a tiny percentage of whom came from infected farms.[8]

Camphillers' ecological sensibilities manifest first in care for particular human beings and particular animals. But they extend out to care for ecosystems at the local, national, and global levels. The Camphill communities in Norway, for example, have catalyzed the spread of pond-based water treatment systems in their nation. Camphill Solborg built its system of three ponds in 1978, incorporating flow forms in order to aerate the water as it passed from one pond to the next—an especially important feature in northern climates, as cold weather can impede the biological activity needed to treat the water. After operating their system for a decade, the Camphillers partnered with water researchers, who discovered that, indeed, flow forms aerated the pond effectively even when all but a tiny corner of its surface was frozen over. The researchers didn't venture an opinion on whether flow forms were superior to more mechanical methods of aeration, though they did note that their "aesthetic appearance" would make water treatment systems more appealing. This research, in turn, led the Norwegian government to pass a law making it easier for people to build constructed wetlands in rural areas without having to install conventional backup systems. Similar systems can be found in dozens of Camphills worldwide, and for a time Camphill Vidaråsen hosted a workshop that manufactured and distributed flow forms throughout Norway.[9]

COMMUNITY-BASED ENTREPRENEURS

Another leading environmental community is Camphill Clanabogan, a fifty-person village in northern Ireland. Clanabogan was founded in 1984, and its special concern for the environment began with the arrival a few years later of Martin Sturm, a young biodynamic farmer, who had grown up in a Camphill in Germany. Like other "staff kids" who remain in the movement, Sturm was entrusted with significant responsibilities at a young age, in this case the care of a "rundown" farm that had not yet been fully developed according to biodynamic standards. As he trimmed overgrown hedges and built lanes to allow tractors to access the fields, he found himself burning enormous piles of wood waste each year. This inspired him in 1996 to ask the community to allow him to install a wood chip boiler using a "biomass" technology that was widespread in Central Europe but unknown in the British Isles. In this system, wood scraps are chipped into pieces of uniform size, which are fed mechanically into a two-stage furnace that chars the wood and burns the resulting volatile gases. The system is sustainable in several respects. So long as the wood is harvested sustainably, it is carbon neutral, as the carbon dioxide released by the burning is absorbed by the following year's tree growth. Two-stage combustion maximizes energy production while minimizing air pollution. And because a single boiler heats an entire village, it can be sized to accommodate a steady energy demand, without the spikes that result when homes (used mostly in the nighttime) and workplaces (used during the day) are heated separately.[10]

Initially, biomass was a tough sell for the Clanabogan community. Sturm persuaded his compatriots by doing diligent research and appealing to their economic self-interest as much as their environmental idealism. From Sturm's perspective, not all students of anthroposophy are zealous environmentalists; for some, "The greater issues are meditation and striving and reading the books." But once his system demonstrated an annual savings of twenty- to forty-thousand pounds, the community empowered him to evangelize for renewable energy on a wider scale. He has been remarkably successful. Because Clanabogan's was the first biomass system in Ireland, the Austrian manufacturer of the furnace was eager to partner with Sturm as a local installer of their systems. Within a few years, he had placed similar systems at the Jerpoint, Callan, and Kyle Camphill communities in the Republic of Ireland, and had overseen the installation of the first ten or fifteen systems for private customers in Ireland. Eventually, Sturm gained the community's blessing to launch his own biomass company with a partner from outside Camphill. They "initially concentrated on gaps in the supply chain of renewable energy equipment connected with biomass and wood chippers," then turned their attention to "helping farmers become sustainable and build sustainable businesses" by creating local supplies of wood chips. Though he devotes more expertise than time to the business, and invests all its profits into its further development and growth, he is conscious of the irony of being both a full-time volunteer and the owner of a thriving business. "That's difficult, certainly, for Camphillers to understand because very few people have a business head among Camphillers." Still, his initiative has allowed several Camphill places to install biomass plants at cost, and its impact on Ireland as a whole is astonishing. Coupled with his work as a lecturer and seminar speaker for Sustainable Energy Ireland, Sturm's Camphill installations have been the catalyst for the installation of more than five thousand wood burners in Ireland over twenty years, a good proportion of them using wood chip technologies similar to that found at Clanabogan.[11]

The biomass initiative reverberates through the ecosystem of Clanabogan. Martin Sturm continually seeks new ways to enhance the environmental impact of his system. During my tour of the village, he enthusiastically showed me a row of pollarded willow trees, which have been bred so that they will regenerate rapidly after pruning every five to ten years. Each tree, therefore, generates a steady supply of burnable wood while continuing to absorb carbon dioxide from the atmosphere. These trees are planted along the boundary separating a pasture from ditches and creek beds, so that they will function as living fence posts, to which electrical fencing can be attached. Sturm explained that "pollarded willows offer a habitat to many different species of insects, bats, and birds." Even before installing the biomass system, Clanabogan built a natural sewage treatment system. And Clanabogan hosts an environmental education classroom for nearby South West College, which ensures that hundreds of young Irish students and environmentalists are not only learning about specific technologies but also discovering the multiplier effects that become possible when new technologies are introduced in the context of an interdependent community and farm.[12]

Other Camphill places in Ireland tell similar stories. When I visited Camphill Ballytobin in the south of Ireland, I joined a group of young architects and activists who were touring Ballytobin's biogas energy plant, which had been installed in 1999 as Ireland's first "Centralised Anaerobic Digestion plant." Despite the similar name, this is a different technology from biomass: the community combines manure from neighboring farms with urban food waste, then uses the resulting combustible gases as fuel for a zone heating system. Since the manure loses some harmful pathogens but none of its value as a fertilizer in the process, it is returned to the participating farms, which get significantly more fertilizer than they gave. The environmental benefit of renewable energy is amplified by the fact that many of the gases that are captured and burned, notably methane, would otherwise generate a greenhouse effect more intense than that associated with carbon dioxide.[13] From the Camphill perspective, one of the most treasured "ecological" effects is the way biogas draws neighbors into the communal and cultural life of Camphill. Our tour, for example, included a lyre performance by a community member, who described the benefits of musical therapy and also explained, with great enthusiasm, that trees that had been cut to make room for the biogas plant had been used to build the community's cultural hall.

The young architects with whom I shared the tour were part of another expression of Camphill's communal ecology. They were participants in a summer school sponsored by Commonage, a social enterprise devoted to the idea of the "commons" that has grown out of the Camphill Movement in the Irish town of Callan. Camphill Callan occupies one of the workhouses erected during the Irish famine of the 1840s; it was a place where hundreds of impoverished people went to work and to die, even as their English overlords continued to export shiploads of meat and vegetables produced in Ireland. Today, it is being converted into living space for Camphillers and organizational space for nonprofits, social enterprises, and government offices. From this base, Commonage sponsors a community arts festival, as well as courses on traditional and sustainable building techniques, such as the use of locally available lime rather than concrete as a building material. For participants in these courses, ecological consciousness is fully integrated with artistic self-expression, the preservation of Irish heritage, and the revitalization of small-town communities.

The youthful energy on display at Commonage is equally evident across the Atlantic at Heartbeet Lifesharing in Vermont, one of the newest villages in the Camphill Movement. Founded in 2000 by Hannah Schwartz and Jonathan Gilbert, Heartbeet is part of a network of food-related social enterprises that have revitalized the northeastern corner of Vermont. These include a forty-year-old cooperative grocery, several organic farms dating to the back-to-the-land movement of the 1970s, and a host of social enterprises created by people who, like Hannah and Jonathan, were born in the 1970s.[14]

Around the time Heartbeet got started, Hannah's friend Tom Stearns—whom she'd met at a biodynamics conference "when we were both super young"—was seeking a permanent home for his organic seed business, which he originally managed out of his truck. Through Tom, Hannah and Jonathan met CSA farmer Pete Johnson, who eventually married Jonathan's sister. Hannah, Tom, and Pete joined with other entrepreneurs to form a business group for mutual education about budgets, payrolls, human resources, and other issues. Heartbeet's budget had tripled in just a few years; the others had experienced similar exponential growth, and "None of us knew what we were doing. Those were the conversations I was needing." Soon the group included dozens of "bread makers and cheese makers and wine makers," all sharing information and resources.[15]

As a community builder who was (initially) neither hiring employees nor selling products, Hannah was an oddity in the group, but her presence helped the entrepreneurs develop more cooperative ways of dealing with their employees. Pete's Greens began offering employees CSA shares as part of their compensation, while Jasper Hill Farm (a cheese business) gives each employee a pig every year, since pigs can be raised on the byproducts of cheese production. Businesses like Jasper Hill Farm, Pete's Greens, High Mowing Seeds (Tom's company), and the cooperative grocery became work sites for Heartbeet's community members with developmental disabilities, who treasure the opportunity for greater interaction with the surrounding community. The cooperative ties have been deepened when people have moved from employment at one of the enterprises to coworker status at Heartbeet, or vice versa, while retaining connections to both.[16]

The cooperative ecology that links Heartbeet to neighboring social enterprises has a special center in the community lunch hosted by the United Church in Hardwick, Vermont. Originally created to address food insecurity, it was struggling to stay afloat for lack of volunteers, when Hannah realized that Heartbeet could take a lead in supporting the effort. Other volunteers might still participate, but Heartbeet offered the "sustainable group of people [so that] no matter who else showed up, community lunch could continue." Soon a great many people were showing up—"the teacher, the co-op member, the lawyer ... the farm intern, all of Heartbeet, the Sterling [College] student ... the stay-at-home mom who is just looking for somewhere to go with her kids, and people who actually need a meal.... It can be up to one hundred people sometimes. People just looking for community."[17]

Superficially, Heartbeet comes across as an embodiment of the environmentalist passions of the millennial generation—the only residents born before 1965 are the recently arrived relatives of the community's founders. But Hannah is grateful to the Baby Boomer back-to-the-landers who first planted organic farms in northeastern Vermont. "When I moved to Hardwick, one of the things that inspired me was seeing war protests and the activism in this town. There are whole groups of hugely alternative individuals who are committed to peace and have such deeply connected shared values with what Heartbeet stands for. So I feel like, although Hardwick continues to have a rough edge, there was also this alternative crowd that had seen multiple renaissances of this town. And stuck with it.... We are standing on the shoulders of giants in this town."[18]

CAMPHILL AND ANTHROPOSOPHICAL ECOLOGY

Heartbeet's pedigree connects it to the earliest expressions of anthroposophical ecology in the United States. Hannah Schwartz grew up at Camphill Kimberton Hills, a community founded in 1972 on land donated by Alarik Myrin. Kimberton Hills lies across French Creek from the other half of Myrin's estate, which is now home to the Kimberton Waldorf School; to Seven Stars Farm—one of the most successful biodynamic dairies in the nation—and to the Kimberton CSA, which was one of the three original CSAs founded in the mid-1980s. Kimberton Hills sponsors its own CSA, Sankanac, and community members say that the community's internal food sharing system was structured much like a CSA in the early 1980s.[19] One of Kimberton Hills's founders, Helen Zipperlen, was an assistant to Eve Balfour in the 1940s, before she joined Camphill, and she has continually inspired the community to expand its farming operations, install solar panels and construct wetlands to treat wastewater, and participate in research on environmental practices. One study showed that Kimberton Hills had the highest share of crops pollinated by native pollinators of several organic farms; another found its section of French Creek had the best water quality of any part of the watershed.[20] And Hannah Schwartz's mother, Sherry Wildfeuer, is not only a Camphiller with more than four decades of community experience but as the editor of the *Stella Natura* calendar is also one of the most influential leaders in the biodynamics movement.

Deep roots make Heartbeet attentive to the intergenerational ecology of Camphill. For more than a decade, the community has hosted "youth" gatherings for young adults connected to anthroposophy and Camphill. In many ways, these gatherings put forward a traditional vision of Camphill and of anthroposophy. While many younger Camphillers, especially those from Europe, have only a glancing acquaintance with Steiner's esoteric teachings, the Heartbeet conferences feature detailed lectures on the symbolic meaning of the first Goetheanum, or the karmic connections linking them to gatherings of anthroposophical followers in the 1960s and during Steiner's lifetime. Both Hannah's father, David Schwartz, a longtime Camphiller, who now lives at Heartbeet, and her mother, Sherry Wildfeuer, are frequent presenters at these gatherings, offering a vivid witness to the movement's continuity. At the same time, participants are introduced to newer therapeutic practices, such as nonviolent communication and HANDLE (Holistic Approach to Neuro-Development and Learning Efficiency), that Heartbeet has embraced even though they are not directly rooted in anthroposophy. The implicit ecological message is clear: an organism with deep roots is better able to spread its branches wide.

Almost every Camphill has at least one innovative environmental project, many of them serving as important links between the community and its surrounding neighborhood. The original Camphill school, outside Aberdeen, participates in a government program that certifies "eco-schools."[21] When a proposed highway threatened to divide them from their neighbors at Newton Dee—a Camphill village for adults with disabilities—they mounted a resistance campaign, ultimately recruiting university researchers to study the impacts of road construction on their community.[22] A few miles east of Belfast, Camphill Glencraig sponsors a "forest school" that introduces students from local schools to the community's biodynamic farming, sustainable forestry, and carbon neutral energy systems, as well as to the rhythms of life with persons with special needs. In a small town in Ireland, the Bridge Community constructed a community path that allows their neighbors to improve their fitness while learning (through interpretive signs) about the plants, animals, and people who share life in Camphill. On the edge of Edinburgh, Scotland, Camphill Tiphereth has developed a rapidly expanding community compost system, for which community members collect yard and food wastes in several urban neighborhoods and process them into high-quality compost. They also have developed a firewood processing business where they purchase sustainable timber, dry and split it, and deliver it to houses in the Edinburgh area.[23] And Kimberton Hills has forged a comprehensive waste management partnership with Trader Joe's in response to the national problem of wasted food. "We pick up food that is near the sell-by date or mislabeled and would usually end up as landfill," explained Diedra Heitzman. "We use what is edible, compost and feed pigs the rest, and recycle packaging." This partnership in turn inspired other nonprofits to follow suit and share in the bounty.[24]

All these inspirational examples notwithstanding, many Camphillers are sheepish about their contributions to environmentalism. When asked about the ways their communities embody anthroposophy's ecological ideals, some Camphillers highlight the beauty of their land, the fact that they "feel that the earth is as important as the people on it," and their commitment to recycling and car sharing. Others complain that not all Camphillers are good recyclers, or they suggest that biodynamic farms and anthroposophical banks are more authentic embodiments of ecological idealism. At Camphill Grangebeg, several people offered strident complaints about the excavation that had been needed to build communal houses on an exposed hillside. "The elementals were extremely upset," observed one community member, "The land has been raped in a sense, brutally." "Our role now is to try and repair that damage and heal the land," added another, by restoring "ancient hedgerows" and other original structures. The community also used straw bale building techniques to create a small gazebo that they see as a gesture of penitence toward the elementals and the first step toward greater harmony between people and the land.[25]

THE SPECIAL GENIUS OF CAMPHILL ECOLOGY

Such apologetic gestures reveal the special genius of Camphill ecology, which always seeks to connect care for the natural world with the other dimensions of their shared life. At Grangebeg, Vicky Syme told me that she has developed a special commitment to the ecological dimensions of Camphill festivals, noting that "Karl König said if we don't celebrate the festivals then the earth will die and become a bleak and barren place." To this end she leads a monthly course, organized around the twelve signs of the Zodiac, with attention to specific festivals; to the four directions of east, west, north, and south; and to the interrelations among plants, animals, and humans. Participants, who might include people from other Camphills, the local Waldorf school, and neighbors, might reflect together on the intertwined meanings of the East, the sign of Taurus, and the festival of Saint John's. Using Goethean techniques of conscious observation, they have generally reached shared insights: "If we are studying the quality of the West, we will have a consensus in the end of what the West means to us. Or if we are studying a plant, the medicinal quality of a plant in this way, most people will agree to the effect that the essence of it has." These reflections in turn have breathed new enthusiasm into the community's actual celebration of specific festivals.[26]

Again and again, Camphillers responded to my questions about ecology by talking about aspects of community life that were not obviously related to the natural world. After asking me for my own definition of the word *ecology* (which is "caring for the interdependent web of life"), one well-known Camphill artist observed that "ecology to me is a massively wide subject" and began reflecting on the ways Camphill has begun to transcend the insularity of its early years. "You can create an ecology within the walls of the community," he observed. The cultural boundaries of early Camphill functioned like a skin that "kept communities vibrant and healthy inside." The parents of the disabled children, keenly aware that there were few good options for their children, created a strong "outer ring... a bit like the outer atmosphere" that defended the community from external threats. In this self-reinforcing context, it was possible to teach by osmosis, as everything in the school environment related to the formal lessons. But now, he went on, increasing numbers of day students and employed rather than residential coworkers have "made the sheath around thinner in many respects." In this context, the ecological challenge is to resist the temptation to rebuild the wall and instead seek a new balance appropriate to the changed reality. Thus, he now uses Old Master paintings—rather than Steiner's writings—to introduce Camphill festivals to newcomers. He accepts that employees will not have as much time to participate in play rehearsals as traditional coworkers, but might agree to be part of an unrehearsed tableau. He also draws on his own experience as an artist: though it is possible to "make very superficially beautiful pictures if you are a control freak," true artistry requires a rhythmic "balance between having control and seriously not having control." For this Camphiller, it is simply not possible to talk about the health of fields and forests without also talking about individual artistry, cultural festivals, the relationship between volunteerism and employment—without, in short, talking about *everything* that must achieve balance in a communal setting.[27]

Another Camphiller affirmed that "You can't separate ecology from ethics and the economy and society and culture." In his view, no one has quite gotten ecology right, neither the deep ecologists nor anthroposophists with their more human-oriented worldview. Humans "are an immensely dominant part of the ecosystem," and it is far too late to imagine that we can save nature by keeping humans out. But it is also too late to imagine that an intentional community can achieve sustainability without engaging the larger society surrounding it. Still, he made clear that Camphill is uniquely situated to think clearly about the interconnections. With no increases in government support since 2006, Camphill communities like his own are seriously contemplating the possibility of their own deaths. The year 2006, he notes, was also the year of peak oil production—which he thinks may not be a coincidence. "Things are changing, whether in the biological environment or the social environment.... I don't think we've got any answers. I think we just have to listen very hard."[28]

While some Camphillers contemplate the possibility of community death, others identify practices surrounding individual deaths as integral to communal ecology. Asked to describe ecological practices at Camphill, one person mentioned the practice of reading to the dead as one that "help[s] us to manage the world in which we are living."[29] At a Camphill community specializing in care for the elderly, a coworker said that "one of our main aims" is to "help people go to a peaceful death." In the context of a society that denies death and is willing to destroy the environment in order to extend human life, anthroposophy offers beliefs and practices that can help people become less fearful of death. This is an especially important gift, she added, for young coworkers, who may never have experienced the death of a friend or relative.[30] Similarly, at a community that works with elderly and physically frail villagers, a coworker described the community's physical environment as especially conducive to conscious dying. The anthroposophical doctor who had previously inhabited the house "had this endearing and touching ability to nurse people through death," and Camphill had continued this by allowing multiple residents to die at home. The result was what the coworker described as a sort of ecological privilege: "This house is more than just bricks and mortar and a bit of real estate. Where I work in that office, the one in the back there, that's a room where Frances died. Where I'm at the desk, the wheelchair was right at the desk with me where Robert died. Just through that door is where Betty died. Upstairs is where my dad died because we had him for the last few years.... It is wonderful! We are just so lucky." Such a household environment creates "opportunities, if you work at it, to experience spiritual realities that you can [otherwise] only read about in books." And this in turn helps heal the larger ecosystem.[31]

Camphill environmentalism offers an intriguing counterpoint to conversations about "scaling up" in the broader environmental movement. At the extreme, "scaling up" might be compared to the evolutionary strategy of invasive species that proliferate rapidly and come to dominate a new habitat. Camphill's approach is more symbiotic. Even when a practice is ecologically sound and economically profitable, as is the case for Tiphereth's composting program, Camphillers will not let it expand at the expense of their community building and therapeutic tasks. A the same time, the program is changing Tiphereth's internal ecology in subtle ways. During my visit in 2013, Camphillers stressed the importance of employing people with special needs in their social enterprises, but by 2016 the social enterprises were primarily how non-disabled coworkers raised money for other community activities in which people with special needs participated. Environmental initiatives are also changing Tiphereth's relationship with anthroposophy, as its residents must wrestle with the paradox of trying to develop biodynamic practices for their own gardens, even as they produce large quantities of fertile, but decidedly not biodynamic, compost from their neighbors' wastes.[32]

I became more aware of Camphill's potential to create ecological symbioses during my follow-up visit to Tiphereth in 2016. I spent one day with the Peregrine Group—a team of persons with special needs, who volunteer at various projects throughout metropolitan Edinburgh. The walls of their gathering space are decorated with commendations from community partners, and on this particular day, we trekked to the "Lost Garden of Pencuik." This stunning walled garden of twelve acres in two terraces, built in 1875, was once the source of produce, fruit, and exotic flowers for much of Scotland. The garden was abandoned after the United Kingdom's entry into the Common Market allowed the importation of cheap fruits and vegetables from sunnier climates. In 2012, a community trust created by local activists Roger and Jane Kelly launched a fifty-year plan, for volunteers to restore the site using permaculture methods. Tiphereth's Peregrines proved to be the backbone of the volunteer team, providing a quarter of all volunteer hours. The Peregrines were appreciated by other volunteers for their community-building spirit. One or two were assigned to cook up a large pot of soup for all to share during the lunch break, and since it was the birthday of one of the Peregrines, there was also cake to enjoy. The Peregrines were also actively involved in one of the garden's main projects: building water-retaining "hügel" beds by piling up old logs, then adding compost. This is a popular permaculture technique that is suited to the Lost Garden, much of which had been converted into a Christmas tree farm and charcoal factory during its "lost" years. It was also a source of pride for the Peregrines, who were able to participate fully in hügel construction and then watch as the beds evolved from season to season. The Lost Garden's ecology thus brought together not only cultivated and wild nature, as all permaculture projects do, but also historical preservation, hard work, and Camphill-style community building.[33]

In a symbiotic ecology, compromise can be a more important virtue than purity. At Camphill Newton Dee, coworker Simon Beckett gave the example of using ice-melting salt. Some environmentalists might say that "under no circumstances will we use salt." But aging people with developmental disabilities are prone to slipping on the ice, and "You've got to think about the ecological impact of someone with a broken hip."[34] Similarly, an Irish Camphill farmer acknowledged that for practical reasons he often uses a mechanical stirrer and sprayer for his biodynamic preparations, though he knows this introduces "Ahrimanic" (that is, excessively materialistic) forces into the farm. But he relishes the way the whole community comes together on Three Kings day to create preparations using gold, frankincense, and myrrh. "Everybody would have a bucket and two or three people would share one bucket, stirring and taking it in turns. And you'd have conversations trying to relate to the land, and ... then go out together with your buckets" to touch the whole community with the preparations.[35]

Camphillers often laugh at the tension between good environmental practice and the regulations intended to protect people with special needs. "Managing to navigate the requirements of licensing and regulations with this whole green movement is quite a journey," mused one resident at Heartbeet. All of the "most un-green parts" of their new community hall, she added, stem from regulations. "You have to have exit signs and all of these crazy requirements that—God—you could never put that hall off the grid."[36]

Jan Bang, a Camphiller who has published one of the most influential and inspiring books on the ecovillage movement, is keenly aware of the ironies. Though his home community has implemented a host of ecological practices that other ecovillages only aspire to, his community mates have steadfastly refused to identify themselves publicly as an ecovillage. The objection, presumably, is that the word *ecovillage* implies a single-issue focus on environmentalism, whereas environmentalism is just one dimension of Camphill life, and by no means the paramount one.[37] At the same time, Camphill's multifaceted example has enriched the ecovillage movement: in the spring of 2015, the Findhorn Community, arguably the world's preeminent ecovillage, launched a program of "care farming," in which local adults with special needs spend one day each week raising vegetables at the community's Cullerne Gardens.[38]

And that's just the point, explained one of the leading stewards of Camphill's legacy. Anthroposophy simply means "being in tune with the spirit," and as such it is an antidote to the "egotistical tendencies" that feed the environmental crisis. "If you are already in tune with what is right spiritually," he explained, "then you look after the environment in the right way, without being just focused only the environment." Too many people, he went on, embrace environmentalism out of fear, or out of a desire to create an "island" that will be safe if "everything sinks." But such attitudes feed back into egotism.[39] A younger Camphiller, who was born into the movement, similarly contrasted Camphill's approach of nurturing the good to the cultural relativism and focus on fighting evil found in many social movements. Founded in a region of Scotland that is home to stone circles that are thousands of years old, Camphill still holds festivals that "celebrate our connection with nature" and cultivate "good in a timeless sense of what is good." And this in turn allows it to draw people of diverse ideologies into ecological practice. While some people who can't place Camphill on a left-right spectrum "see [it] as being unpolitical, even apolitical," he thinks it represents an entirely new form of politics: "Camphill wouldn't build a parliament with two sides like that. It would be an octagon or something bananas with lots of different levels and you'd be able to move through it."[40]

Indeed, elaborated a Camphiller and Christian Community priest, Camphill's current ecological endeavors are a logical continuation of its founding task of transforming social attitudes toward developmental disabilities. Drawing on a karmic logic that is common in anthroposophy, he explained that "those whose body is disabled but whose spirit is probably further advanced than any of ours" have incarnated in this way in order to serve as teachers to the rest of us. After Hitler murdered thousands of people with disabilities, the spirits of those people began guiding young people to Camphill, with "the task to make the destinies of disabled people not only known but also appreciated," so that they would receive full civil rights. With that task largely achieved, Camphill is now in a position to create a threefold alternative to the ecologically destructive booms and busts of capitalist economies. And this will happen, he concluded, only if Camphill allows its disabled residents to become the teachers of the young idealists, who come to Camphill in search of an ecological society.[41] Camphill's greatest contribution to ecology, in short, will come only as it deepens its core identity as a community nurturing diverse abilities.

Ecology

The Boundaries of Anthroposophy

The preceding chapters have demonstrated that anthroposophy has profoundly shaped the environmental movement throughout its evolution. Without the yeasty contributions of anthroposophical initiatives, there might have been no organic agriculture, no campaign to ban DDT, no community supported agriculture, and no environmental banks. At a minimum, each of those pillars of environmentalism would be profoundly different without anthroposophy. And yet it is equally true that most people who consider themselves environmentalists are unaware of Rudolf Steiner's spiritual science. Among those who are aware, some regard Steiner's ideas as off-putting, if not downright dangerous. Again and again, anthroposophy has given birth to new practices that have expanded rapidly, without conveying much awareness of their anthroposophical roots. It is thus insufficient to demonstrate that anthroposophy *is* connected to the larger environmental movement: we must also explore the dynamics that limit the connection. If a healthy social movement is like an ecosystem—an interdependent web of entities evolving in mutual relationship—what boundaries define anthroposophy's ecological niche? Are those boundaries tough enough to preserve anthroposophy's uniqueness, yet porous enough to allow for genuine relationship?

Anthroposophy, and indeed every aspect of environmentalism, faces a paradoxical challenge in relating to the other parts. Since environmentalists think in terms of relationships and connections, they continually seek to build bridges between their own specific initiatives and those of others. But when a subgroup of environmentalists imagines that their specific insight is the key to the movement as a whole, inclusive and ecological solutions can become dogmatic monocultures. Consider these four claims, all common within the environmental movement but framed here in their most dogmatic form:

1. Environmentalism is about good science. Science has proved that catastrophic consequences will follow if global temperatures rise more than 2 degrees Celsius—and you cannot negotiate with science.
2. Environmentalism is about social justice. Capitalism, patriarchy, and racism are at war with all life, and they must be abolished along with all social hierarchies.
3. Environmentalism requires that we treat all living beings with equal regard and end the anthropocentrism that sets humans apart from other creatures.
4. Environmentalism is about balance. One-sided ways of thinking or acting, even in the name of environmentalism itself, can only lead to disaster.

The fourth of these claims represents a dogmatic version of the alchemical worldview that informs biodynamics and other anthroposophical initiatives. In keeping with this worldview, most students of anthroposophy would respond to the previous points with "yes, and": Yes, materialist science has revealed catastrophic dangers, *and* spiritual science is also needed to fully understand the situation and its possible solutions. Yes, capitalism with its one-sided emphasis on economics threatens life on earth, *and* capitalism could have much to offer that is positive if it were folded into a more balanced, threefold social order. Yes, all creatures have equal value when seen from a certain perspective, *and* humanity has a unique role in becoming the planetary consciousness that can see this.

Anyone who dogmatically and one sidedly accepts any of the first three positions will necessarily reject anthroposophy's nuanced response, and this rejection creates one boundary between anthroposophy and other strands of environmentalism. This boundary is maintained by the handful of organizations devoted to criticism of anthroposophy. (In the English-speaking world, the most prominent of these is People for Legal and Nonsectarian Schools, which maintains a website called waldorfcritics.org.) Since these critics have occasionally forced the closure of anthroposophical initiatives, many students of Steiner are highly aware and wary of them. But relatively few environmentalists hold the first three positions in dogmatic form, and even fewer have devoted significant energies to attacking anthroposophy. The more serious challenge for anthroposophy is that people who care deeply but nondogmatically about science, social justice, or nonhuman nature may hear anthroposophy's "yes, and" as "no, but"—as a one-sided rejection of science, social justice, or equal regard for all creatures. Or these people may realize that anthroposophy is seeking a balance but still judge that it is tilted too far away from their cherished values. Such judgments are not necessarily problematic: they may create friendly boundaries that preserve diversity while allowing for mutually transformative dialogue. But this is possible only if outsiders to anthroposophy see it for what it is.

Too often, outsiders—including friendly outsiders—fail to recognize anthroposophy's alchemical balance. Instead, they perceive anthroposophy as weird, one-sided, or on the "fringe" of mainstream society. Some environmentally conscious consumers, for example, prefer biodynamic produce because they perceive it to be further removed from mainstream agriculture than other organic methods, and its producers are less likely to compromise on standards. This emphasis on the extremity of anthroposophy does not fit with the self-understanding of its practitioners, for whom it is better described as a way of working creatively with polarities: spirit and matter, East and West, tradition and progress, socialism and capitalism, wild nature and human culture. Even when contending with the polarized demons of Lucifer and Ahriman, many students of Steiner would say the best strategy is not to banish them but to hold them in close and creative tension.

Indeed, many environmentalists have been more extreme than Steiner, in the sense that they have rejected phenomena—modernity, Christianity, capitalism, materialist science—that he was willing to engage as one side of a polarity. Such people have sometimes forged alliances with anthroposophy in order to gain access to its agricultural practices or its holistic model of education. Yet these allies have sometimes turned against anthroposophy when they realized it was not willing to go as far as they felt necessary. What's more, the anthroposophical practice of integrating polarities has led some students of anthroposophy to stake out positions that seem more extreme than those of its one-sided allies. Because Lord Northbourne saw science as subordinate to spirituality, for example, he had no need to quibble with the details of the materialistic scientific paradigm, while Steiner's tendency to frame spiritual teachings in scientific terms left him vulnerable to charges of "pseudoscience."

To find the boundaries that define anthroposophy's ecological niche, this chapter will engage criticisms of anthroposophy from the perspectives of mainstream science, social justice, and "Gaian" biocentrism. It will identify ways in which the anthroposophical approach is more balanced than some critics suppose, as well as ways in which it may be less balanced than students of anthroposophy imagine. It will conclude by considering the extent to which students of anthroposophy may express their own dogmatic or monocultural tendencies, seeing their movement as the sole source of practices needed to restore ecological harmony between humans and nature. In practice, some students of anthroposophy do too little to build partnerships. But where such partnerships exist, anthroposophy's sense of alchemical balance can provide a safeguard against practical and ideological monocultures.

ANTHROPOSOPHY AND MAINSTREAM SCIENCE

Let us turn, first, to the boundary separating anthroposophy from mainstream climate science. Many environmentalists assume that a sharp line separates "good science" from fundamentalist "denialism." These environmentalists may be shocked to learn that anthroposophy does not fully accept Darwinian evolution, that biodynamics assumes that stars and planets affect plant growth, and that the biodynamic preparations are so diluted that no atom of the original substance may remain in the spray administered to a given field. Such characteristics are sufficient to mark anthroposophy as "unscientific" even in the minds of people who are not otherwise hostile to it.

Students of Steiner, by contrast, regard the "scientific" character of Steiner's worldview as one of its leading qualities. Anthroposophy, they insist, is not a religious faith but a "spiritual science." Steiner's approach to spirit was shaped by his familiarity with laboratory experimentation, as he was trained not in the classical gymnasium but in a more scientifically oriented technical school. Steiner's scientific approach, his students insist, sets his work apart from his theosophical precursors and earlier esoteric traditions, and makes anthroposophy a distinctively "modern" spiritual path. In fidelity to Steiner's identity as a scientist, his followers rarely denounce mainstream science: even when Herbert Koepf described conventional agriculture as a "threat … to life on earth," for example, he also praised "the independent application of the scientific intellect to the problems of agriculture" as "a step forward in human evolution."[1]

Neither Steiner nor his students use the term *science* in quite the same sense as other people. To clarify their perspective, one must first distinguish the related but distinct concepts of "spiritual science" (or "spiritual research") and "Goethean science." The former designates the clairvoyant practices that Steiner claimed to have refined to a high degree. He drew on spiritual science when he gave indications about karmic connections between individuals, when he described previous epochs of cosmic history, and when he gave instructions for making biodynamic preparations. Steiner taught that anyone could become a spiritual scientist simply by engaging in meditative exercises that involved reflecting on mental concepts *in themselves,* rather than as mirrors of external reality. In *The Philosophy of Freedom,* published before Steiner emerged as a theosophical teacher, he presented such reflection on mental concepts as a way to overcome the Kantian division between subjective experience and objective reality.

In 1911, Steiner explained to a nonanthroposophical audience why spiritual science is "scientific." When we reflect repeatedly on mental concepts ideally "through meditations upon the same content which are repeated at definite intervals," and in seclusion from "all external sense impressions"—they cease to be "cognitional elements" and become instead "operative forces" that act as "spiritual seeds ... within the soil of the mind's life." As examples of mental concepts that could act in this manner, Steiner mentioned the centaur (as an image of the ideal human in relation to the animal body); the staff of Mercury; and the *Urpflanze,* or archetypal plant, that Goethe claimed to have seen as a result of botanical meditations. Such symbols put us into contact with a "supersensible" world that we can then study in the same way that ordinary scientists study sense experiences. Steiner argued that it was only prejudice that would deny the label of "science" to supersensible research. He also encouraged people to treat the findings of spiritual researchers as hypotheses, suitable for testing in the sense world (which is what participants in the Agricultural Experimental Circle did with the teachings of the Agriculture Course).[2]

Though Steiner suggested that Goethe was engaged in spiritual research when he glimpsed the *Urpflanze,* Goethean science is ordinarily more mundane. It is a method that seeks to achieve objectivity not by bracketing out subjective consciousness but by disciplining our consciousness so that it is capable of observing things in themselves. When other scientists were pioneering techniques of "blind" experimentation, Goethe argued for an alternative strategy for overcoming the "thousand errors" that stem from our "natural" tendency to perceive objects "in relation to ourselves." True scientists, he said, must cultivate a "quasi-divine" capacity to "seek and examine what is and not what pleases." This implied a holistic approach: the botanist was not to look at each plant in isolation but in "relation to the remaining plant kingdom." It implied collegiality, for each observer notices slightly different phenomena. But it did *not* imply hypothesis-driven experimentation. "We should not try through experiments to directly prove something or to confirm a theory," for such an approach diverts our attention from "the thing itself" to our ideas about it. Goethe regarded the experimental focus on "isolated facts" to be misleading, because "in living nature nothing happens that is not in connection with a whole." He urged scientists to conduct an open-ended series of experiences that would ultimately grow into "one single experiment, one experience presented from manifold perspectives," allowing the experimenter a higher level of awareness.[3]

For students of anthroposophy, Goethean science dovetails with Steiner's critique of Kantianism, articulated in his earliest published works. As Owen Barfield explained it, when materialistic science brackets out subjectivity in order to get at "objective" reality, it fails to consider the fact that we know of no reality apart from consciousness. A fuller understanding of the evolution of consciousness, rooted in close observation of our own thinking, can bridge the Kantian gap between phenomenal "appearances" and things in themselves.[4]

Few scholars outside the anthroposophical subculture would identify Goethe as a major contributor to the history of science, except insofar as his theory of the metamorphosis of plants anticipated Darwinism. Today, most Goethean scientists are either students of anthroposophy or affiliated with anthroposophical initiatives—and they are rather more numerous than spiritual researchers claiming clairvoyant insights. These contemporary Goetheans portray Goetheanism as a phenomenological and participatory path not taken in the history of science. "It is impossible," explains David Eyes, "to divorce oneself from participation in nature, contrary to the method of contemporary science."[5] One scientist who has integrated a conventional scientific training with Goetheanism uses metaphors of vision and hearing to make this point. Goethean science, he told me, requires one to "listen to the growth of plants," rather than merely looking at them from a distance. In "ordinary science," he added, we fit our objects to our methodologies, "whereas we adapt or try to adapt our methodology to the object of our research in Goethean science."[6] Some propose Goethe as the great rival of Newton, noting that Goethe's work in botany made him attentive to the interconnections among phenomena, even as Newton's work on physics tempted him to reduce all phenomena to a few root causes. Goethean holism is thus the antidote to Newtonian reductionism. Others present Goethe as a "vitalist," willing to ascribe to "life forces" a causal efficacy transcending that of mere physical or chemical processes.[7]

Goetheans rarely demonize materialist science, though they may reject its one-sided application. Casual admirers of Steiner are often more stridently antimaterialist than his serious students. Thus, while Paul A. Lee, who knew Goetheanism as mediated by Alan Chadwick, described a grand "battle" between physicalism and vitalism, other practitioners stress that "the workings of nature reveal themselves" to both "our outer senses" and "our inner being."[8] Goetheanism can function as either a complement or an alternative to mainstream science, depending on the circumstances. The opponents of Goetheanism, for their part, are more inclined to ignore its adherents than to seek either to vanquish or harmonize with them.

In part, this reflects divergent notions of scientific progress. Mainstream experimentation relies on the notion of falsification, a point that Goethe seems to have misunderstood or ignored. While he faulted experiments for seeking to "prove" theories and thus serving the theorists' self-interest, in fact those experiments are ordinarily designed to *disprove* theories and force theorists to abandon preconceived notions. The consequence of the falsification regime is that it predisposes experimenters to regard older ideas and worldviews as unworthy of being remembered. For them, scientific progress is a matter of continual self-correction. For Goetheans, by contrast, science is more cumulative. Older ideas—theories of the four elements, the four bodily humors, or the seven planetary spheres, all integral to biodynamics—represent observations of past observers and are worthy of being included in a holistic picture of "living nature." Critics who fail to note this difference between Goethean and mainstream science often wind up imagining that anthroposophy is hostile to the mainstream, failing to see how it makes a both/and approach possible.

Anthroposophy's both/and approach to science also reflects Steiner's lifelong fascination with Ernst Haeckel (1834–1919), a biologist known for his work on evolution and for coining the term *ecology*, which he defined as the "science of relations between organisms and their environment."[9] Haeckel's bestselling book on evolution was published when Steiner was seven years old, and controversy over it raged into Steiner's young adulthood. Steiner entered the controversy as a defender of Haeckel, though not an uncritical one. He valued Haeckel for introducing the idea of evolution and for insisting, against Kant, on the fundamental unity of the world. Steiner thought Haeckel's version of world unity was too materialistic, but he nevertheless devoted an entire chapter of his *Riddles of Philosophy* to Haeckel's ideas. For Steiner, Haeckel and Hegel represented two equally appealing proposals for a unified world, superficially contradictory but in fact enabling "us to recognize how the striving shoots and sprouts of life are sent out from very different corners of the universe."[10]

Steiner's *Riddles of Philosophy* responded to Haeckel's *Riddle of the Universe*, a manifesto for a quasi-religious political movement that Haeckel called "monism." Like other environmental philosophies, Monism did not fit easily within categories of Left and Right: Haeckel's eugenicist proposals helped prepare the way for National Socialism, but he also used words like "love" to describe the fundamental character of nature. As the monist movement developed, he became increasingly friendly to the vitalist view that the world is permeated with living forces that cannot be reduced to the mechanistic level. He even suggested that matter and spirit might be equally valid ways of describing the basis of world unity. All of these ideas found an echo in anthroposophy.[11]

The possibility of a both/and approach—of following Goethe's guidelines while being in conversation with the scientific establishment—has inspired anthroposophical scientists from Steiner's day to our own. Steiner admonished many of his students to pursue graduate degrees in science, seeking always for correspondences between what they were learning in the laboratory and what they could glean through spiritual research. Anthroposophical doctors receive dual certification, obtaining conventional MDs while also learning homeopathy and reflecting on karmic influences on human health. Ehrenfried Pfeiffer's use of controlled field studies, as well as his disciplined development of the subjective technique of sensitive crystallization, reflects this ethos.

Both Goetheanism and spiritual science influenced the ways students of anthroposophy engaged with scientific developments in the middle of the twentieth century, a time when ecological science was emerging *and* increasing specialization threatened ecological holism. In the face of public criticism of nuclear power, one anthroposophical writer expressed cautious sympathy, suggesting that Goethean observation might allow for a "clearer picture" of the situation. Might the fact that radioactivity damages living cells indicate a kinship between nuclear forces and life forces, since "only like can affect like"? Might the fact that atoms are not directly observable—seemingly a problem for Goethean scientists—be an invitation for Goetheans to look for something in the inner experience of humanity that corresponds to atomic phenomena? He concluded by suggesting that, while nuclear powers currently "threaten life itself with destruction," further spiritual development may "transform the anti-life powers coming from nuclear reactions into a process in which their true origin and world purpose will become apparent."[12]

Biodynamic conferences in the early 1960s celebrated the new science of ecology as a sign that the age of materialism might be ending. One medical doctor called for the development of a "human ecology" that would revive the ancient Hippocratic emphasis on knowing the whole human being as the foundation of medicine. Because "the history of mankind is largely the history of his use of the land," he added, there can ultimately be no separation between the fields of agriculture and of medicine.[13] Another speaker characterized ecology as "an attitude of wonder" that says, "Let's see what nature is doing here." This approach, he went on, contrasted with "the arrogant attitude of the materialists" and offered an antidote to the disciplinary fragmentation of university science.[14]

Herbert Koepf repeatedly warned about the dangers of scientific specialization. Agricultural economists, he noted, made much of the fact that farm productivity per hour of labor had increased fivefold between 1921 and 1966, yet farm laborers received half the compensation of factory workers. But the only solution they could imagine, using the tools of their discipline, was "to produce ever higher yields at lower relative costs per unit," while neglecting the long-term health of the soil. Participants in a conference on animal waste disposal similarly ignored the soil when they assumed that their task was merely "*to dispose of their wastes* at minimum labor, and minimum costs."[15] Expanding on these insights, Koepf charged that when scientists deal with a living system by "*taking … [it] to pieces and utilizing its parts*," they contribute to "the pollution of our environment, the impairment of the productivity of our soils, the wildlife, the water supplies, etc." Stressing that "nobody would want to turn back the wheel of progress," Koepf praised the increasing numbers of scientists who were insisting that "the biological processes in the soil must be put to work" in order for plants to be properly nourished.[16]

Perhaps the most influential interpreter of Goethean science in relationship to environmentalism in the 1960s and 1970s was John Davy, the science journalist (and Emerson College vice principal) who was Rachel Carson's British champion. Writing in an anthroposophical journal in 1962, Davy noted that 1961 had been the centennial of Rudolf Steiner's birth and the four hundredth anniversary of Francis Bacon's. Bacon, according to Steiner, had initiated the age of the consciousness soul—

a problematic but necessary phase in human evolution—with his emphasis on sense-based science. Davy suggested that this age had come to maturity in the twentieth century, as Baconian scientists realized that they were working with models rather than with nature itself. The consequence was that science became more concerned with what works than what is true. The problem with this development, from an anthroposophical perspective, was that our concepts are *not* merely tools: they are spiritual realities. Davy urged scientists to cultivate a "feeling of *responsibility*" to their thoughts as well as their deeds, and to see the goal of science as "acquiring new faculties" rather than merely "performing new experiments." He alluded to the new sense of responsibility felt by scientists in the wake of Hiroshima as a step forward.[17]

Six years later, in a forward-thinking newspaper column that dealt not only with DDT, lead poisoning, and soil depletion but also with global warming (Davy predicted a rise of two degrees Celsius by the end of the twentieth century), Davy analyzed Bacon for a general audience. Environmental problems, he said, stemmed from Bacon's misogynistic advice to "torture nature's secrets from her." In keeping with anthroposophy's emphasis on balancing polarities, Davy refused to condemn Bacon outright. Materialist science was necessary, because "if we had not learned to kick nature in the teeth, we might never have emerged from the medieval womb." But his hope lay in a counterbalancing factor: the "social concern" of the nineteenth century was expanding to include "effective provision for the welfare of the planet."[18]

In later essays Davy explained the spiritual significance of this new consciousness. The environmental movement, he wrote in 1971, was a hint that humanity was beginning to step beyond the age of the consciousness soul. "The twentieth century, for all its apparent darkness, violence and corruption, is bringing events and experiences which are gradually educating many human beings to a deeper and truer experience of this situation.... The crises are ... gradually dissolving the veils which are still obscuring the Virgin Sophia."[19] In 1980 he faulted New Age champions of spiritual science for not taking the environmental crisis seriously enough, then suggested that environmental conscious-ness was drawing humanity back to the "original way of science," which was to "ask nature to be our teacher." While the Baconian impulse had led scientists to the "subnature" of atomic particles, "thinking *with* nature, with the rhythms of growth and the seasons, brings a different experience.... We can begin to ... seek for a realm above the physical, a world of constant living activity."[20]

Carsten Pank, writing on the tenth anniversary of *Silent Spring,* offered an account of the special contribution biodynamics could make to the broader environmental movement. The important thing, Pank said, was that biodynamics was "very scientific ... a new, a modern, a rational method of farming." When Robert Rodale described the organic approach as "old-fashioned natural methods," he played into the hands of critics who claimed that turning the clock back would lead to wide-spread starvation. But that had "nothing to do with Bio-Dynamic farm-ing," which did not want to "revert to old-fashioned methods" or to "get used to reaping smaller yields" but to heal and transform the soil.[21]

John Davy's father made a parallel argument about another leading environmentalist, who might, like Rodale, appear more mainstream than Rudolf Steiner. E.F. Schumacher, generally regarded as the father of environmental economics, published *Small Is Beautiful* in 1973. He was a member of the Biodynamic Association, as well as a president of the Soil Association, but did not mention Steiner in his published works. When he died, Charles Davy argued that Schumacher's objection to anthroposophy was that it was too balanced, not too extreme. Citing Schumacher's late-in-life conversion to Roman Catholicism and his belief that Western culture had taken a "wrong turning" at the time of Descartes, Davy suggested that Schumacher "could not accept Steiner's view of the rise of modern science as reflecting a necessary phase in the evolution of human consciousness."[22] Davy's insight was that Schu-macher was aligned more closely with the perennialism of Lord North-bourne—who profoundly influenced Schumacher—than with Steiner's views on the evolution of consciousness.

More recently, students of anthroposophy have sought middle ground between the polarities of Darwinian evolution and creationism. Writing in *New View,* Paul Carline argued that both sides of that debate had "hijacked" key terms—the Darwinists by assuming that theirs was the only evolutionary worldview and the creationists by assuming that only "young Earth" theories were compatible with a sense of divine purpose in the world.[23]

Within the anthroposophical movement today, Goethean science inspires a sparkling array of research programs, many of them linked to the new fields of ecology, complexity studies, and quantum physics. At the Mandaamin Institute in Wisconsin, Walter Goldstein and his colleagues seek to develop strains of wheat that do not cause gluten intolerance and high-protein corn varieties that are capable of fixing nitrogen in the soil. Eschewing genetic engineering, the scientists at Mandaamin believe this can be achieved through a renewed practice of traditional breeding, done in true partnership with plant species. Domesticated plants and animals, the Mandaamin website declares, "are not gadgets" but rather beings with "abilities to change, adapt, self-regulate, grow, and reproduce.... They have a long history, rooted in the wild." For this reason, "Breeding should be done in a spirit of respect and a kind of working dialogue with our domesticates, to enhance their gifts; not to violate their integrity, nor force them to be unbalanced organisms."[24] This approach shares some assumptions with the contemporary philosophical tradition of new materialism, which holds that all beings have their own agency and capacity to shape history.[25] At Mandaamin, this is a practical guide to action.

Another scientist left a conventional career in neuroscience to launch Ananné, a social enterprise making skin care products inspired by a Goetheanistic encounter with the healing powers of nature. Both Goethe and Steiner, he explained to me, lived in a world in which scientists could engage diverse philosophical perspectives on their work, while in mainstream science today "the rules are so set" that "you disqualify yourself" if you question the presuppositions. He went on to explain that the best way to identify the healing qualities of plants is through a radically open-ended practice of observation. Initially, you may have no evidence at all of what a plant might be good for, so you simply "look at the environment of the plant, its growth, movement, and colors" and whether it has "five petals or twenty-six petals or whatever." Gradually, you "listen to the thoughts that the plant might inspire within you." If this leads to an intuition about the plant's use, you can then use conventional experimentation to test that intuition. The great advantage of the Goethean approach, he stressed, is that it "nourishes the formation of ideas within yourself," while conventional science offers tools for testing ideas that have already been formed. But he added that anthroposophy doesn't always provide a congenial environment for "doing my kind of science." In his experience, scientists connected to anthroposophy sometimes allowed preformulated concepts found in Steiner's writings to stand between them and actual phenomena. He has generally found emergent scientific fields, such as consciousness studies, to be more conducive to genuine open mindedness than either the anthroposophical subculture or mainstream scientific departments.[26]

Though both of these researchers hold conventional doctorates, Goethean research is not limited to full-time researchers or individuals with crossover credentials. At Camphill Glencraig in Northern Ireland, one farmer explained that his lifetime of biodynamic research began when, at age eighteen, he was placed in charge of a Camphill farm in England. Because he had not attended agricultural college and didn't know all the "rules," he felt free to try new approaches, formed on the basis of his observations. He noticed that many lettuces and cabbages produced "very nice" heads, hard and well-formed. But later on they produced only "sickly little flowers," as the heads rotted away. From a conventional perspective, and even from the perspective of many biodynamic farmers, this was not a problem, since cabbage and lettuce have no uses beyond the head stage. But the farmer realized that implicit in biodynamics was a respect for all the forces inherent in a plant. "Every plant has the capacity of opening its bud and sending forth a blossom and then a fruit." By honoring plant capacities that are not useful to us, we create a reciprocal relationship with the plant that is ultimately of mutual benefit—for the nutritional value of a plant, he is convinced, derives from all of its formative forces. "The plant has got its right," he summed up, "to be a cabbage, to be a carrot."[27]

Goethean scientists have also engaged the issue of genetically modified organisms. The Nature Institute has published widely on this topic, and in 1996 the Anthroposophical Society's School for Spiritual Science set up the International Forum for Genetic Engineering, or *If*gene, to promote dialogue and debate. Though most students of anthroposophy oppose genetic engineering, *If*gene sought to "face up to [it] as something that really does belong to the destiny of mankind." In addition to sponsoring dialogues between opponents and proponents, *If*gene encouraged debate on some uniquely Goethean questions. Since genes cannot be directly observed, Goetheans take diverse positions on whether they truly exist. Some accept "genes as fact," but interpret them differently than conventional scientists; others see them as "physical objects necessary for reflecting events in the realm of the etheric," and still others, following Steiner's notion of subnature, view "DNA, not as a phenomenon, but as a concept created by Ahrimanic beings who try to prevent us from having a true connection with nature."[28] *If*gene participants also explored the possibility that, just as Goethean science has long promoted a holistic approach to living organisms, it might be able to "re-enliven" molecular biology.[29] None of this prevented Demeter from issuing a statement that repudiated genetic engineering on multiple grounds: as inconsistent with the "farm organism" principle, as oriented toward centralized global markets and large-scale production rather than local economies and small farms, as inimical to biodiversity, and as a violation of the precautionary principle.[30]

ANTHROPOSOPHY
AND THE ANTIHIERARCHICAL LEFT

Anthroposophy, in short, meets the criticism that it is unscientific by offering an alternative, Goethean paradigm for scientific research. Its response is more muted and more anguished to critics who argue that anthroposophy promotes a hierarchical or even racist worldview. These critics typically have roots in the socialist, feminist, and antiracist Left. Some believe that environmentalism as a whole is tainted by hierarchy; many more seek to draw a clear line between a progressive environmentalism allied with other leftist causes and a dangerous and reactionary "ecofascism." People who place anthroposophy on the wrong side of this line seek to alienate it from its strongest environmental allies.

For leftist environmentalists, the root of all (or most) evil is oppressive hierarchy: one group exerting power over another. Dominant groups use a binary logic to assert that their power is both natural and justifiable because they possess more intrinsic value than subordinate groups. The mutually reinforcing binaries that structure the social world—male over female, white over black, heterosexual over homosexual, human over animal—are often sustained by an underlying binary of spirit and matter, mind and body. Subordinate terms within social hierarchies are seen as mired in materiality, while dominant terms are seen as capable of transcending earthly limitations. Environmentalism is thus the linchpin of the Left: only by loving the material world, on its own terms and without reservation, can we overcome the antimaterialist ideology that underwrites racism, sexism, homophobia, and capitalism.

This line of argument informs many contemporary "ecotheologies." As early as 1972, Rosemary Radford Ruether blended feminism and environmentalism by positing a "set of dualities" that generate alienation everywhere: "the alienation of the mind from the body; the alienation of the subjective self from the objective world; the subjective retreat of the individual, alienated from the social community; the domination or rejection of nature by spirit."[31] More recently, Sallie

McFague has presented ecotheology as an antidote to "two-world thinking." She affirms flatly that "there is only *one* world.... We *have* a place and a vocation: our place is planet Earth."[32]

Superficially, anthroposophy may seem to be a hierarchical, two-world spirituality. Steiner published a book on *How to Know Higher Worlds,* and Ruether or McFague might reject the idea that there are other worlds, that they are higher, and that our relationship with them should be one of "knowing." Yet many admirers of Steiner portray anthroposophy as a one-world philosophy. "The essence of [Steiner's] message," declares filmmaker Jonathan Stedall, "is that there is only one world, part seemingly hidden and part revealed, and that we human beings are not alone ... in the universe at large."[33] A biodynamic educator told me that he stressed Steiner's teaching that "There is no spirit without matter, there is no matter without spirit."[34] So is anthroposophy better understood as a one-world or a two-world philosophy?

Steiner saw himself as a philosophical monist. His early philosophical work rebutted the dualism embedded in Kant's distinction between things in themselves and our experience of them. But for Ruether and McFague, Steiner's alchemical balancing of polarities might be tantamount to dualism. And this raises vexing questions about their argument. Is the distinction between spirit and matter problematic in itself, or does it only become problematic when the two are separated or placed in a hierarchical relationship? Does the introduction of a third term between spirit and matter exacerbate the problem or soften it? Should forms of monism that treat either *only* matter or *only* spirit as ultimately real be seen as antidotes or as means of sharpening dualistic hostility to the excluded term? Complicating all these questions is the tendency of orthodox Christians to demonize metaphysically dualist traditions, some of which are admired by students of Steiner. History provides ample evidence that violence directed against the "other" is not the monopoly of any single metaphysical position, yet the tendency to equate esoteric or New Age spiritualities with Gnosticism and thus with fascism persists in both church and academy.[35]

It is easy to situate anthroposophy in relation to these vexing questions. Anthroposophy distinguishes spirit from matter and uses vertical metaphors to describe their relationship, but it refuses to separate them. Steiner's monism is thus a monism of spirit *and* matter, working in creative polarity. Steiner regarded the unity of the world not as something given but as something to be achieved through spiritual activity.[36] His view is expressed in Raphael's painting "The School of Athens," which depicts Plato and Aristotle side by side, the former pointing up to heaven and the latter gesturing toward the earth. For Steiner, humans are called to experience the spirit as it works within the material world, embracing both the downward flow of spirit into matter and the upward rise of matter toward spirit. Matter itself is "a transformed portion of the original spiritual element," not something opposed to spirit. Steiner portrayed "higher" spiritual beings as serving or sacrificing on behalf of those lower than themselves, "renouncing any benefits, any gratification or pleasure" of their higher place.[37]

Anthroposophy often wards against dualism with intermediate terms. For Steiner, the human soul occupies a middle ground between spirit and body. He traced the problem of dualism to the rejection of "body, soul, spirit" anthropology at the Council of Constantinople in 869 CE, which eliminated the "interworld between and linking spirit and body."[38] And by positing two distinct diabolical personalities, the materialistic Ahriman and the spiritualizing Lucifer, he suggested that the path of virtue lies midway between the extremes. Anthroposophy is so antithetical to one-sided monisms of either spirit or matter that students of Steiner occasionally demonize materialism and spiritualism in the same way that orthodox Christians demonize dualism.

It is not easy to determine whether anthroposophy avoids the problems that Ruether and McFague ascribe to dualism. Steiner's vertical metaphors are off-putting but also fascinatingly complex. In the Agricultural Course, he asserted that the brain, with its lofty spiritual functions, is actually "a highly advanced heap of manure,"[39] and in his sevenfold hierarchy of human nature, the highest level is directly evolved from the lowest. Farmer Andrew Marshall, who called my attention to this aspect of Steiner's anthropology, acknowledged that hierarchy is "challenging," but offered an intriguing defense: "People don't want the spiritual world to be structured.... But the physical world would be nebulous if the spiritual world was nebulous. We'd live in a big jelly."[40] Fifty years earlier, George Corrin offered a similar caution: without a sense of hierarchy, people often reduce all phenomena to the lowest—that is to say, the material—level. In conventional agriculture, he observed, animals are treated like plants: chickens are not allowed to walk or stretch their wings, pigs are fed chicken manure that could have been used to fertilize plants. Plants are reduced to minerals by being given chemical fertilizers; minerals are reduced even lower when atomic reactions convert matter into energy; and humans are often treated like animals. "The situation has arisen," Corrin admonished, "because we have not kept before us a *whole* view of the different kingdoms of nature." The only antidote, he concluded, was to honor the integrity of each kingdom.[41]

One way to determine whether anthroposophy's version of spiritual hierarchy is problematic is through a pragmatic test: does it contribute to injustice? Clearly, it does *not* contribute to neglect of material ecosystems. But people who come to anthroposophical initiatives with antihierarchical sensibilities often struggle to discern where anthroposophy stands with regard to sexism and racism. Depending on their experiences, they may reach divergent conclusions. Some are put off by the heavy reliance on European mythologies in the Waldorf curriculum and the seasonal festivals; others notice that some schools have embraced other cultural traditions with equal enthusiasm. Some observers immediately notice the prevalence of German people in anthroposophical initiatives, or the fact that (in the United States) many initiatives are located in racially homogeneous communities. Others give more weight to the recent growth of anthroposophical initiatives in the global South or the fact that so many students of anthroposophy have married across national and linguistic lines. Still others wonder if there is a racial subtext to the prohibition of black crayons in many Waldorf schools.[42]

My own first impressions of anthroposophy were shaped by antihierarchical sensibilities. I noticed that most students of anthroposophy use "man" where I would use "humanity." Anthroposophical liturgies remind me, and many observers, of the pre–Vatican II Roman Catholic mass. And anthroposophy's version of Christianity makes little use of the Hebrew Bible, something I was taught to see as evidence of anti-Judaism. I gradually learned that many students of Steiner are of Jewish heritage and value that heritage, even if they also regard the "mystery of Golgotha" as the fulcrum of cosmic history. I learned that the Christian Community has always ordained women priests and that women served on the Anthroposophical Society's earliest executive council. And I learned that gender-exclusive language is slowly fading from the anthroposophical scene.

Outsiders who ask questions about puzzling experiences will encounter varying degrees of defensiveness, depending on which students of anthroposophy they ask. But they will eventually discover that the anthroposophical movement, despite its alliances on the left, is more committed to restoring balance than to resisting evil. As a consequence, students of anthroposophy will extend generosity, even reverence, to cultural phenomena that leftists regard as evil. For those with a dogmatic commitment to the leftist worldview, this is an unbridgeable ecosystemic barrier, and it is reinforced by websites and organizations that characterize anthroposophy as "a blatantly racist doctrine which anticipated important elements of the Nazi worldview by several decades" and which continues to "collaborate" with "a specifically 'environmentalist' strain of fascism."[43]

These charges are one sided and disconnected from anthroposophy's present complexity, but they point to phenomena that cannot be ignored. Steiner had much to say about race—though far less than he had to say about education or agriculture or medicine or reincarnation—and some of what he had to say concerned the spiritual significance of racial difference. Steiner was critical of Adolf Hitler (just as Hitler was critical of him), and many of his students were appalled when the Nazis gained power in Germany. Yet when Hitler threatened to suppress the Anthroposophical Society, its executive council—which had recently expelled much of its membership—chose to collaborate rather than resist. Marie Steiner, Günther Wachsmuth, and Albert Steffen knew of Hitler's violent intentions toward the Jewish people, since Hitler's attacks on anthroposophy included the accusation that anthroposophy was aligned with the Jews. Rather than standing in solidarity with Hitler's other targets, they disavowed any sympathy for Judaism and assured Nazi leaders that both they and Steiner were of pure Aryan heritage.[44] The society was eventually suppressed anyway, but a few of its members remained faithful to the Nazi creed and participated in neo-Nazi organizations almost up to the present day.

Examining the racial teachings found in *How to Know Higher Worlds* is helpful for understanding what this history means for anthroposophy today. As a "basic" book that newcomers were (and are) encouraged to read on joining the society, *Higher Worlds* provides a framework that Steiner presupposed when he addressed racial topics in lectures for society members. It contains a capsule version of Steiner's core teaching alongside the interpretive principles that most students of Steiner, past and present, apply when engaging Steiner's other racial comments.

A few passages tell the story. In the first chapter, Steiner identified the "inner qualities" necessary for a student to embark on the path of spiritual science. One is a mood of reverence: "We will not find the inner strength to evolve to a higher level if we do not inwardly develop this profound feeling that there is something higher than ourselves." Steiner contrasted this mood with the critical spirit of modern civilization, which he admitted had given rise to "the greatness of our culture."[45] The practice of reverence was thus enclosed within a larger alchemical balance. Reverence infuses the way students of Steiner study his lectures: they work through them slowly, discuss them in groups, and incorporate their content into their meditative practice.

Many refuse to comment on particular lectures unless they have worked with them in this manner, even if the lectures contain passages that an outsider would regard as patently offensive. Steiner's use of a vertical metaphor to describe the practice of reverence is also significant: students of Steiner resist the notion that the only way to defeat racism is to uproot any distinction between "higher" and "lower."

Steiner also articulated the "fundamental principle" that one can advance spiritually only through devotion to "the ennoblement of humanity and world evolution." He reiterated this in a frequently quoted form: "For every single step that you take in seeking knowledge of hidden truths, you must take three steps in perfecting your character toward the good." He called this the "golden rule of the occult sciences," implying that disastrous consequences might follow upon its violation.[46] In keeping with this principle, students treat the fruits of Steiner's spiritual research as potentially dangerous. It does not surprise them that Steiner's teachings can be interpreted in ways that support racial discrimination; that is what one would expect to happen when such "hidden truths" are handled by people who are not on an ethical path. Students of Steiner also conclude from this principle that any interpretation of Steiner's teaching that is not conducive to ethical development is a false interpretation, however plausible it might seem on the surface.

The further inference that racist interpretations are necessarily false is justified only if opposition to racism was part of Steiner's ethics. And indeed, he included racial prejudice in a list of negative qualities that spiritual students must ward against: "In addition to anger and irritation, we must also struggle against other traits, such as fearfulness, superstition, prejudice, vanity, ambition, curiosity, the urge to gossip, and the tendency to discriminate on the basis of such outer characteristics as social status, gender, race, and so on."[47] Most contemporary students of Steiner read this as a straightforward condemnation of racism and sexism.

But Steiner also warned his readers not to imagine "that to fight against discrimination based on social status or race means becoming blind to the differences among people. The fact is that we learn to recognize these differences for what they are only when we are no longer caught up in prejudice."[48] Here Steiner introduced a subtle dimension of his condemnation of prejudice: we are not only to avoid the prejudice that might cause us to treat people unequally but *also* the prejudice that might cause us to imagine that racial differences do not exist at all (or, perhaps, in contemporary language, the prejudice that race is merely a social construction). Steiner was thus neither a *racist*, if that term implies a willingness to treat people differently on the basis of race, nor an *antiracist*, if that implies a social constructivist view of racial differences. He was what is sometimes called a "racialist": he believed that racial differences are real but *not* a basis for differential treatment of individuals. Steiner's racialism was part and parcel of his larger understanding of the interplay between spirit and matter: as he explained later in the book, "folk souls" and "race spirits" are "real beings" who "make use of individual human beings as physical organs."[49] The distinction between racialism and racism provides an interpretive key for Steiner's other comments about race.

Steiner's racialism was shaped by the "root race" theory of Madame Blavatsky—though Steiner insisted that he did not teach theosophical concepts unless he had verified them through spiritual research. According to this theory, human evolution has passed through multiple racial phases, each with its own cosmic or earthly geography. The timescale of this evolution was vast, and both Steiner and Blavatsky were clear that root races were not identical to the racial groupings visible in the world today. After his split from theosophy, Steiner often referred to "epochs" rather than "root races" to underscore the spiritual character of the concept, and replaced Blavatsky's "Aryan" race with the "post-Atlantean" epoch. The passage from one age to the next involved evolutionary progress, meaning that cultures associated with a later epoch were seen as more advanced, but this progress was more cyclical than linear. Steiner ascribed a progressive descent into materialism to the first five post-Atlantean epochs, as humans gradually shed the natural clairvoyance of their ancestors. Things began to turn around in the current, "Christian" era, which Steiner identified as the time when racial differences would begin to disappear, because "the Christ concept supplied an ideal that counteracts all separation."[50]

Both anthroposophy and theosophy were shaped by broader cultural currents, so much so that one of anthroposophy's sharpest critics has rightly concluded that anthroposophy was tied to fascism through "its familiarity, its participation in and influence by central cultural currents of the era."[51] During the heyday of scientific racism, biological categories were replacing religious ones in the Western understanding of human diversity. Blending scientific curiosity with imperial self-interest, European researchers exaggerated the significance of superficial physical traits. Many, including Ernst Haeckel, departed from the biblical theory of monogenesis (all humans descended from Adam and Eve and were thus of one family), postulating instead that racial difference emerged simultaneously with humanity itself. Most mainstream scientists also favored eugenics, or the progressive improvement of the human race using principles derived from genetics.

Rudolf Steiner related to scientific racism as he related to most cultural currents: with a balanced mixture of affirmation and critique. He deplored eugenics, lambasting a London congress ("chaired by Darwin's son," he pointed out) that compared the skulls of rich and poor people. He supported the eugenicists' goal of evolving a more perfect humanity but thought that this could be done by spiritual rather than material means. In keeping with his principle that ethical development must take place alongside spiritual development, he claimed that Atlantis had fallen because its inhabitants had engaged in unethical eugenic experimentation.[52] Steiner's critique of materialism notwithstanding, he shared the mainstream scientists' assumption that physical differences can be important. This view was consistent with his ecological holism, according to which every element of a complex system carries significance. In a 1923 lecture on "Color and the Human Races," Steiner affirmed that it is only possible to "rightly understand the spiritual element if one first studies how the spirit works in man precisely through the skin-color."

This lecture was framed as a critique of materialism: he parodied scientists who shouted "Give us corpses!" in hopes that experimentation on them would unveil the secrets of humanity. But Steiner echoed the materialists' assumption that certain races (notably Native Americans) were dying out, and that racial mixing and geographical mobility sometimes contributed to racial decline. For him, these were neutral facts that cried out for spiritual interpretation, not products of European bias. Part of his spiritual interpretation was that whites, in India and Europe, were currently at the forefront of human evolution.[53]

Steiner's racial teaching was also influenced by the German and Austrian experience during the First World War. As a young man, Steiner participated in pan-German nationalist organizations, and throughout his life he remained convinced that Central Europe had a unique contribution to make to spiritual evolution. He regarded his home region as the alchemical balancing point between the dusty materialism of the Anglo-American world and the airy spirituality of the East. The traumas of war intensified his devotion to Central Europe and to the cosmopolitan Vienna of his youth. Steiner rejected socialism and fascism, English imperialism, and Slavic nationalism as one-sided threats to alchemical balance. He despised Woodrow Wilson for endorsing the national ambitions of ethnic communities that had previously been included within the Austrian empire. Many passages that defenders of Steiner cite as evidence of his opposition to nationalism were actually pro-Austrian attacks on Slavic self-determination.[54] On the other hand, some seemingly racist passages display more hostility to Wilson (himself a racist) than to any racial group.[55]

All of this creates a dizzying context for interpreting Steiner's racial teachings. Steiner's students understood, and still understand today, that his comments about racial groups did not apply perfectly to individual members of those groups, who might pass through multiple races in their karmic history. They understood that, when Steiner used a racial category, he was sometimes referring to far distant events in cosmic history. They understood that, for Steiner, evolutionary progress was always tangled up with regress: groups characterized as having been "left behind" might retain spiritual gifts needed for subsequent eras. They understood that, for Steiner, race was of profound spiritual significance but also in the process of losing that significance. And, following Steiner, they understood that declining significance in terms that placed Christian Europe at the center of the contemporary human story.

All of this would have been in the background when attendees of Steiner's Oslo lectures on folk souls heard him—to take one hotly debated passage—explain that "the black race" was especially shaped by forces associated with childhood, "the yellow and brownish races" in Asia by "the characteristics of youth," and Europeans by the "ripest characteristics" of adulthood." He went on to say that Native Americans are shaped by "those forces which have a great deal to do with the decline and death of man," adding that "the American Indians did not die out because it pleased the Europeans that they should do so, but because they had to acquire those forces which lead them to die out." Steiner also reminded his hearers that race would cease to exist in the next cultural epoch, that he was referring not to the "forces which constitute [a person's] essence as a human being" but only to "the physical organizing forces," and that since all people will "pass through the various races" we "should not be prejudiced" by the apparent advantages of the Europeans.[56]

Taken in context, these passages do *not* suggest that Steiner advocated racially discriminatory policies. But their implications are ambiguous. When Steiner said that American Indians did not die to please the Europeans, was he trying to counter the prejudicial assumption that innate inferiority caused Native American deaths? Or was he trying to absolve European invaders from the guilt of genocide? Did Steiner intend to endorse European ascendancy over other cultures, or merely to find spiritual meaning in the seemingly self-evident fact of European dominance? If Steiner assumed that nonwhite races were dying out, might his prediction of a nonracial future be tantamount to a vision of a monolithically white future?[57] Most contemporary students of Steiner categorically reject any interpretation that implies a negative judgment about non-European peoples. Using their hermeneutic of reverence and ethical development, they either decline to interpret these passages altogether, or else see them as pointing in some mysterious way to future spiritual tasks associated with *all* races.

In the 1920s and 1930s, many but not all students of anthroposophy likewise refused to interpret Steiner's words as condoning prejudice. In England in 1938, George Kaufmann Adams prepared a study guide for anthroposophists who were reading the lectures on folk souls; he began by reminding them that "We want to be imbued with the feeling that what we do is for the benefit of all mankind."[58] In Munich, Traute Lafrenz participated in the White Rose network of underground resistance to Hitler, alongside allies following many alternative spiritual paths. Ita Wegman and her supporters opposed the Third Reich, regarding the collaboration of other anthroposophists as a betrayal of Steiner. They helped ethnically Jewish anthroposophists, developmentally disabled children, and the doctors and teachers who worked with them find places of safety from Nazi violence. But they rarely aligned themselves with left-wing opponents of Hitler. Their "spiritual resistance" confirmed the character of anthroposophy as a political third way, not reducible to the categories of left and right.[59] Since Ita Wegman and her friends were expelled from the Anthroposophical Society at the beginning of the Nazi era, their story is virtually unknown to those who portray anthroposophy as "ecofascist." One could perhaps argue that the society's schism created an alchemical imbalance within the movement, rendering some anthroposophists more vulnerable to the distorted teachings of Hitler.

In the face of the anthroposophical movement's mixed history, many antiracist activists would like to see contemporary students of Steiner disavow certain passages as either prejudiced or too ambiguous to be helpful. Because such disavowals are incompatible with the hermeneutic of reverence, many students of anthroposophy refuse to offer them, including some of Ita Wegman's most zealous admirers.[60] But disavowal has been the implicit policy of the Anthroposophical Society.

Critics fault the society for publishing editions of Steiner's works that have the most troubling passages excised, but this reflects the society's unwillingness to defend such passages. In 2000, the Council of the Anthroposophical Society in the Netherlands issued a 720-page report in response to allegations of racism, in which they acknowledged the existence of sixteen passages in Steiner's works that "could be a violation of the prohibition of racial discrimination under the Civil Code of the Netherlands" if actively promoted today. The commission described these passages as "either careless, problematic, or seriously discriminatory," singling out for special disapproval a passage in which Steiner belittled African novels and said that a pregnant white woman who read a novel by a black author would have a mulatto baby. They identified another sixty-seven passages that could easily be misinterpreted. At the same time, they called attention to Steiner's criticism of racial prejudice and blasted the "selective indignation" of his critics.[61]

Anthroposophy today remains culturally Eurocentric to a degree that can be jarring to anyone formed by American multiculturalism, and as a consequence many people remain uneasy in the anthroposophical milieu. Yet other people, of all races and ethnicities, have found a welcoming home within the anthroposophical movement. Though the global spread of anthroposophy initially followed the migration patterns of German and English speakers, there are rapidly expanding initiatives today in China, India, Brazil, and Vietnam. Triodos Bank encourages the cultural diversification of Europe by providing loans to immigrant faith communities. The current president of the Camphill Association of North America is a gay Filipino. Persons of Jewish descent are included in movement leadership at the highest level, including the executive council of the international society. Given these realities, it is hard to credit one critic's assertion that anthroposophy is "loyal to an unreconstructed racist and elitist philosophy," hiding its true agenda behind "a public face that is seemingly of the left."[62]

That critic is correct that the anthroposophical movement has refused to call Steiner's spiritual authority into question by condemning any of his specific teachings. There is no anthroposophical counterpart to Lutheran statements that "reject [the] violent invective" of "Luther's anti-Judaic diatribes."[63] In part this is because Steiner, unlike Luther, never advocated racial or ethnic violence. In part it is because the anthroposophical community is divided about how to interpret the passages on race and how to respond to external critics. Some students of Steiner would insist that *all* of his statements about race, if properly interpreted, carry antiracist implications; others privately acknowledge that his clairvoyant insights were sometimes mistaken. Many leaders of the Anthroposophical Society have encouraged dialogue with critical outsiders, for example, by making Helmut Zander's books available at the Goetheanum bookstore, but others leaders have denounced this as a betrayal of anthroposophy.[64]

In any case, the crucial ecosystemic boundary is that of racialism. Many serious students of Steiner continue to believe, and seek to demonstrate in their personal practice, that it is possible to oppose racial prejudice while ascribing a real if declining spiritual significance to racial differences. Most mainstream antiracist activists, by contrast, remain convinced that race is, in the words of the PBS series, a "powerful illusion" that has no basis in biology, much less spiritual history. For environmentalists who regard any deviation from leftist orthodoxy as evidence that a person or movement is "right-wing," this is an unbridgeable divide.[65] A more open dialogue would require leftist environmentalists to acknowledge anthroposophy's identity as neither left nor right, and it would require students of anthroposophy to consider the possibility that their hermeneutic of reverence for Steiner might require a dose of antiracist critique.

ANTHROPOSOPHY AND GAIANISM

As I have shown, scientific and leftist critics perceive anthroposophy in ways that students of Steiner would not recognize. Critics see anthroposophy as unscientific; participants view Goethean science as sophisticated and reconcilable with the authentic insights of conventional research. Critics see anthroposophy as hierarchical and racist; students of Steiner believe their spirituality can be the basis of human solidarity. I now turn to a case in which there is a shared understanding of the terms of disagreement.

Many of anthroposophy's alliances are with people and movements that might be characterized as "Gaian." "Gaianism" is the view that the whole world constitutes a living organism, all of whose components have equal and intrinsic value. Some Gaians (especially within the neo-pagan and New Age movements) regard Gaia as a spiritual personality, who is worthy of worship; others use Gaia as a metaphor for the web of symbiotic relationships linking planetary phenomena. Religious studies scholar Bron Taylor has helpfully categorized both sorts of Gaianism as examples of "dark green religion," or the view that "nature is sacred, has intrinsic value, and is therefore due reverent care."[66] This affirmation is typically accompanied by denunciations of "anthropocentrism," or the view that humans are unique and worthy of heightened respect. A few Gaians portray humans as parasites and advocate for sharp reductions in the human population; many more insist that humans have equal value with other living creatures. Gaianism is closely connected with the ecovillage movement; indeed, the Global Ecovillage Network receives its primary financial support from the Gaia Trust, a charity whose mission "is to promote a new, global consciousness which sees our entire planet as a living organism with Humankind as an integral part of the entity."[67]

Through the influence of George Trevelyan, anthroposophy laid foundations for spiritual Gaianism; indeed, back in the 1920s, the Natural Science Section of the Goetheanum named its yearbook *Gaia-Sophia.* Still, most Gaians and most students of Steiner would agree that anthroposophy is *not* a form of Gaianism. As the name suggests, anthroposophy is wisdom that centers on the human being. Steiner posited a spiritual continuity connecting humans to animals, plants, and minerals, but he also portrayed humans as the highest level of this fourfold hierarchy.

Like animals, plants, and minerals, humans have a physical body; like animals and plants they have an etheric or "life" body; like animals, they have an astral body. But in our currently earthly incarnation only humans have an "ego" that integrates and directs all the lower levels. (The other kingdoms of nature will gain the capacity to incarnate their egos in subsequent phases of evolution.)[68] In the Agriculture Course, Steiner emphasized the cosmological context for farming but also placed humans at the center of the cosmos, insisting that "as everywhere in Spiritual Science, here too we take our start above all from man himself. Man is the foundation of all these researches."[69] Ehrenfried Pfeiffer echoed this sentiment in a quote that is prominently featured on the Pfeiffer Center's website: "The human being, who guides and directs the beginning, the course and the end of the natural growth process, is the strongest force of nature. His capacity is the final decisive factor."[70]

Just as Steiner's teaching about the spiritual significance of race creates an ecosystemic boundary between anthroposophy and antiracist environmentalists, so too does his insistence on the distinction between humans and animals, and his concomitant endorsement of animal agriculture, create an ecosystemic boundary between anthroposophy and Gaianism. Many Gaians are either vegan or aspire to veganism as an ideal; it is a common practice at Gaian ecovillages for community meals to be free of animal products. Many ecovillages have extensive vegetable gardens but no livestock. Even vegan students of anthroposophy, by contrast, are often involved in the practice of animal agriculture, and within anthroposophical communities veganism is less common than the "Wise Traditions" approach, which opposes processed foods but endorses such traditional animal products as raw milk, lard, and grassfed meat.[71] Yet Gaians who do use animal products often recognize the biodynamic movement as the leader in developing ethical practices for animal agriculture.

Steiner's distinction between humans and animals is a surprising starting point for ethical agriculture. In the early years of the anthroposophical movement, some leaders used human uniqueness as a rallying cry in their battle against materialist theories of evolution. Hermann Poppelbaum, who served on the society's executive council and led its natural science section during the 1960s, began writing on animals in the 1920s in order to rebut a German biologist, who taught that some animals are actually more highly evolved than humans. Poppelbaum accepted this notion but turned it against itself: "more formative intelligence" had "been poured out into the animal than into the human body," but this was because animals had descended earlier into material hardening. In humans, the "cosmic intelligence" was "held in reserve" so that it could "emerge again in a mental form in the human faculty of thought." As evidence, Poppelbaum noted that young chimpanzees looked almost human, while adults had a "hideously repulsive, almost dog-like profile."[72]

Though Poppelbaum's description of the adult chimpanzee sounds harsh, his other writings contained tender descriptions of animal species.[73] He taught that humans should feel grateful to the animals for their role in our own evolution: "To be human is to know the animals and all the creatures on the earth. It is to recognize man's responsibility towards these beings, once of the same order as himself but now obliged to live beside him in an incompleteness which never ceases calling to man."[74] Poppelbaum's view of evolution remains widespread in the anthroposophical movement. One Goethean scientist, for example, told me that while each animal species has something "that they do exceptionally well," the unique gift of humans is our "universality."[75] Another scientist explained that, while the lack of instinct can separate humans from the world, it also gives us the opportunity to consciously "turn to the rest of the world in an effort to understand it in its own right."[76]

Other early anthroposophical writers insisted that *loving* animals was the way to avoid descending into animality. Richard Karutz used an East African legend to make this anthroposophical point. According to the legend, cows lived among humans until one man decided that he would kill his cow. He pretended that his son was sick and persuaded the cow to offer first milk, then blood, and finally bone marrow in order to heal the son. At this point, cattle changed form and lost their ability to speak. For Karutz, this is a parable of the evolutionary process as described by Steiner: before cows or humans assumed physical form on earth, they lived together in a "Paradise-community of man and beast." The cows, like other animals, preceded humans into the material world, and in this sense the cow "is 'the Mother of Man.'" Because animals prepared the way for our own incarnation, we humans should "understand and love the animal," retaining a "spiritual kinship of all that has become." If we fail to do this, Karutz warned, we will lose our mission and our future.[77]

Karutz also shared a poem by the anthroposophical poet Christian Morgenstern that is still quoted by students of Steiner today—indeed, the people of Camphill Village Kimberton Hills have used a musical setting of it in their Easter festivals.[78] It suggests that not only the animals but even the plants and minerals deserve gratitude from humans because their sacrifices contributed to human evolution:

> I give you thanks, cold silent stones
> And kneel in quiet awe before you.
> From you, the plant in me has grown.
> The washing of the feet, the washing of the feet, the washing of the
> feet.
> I give you thanks, green grass and flower
> And bend in reverence before you.
> You let me win the beast's swift power.
> The washing of the feet....
> I thank you all, plant beast and stone
> And bow in gratitude before you.
> Through you my human crown is won.
> The washing of the feet....

Later anthroposophical writers added a few twists to these ideas. In the 1950s, Ernest Lehrs argued that the formation of Christian communities that are freely bound together can liberate animals from the unfree bondage of instinct.[79] In the 1990s, when the reality of mass extinction became apparent, Virginia Gilmer defended animals on the grounds that they take on themselves "the animalistic passions and violence" that would otherwise infect humanity. Humans should thus resist the extinction of tigers, lest we all become more tiger-like. Gilmer also affirmed that since "we are connected inseparably" with the animal kingdoms, we are in a sense as endangered as they are.[80] And in 2015, Michael Ronall reinterpreted the hierarchy of minerals, plants, animals, and humans to make clear that all possess inherent worth: "Given our competitive habits, it is worth noting that a *lower* status on this ladder does not mean a *less worthy* one. At each step in the metamorphosis from mineral to plant to animal to humanity, something is lost while something else is gained, so that the entire hierarchical network is interdependent."[81]

The latest and most comprehensive entry in this conversation is Douglas Sloan's *The Redemption of the Animals,* published in 2015. An emeritus professor at Teachers College, Columbia University, who also directed the master's program in Waldorf education at Sunbridge College, Sloan places Steiner's teaching about animals into dialogue with Darwinian theory, research on animal behavior, and the animal rights movement. He makes much of Steiner's claim that animals possess species-wide "group souls" rather than true individuality. Drawing on a few neglected passages from Steiner's lectures, Sloan suggests that this may not apply to apes and to other species that have demonstrated capacities for self-recognition, language, problem solving, and a biographical sense of self.[82]

For Sloan, these exceptional species prove Steiner's general rule: most animals lack individual egos and are instead guided by the embodied wisdom of instinct. While many animal rights activists, following Peter Singer, regard any suggestion of a qualitative distinction between humans and animals as evidence of an oppressive "speciesism," Sloan cautions that "Difference does not have to mean despotic dominance." By recognizing that humans are both like and unlike animals, Steiner showed that "Human differences of kind from the animals entail ever-greater responsibility on the part of the human, while

similarities simultaneously serve to reinforce our human-animal kinship." In particular, Sloan suggests that animals' tendency to live
entirely in the present makes them more vulnerable to pain and suffering than human beings, while humans' unique capacity for self-trans-
formation gives us a unique potential for evil, including evil directed
against animals and ecosystems. We thus have a special, twofold
responsibility to animals: in the "far distant future" we will help them
attain their next stage of spiritual evolution, and "In the meantime our
responsibility is to provide them with every love and kindness of which
we are capable in order to relieve their present suffering." Sloan's
approach reflects the persistent anthroposophical concern for alchemi
cal balance and finding the middle path between extremes.[83]

Anthroposophical themes of gratitude and connection to the animals find concrete expression in the biodynamic approach to animal
agriculture. Anthroposophical beekeeping, for example, seeks to "start
from the bee" by using structures modeled on nature and allowing bees
to create their own new hives by swarming whenever possible. A biodynamic cattle farm can be immediately recognized because virtually all
of the cows have their horns. Conventional farmers dehorn cattle so
that they won't injure themselves in crowded spaces; biodynamic farmers renounce overcrowding in order to protect the cows' natural dignity
and, according to Steiner's teaching, their access to cosmic forces. They
also experiment with alternative weaning practices intended to foster
positive relationships between cows and calves, without foregoing milk
production for human benefit. At Camphill Kimberton Hills, for example, farmers wait three days before weaning, so that calves can experience a maternal bond and receive the immunological benefits of their
mothers' milk. They have also explored the nurse cow system, in which
a few cows are designated as foster mothers, and fence-line weaning, in
which mothers and calves can interact across fences that prevent them
from nursing. Perhaps most importantly, they extend their Goethean
attention to the farmers' own feelings. As one farmer put it, "I love these
cows and love is resistant to reason, resistant to economic incentive,

feasibility, practicality." And so the experimentation and discernment continues.[84]

One farmer told me that biodynamics "is about healthy relationships." Though others might adopt veganism as an expression of their concern for animals, for him the ideal is to participate in the full life cycle of each animal, from birth to butchering. People say that his pigs "are just different," and the reason is that "I really love the pigs. I spend a lot of time with them. Like any good parent … you set up boundaries, you know what your child is capable of and what they aren't capable of, and you maintain those loving boundaries. With the pigs and the cows, I have a very specific intention. I'm trying to let the pigs be pigs and I'm trying to let the cows be cows."[85]

Such attitudes set biodynamic farmers apart from the "light green religion" that Bron Taylor characterizes as the view that "environmentally friendly behavior is a religious obligation," even though nature lacks intrinsic value. Typically, light green religionists value nature insofar as it was created by a transcendent God, or because it serves human needs. Such a formulation implies a separation between humans and nature that anthroposophy rejects. Yet students of anthroposophy refuse to endorse the sharp critique of biblical "dominion" that is a staple of Gaian philosophizing. Reviewing a 1970 environmental book that "point[ed] an accusing finger at the book of Genesis," anthroposophical reviewer George Corrin argued that Christian notions of dominion are no more problematic than the Darwinian picture of humanity as "the most cunning animal in the animal world." As an alternative to both, he urged that we "see our *unique* place in the evolution of the cosmos, at the same time recognizing the necessity of interrelationships with all forms of life."[86]

In my conversations with biodynamic farmers and other students of Steiner, most distanced themselves from critiques of anthropocentrism. "There seems to be quite a bit of the … environmental conservation movement that can view humans as just a plague on the earth," observed Thea Maria Carlson of the Biodynamic Association in America. But biodynamics, she went on, demonstrates that "Humans do have an important role in creating ecological health." On a healthy farm, she explained, "the farmer is working consciously with the unique characteristics of the land," bringing plants and animals into mutually beneficial relationships "that wouldn't happen by chance." The real problem, she went on, is not anthropocentrism but a "mechanistic view of the world" that fails to "perceive and understand how the living organisms in their relationships develop."[87] Describing his debate with Gaian scientists, a prominent Goethean scientist quoted Lynn Margulis's attack on the "pox called man," and said that acknowledging simple facts about "the way we are" is a "threshold" these scientists won't cross. (He also acknowledged that "sometimes anthroposophists ... elevate [humanity] onto a throne ... in a really off-putting way.")[88]

Some biodynamic practitioners make a pragmatic case for a human-centered worldview: like it or not, humans are currently the most important force shaping ecosystems on Earth. One Camphiller, who declared he had "issues" with both Gaian deep ecology and Steiner's anthroposophy, explained that "Unfortunately we are an immensely dominant part of the ecosystem. We have to look that one in the teeth."[89] Farmer Andrew Marshall mused that "we are going beyond the tipping point. If we left nature to itself, it would not be able to put itself back together at this point." Thus humans must embrace the new role of "nature's executive functioning."[90]

Gaians might be able to accept this line of reasoning. Many accept that planet Earth has entered an "Anthropocene" geological era but regard this as cause for mourning and repentant action. Students of anthroposophy also mourn the loss of species, but embrace the Anthropocene as a step forward in Earth's evolution. At Hawthorne Valley, farmer Steffen Schneider reasons that if the world is being reshaped by human activity, it is high time for environmentalists to cultivate such "uniquely human possibilities" as mindfulness.[91] Rachel Schneider adds that "To base your entire agricultural practice on a mimicking of nature is not sufficient." If the farm is a living organism, it can also "grow to be an individuality, a spiritual individuality, the same as a person." But this will happen only if humans take on the task of "coevolving" with both the farm and the planet.[92] Down the road, a nearby Goethean scientist suggested that perhaps the central task of human evolution is "to let these other beings actually reveal sides of themselves that can only be revealed in human consciousness." He described this idea as "a thought that is almost overwhelming."[93]

Students of Steiner also embrace the Anthropocene as a confirmation of Steiner's teaching that the earth itself is "the reincarnation of an ancient planet," and that human evolution has extended overall several distinct planetary incarnations.[94] This cosmology might seem to be the polar opposite of Gaianism. For Gaians, the earth is the ultimate object of devotion, and humans are merely one component of it. For Steiner, human evolution is the ultimate value, and the earth is merely one stage in that process. But from a practical standpoint, the salient feature of Steiner's cosmology is that the whole earth is inseparably caught up in human evolution. Animals, plants, and minerals, as well as angels and other spiritual personalities, have been evolving alongside humanity across the successive planetary incarnations, in complex interaction with one another. Mediated by such individuals as George Trevelyan, such anthroposophical notions laid the foundation for spiritual Gaianism.

It is thus unsurprising that many farmers today place themselves in both the anthroposophical and the Gaian camps. At one biodynamic farm, a farmer surprised me by describing himself as a "nature worshipper." I asked if he would describe anthroposophy itself as a nature worshipping tradition. "It is both a nature-worshipping stream," he mused, and "a spirit-worshipping stream." The same could be said, he continued, for Christianity, even though "The church has polarized the earthly part as the forbidden fruit." Identifying himself with the Franciscan tradition within Christianity, he argued that both Franciscanism and anthroposophy teach "the mutual relationship between what we call the physical world and the spiritual world. They are not separate. They belong together.... Even the organic movement and most people will treat carrots as a commodity.... But in my heart, the carrot is a being. It is a lovely being that can nourish."[95] Compared with the boundaries separating anthroposophy from mainstream science and leftist environmentalism, this boundary is permeable indeed.

FROM SELF-REINFORCEMENT
TO SELF-DISPERSAL

Thus far I have emphasized the ideas—about science, hierarchy, and humanity—that distinguish anthroposophy from other strands of environmentalism. The final boundary I will discuss is more intimately connected to the social structures organizing anthroposophical initiatives. This is a more literal boundary, in that it has to do with the patterns that cause many students of Rudolf Steiner to spend more time interacting with one another than with other environmentalists. Especially in its early years, anthroposophy was an intensely self-reinforcing spirituality that encouraged participants to devote their personal energies and material resources to the building up of a tight-knit community. Since 1970, the pendulum has swung toward self-dispersal, as people with little personal connection to anthroposophy have come to dominate many anthroposophical initiatives. But other expressions of environmentalism—including, for example, the mainstream organics movement—are even more self-dispersing. Against that backdrop, anthroposophy can be perceived as an isolated subculture, or even as a "sect." Such perceptions cause considerable distress to students of anthroposophy, who nevertheless disagree about whether the current moment calls for even more self-dispersal, or for a return to the self-reinforcing patterns of previous decades.

When confronted with critics who describe anthroposophy as a "sect," many people point to the statutes Steiner established for the General Anthroposophical Society when it was reconstituted at Christmas 1923. "The General Anthroposophical Society is in no sense a secret society," began the fourth statue, "but an entirely public organisation. Without distinction of nationality, social standing, religion, scientific or artistic conviction, any person who considers the existence of such an institution as the Goetheanum in Dornach ... to be justified, can become a member of the Society. The Anthroposophical Society is averse to any kind of sectarian tendency." Other statutes struck similar notes, calling for "assistance to every human being" and for the exclusion of "dogma in any sphere."[96]

Steiner's nonsectarian intentions were qualified by his commitment to esoteric research, which is by definition not fully public, since its deeper expressions are accessible only to those with preliminary spiritual experiences. While membership in the society itself was open to all who thought it should exist, these members gave financial support to a School of Spiritual Science, whose First Class was open only to those who passed through a period of probation. (The anticipated second and third classes were never established.) The society's statutes drew a subtle distinction: while society publications would be "open to the public," those emanating from the School of Spiritual Science would carry a disclaimer indicating that "No person is held qualified to form a judgment on the contents of these works, who has not acquired—through the School itself or in an equivalent manner recognised by the School—the requisite preliminary knowledge."[97] This policy, reflected in the decision to keep the content of the Agriculture Course secret for many years, created a twofold boundary. On the one hand, those who were given access to esoteric knowledge were bound more tightly to the society—especially since some of the esoteric content they were given had to do with the ways they had been karmically bound to one another over multiple lifetimes. On the other, outsiders who might have sympathized with aspects of anthroposophy were denied the chance to explore those aspects on their own terms.

From the beginning, anthroposophy has thus been characterized by a double gesture, reaching outward to the world through practical initiatives intended to foster "a social life based on brotherly love," but also looking inward through spiritual research that is accessible only to the initiated. Members of the Anthroposophical Society have struggled to find the right balance between these tendencies. Early on, they debated whether to publish lectures originally intended for restricted audiences; both early and late, they debated how much time and energy to devote to practical initiatives and how much to "core" anthroposophy. It is common, in anthroposophical circles, for people to insist that Steiner himself bore no responsibility for sectarian tendencies within the society, which they ascribe either to proclivities inherited from the Theosophical Society or to the misunderstandings of his students. But finding the right balance was as difficult for Steiner as for any of his students.

Just before the reconstitution of the Anthroposophical Society, Steiner gave a series of lectures on "Awakening to Community" that continue to be among the most commonly studied. He made an inspiring case for renewing the "universally human character" of anthroposophy, and for avoiding "separatism" and "sectarianism." He singled out the Waldorf school as a positive example of an "institution set up [not] to teach anthroposophy, but to solve the problem of how to teach for the best development of the whole wide range of human capacities," and urged his students to create other institutions along similar lines. But he criticized other, unnamed initiatives that "did not, in fact, spring directly from an anthroposophical spirit, but [were] instead founded and carried on alongside and unrelated to it." He faulted their leaders for the way they related to the society: "A person can be the most excellent Waldorf School teacher imaginable.... without necessarily doing the right thing by the Society as a member. I am not saying that this is true in any given instance, just that it could be true." He then turned to a similarly ambiguous criticism of The Coming Day and the Christian Community, stressing that "the failure to give the parent entity what it needs in order to foster all its offspring properly is cause ... for really deep worry about the Anthroposophical Movement."[98]

Steiner raised an essential challenge for any spiritual movement that seeks to share its gifts freely with the world: how to balance the sharing of gifts with care for the wellsprings from which they arise? He strove to honor the complexity of the question and to soften what he regarded as necessary criticisms of his students. But because he spoke in a tone that was both authoritative and ambivalent—claiming a unique right to judge but failing to render an unequivocal judgment—he left his students perpetually off balance. To this day, this text is cited both by those who fault the society for "sectarianism" and by those who worry that it directs too much attention to the practical initiatives and not enough to spiritual research. These debates, in turn, are incomprehensible and off-putting to outsiders, who are drawn to anthroposophy through the initiatives.

The challenge of balancing practical initiatives with core anthroposophy is compounded by a tendency that is, ironically, inherent in the initiatives. Precisely because there are so many initiatives, it is possible for devoted students of Rudolf Steiner, and even some people with little interest in Steiner, to live their lives entirely within the orbit of anthroposophical initiatives. One might study at an anthroposophical school, receive therapies from an anthroposophical doctor, attend eurythmy performances, worship in a congregation of the Christian Community, and—of course—eat biodynamic food. Each choice might be intrinsically meritorious, yet the person who chooses all of them will begin to speak in anthroposophical jargon that is difficult for others to understand, and may lose touch with important conversations in the larger society.

The anthroposophical movement's early tilt toward self-reinforcement harmed some of Steiner's most devoted students. The investors who lost their fortunes in the collapse of The Coming Day would not have invested those fortunes if Steiner had not instilled in them a sense of all-encompassing devotion. Less wealthy anthroposophists gave countless hours of labor to such tasks as the construction of the first Goetheanum. Practices that bound people tightly to the movement made it difficult for them to extricate themselves, even if it became unhealthy for them. Within the Camphill movement, for example, this has been the case until recently. People worked without salaries (and thus without paying into governmental pensions) on the understanding that the movement would care for them throughout their lifetimes, but there was no guarantee of support for people who chose to leave, or were forced out. (Most Camphill places now have formal systems for retirement savings and for offering automatic "leaving money" to co-workers who depart.)

From the beginning, anthroposophy attracted vulnerable people. Some had had intense, perhaps frightening spiritual experiences and longed for reassurance that they were not insane. Bereaved parents and spouses longed for a spiritual connection with their relatives. Many early anthroposophists had family members with intellectual disabilities or mental illnesses; they had seen those loved ones rejected by the larger society, then embraced with warmth and understanding in anthropo-sophical curative communities. Still others had experienced social ostra-cism because of their Jewish heritage. Anthroposophy gave these people a sense of connection and meaning but not without a price. That price included extensive investment of time and money, a willingness to be criticized by Steiner, and a willingness to take seriously ideas that their friends and family were likely to reject as bizarre. Steiner himself paid a similar price. He also lost money to The Coming Day, he also embraced ideas that he found discomfiting, and his unwavering commitment to movement leadership alongside spiritual research led him to an early grave. Steiner's personal suffering did not change the reality that, while preaching a message of spiritual freedom, he encouraged his students to subordinate their self-interest to the development of his movement.

Self-reinforcement also caused lingering harm by creating a picture of anthroposophy as a secretive sect in the minds of some outsiders. The undeniable fact that in the early years the anthroposophical movement had teachings and practices that it did not divulge to the public makes it easier for critics to imagine that it is still keeping secrets. Even critics who claim to be concerned primarily with "pseudoscience" or racism may actually be motivated, more viscerally, by concerns about secrecy, transparency, and the defensive attitudes they may have encountered among committed students of Steiner. Yet the self-reinforcing patterns evident in anthroposophy's history can be found in the early years of virtually every spiritual movement that has lasted more than a generation. Genuinely new ideas cannot enter the world without a struggle. Ideas that ultimately change the world are initially rejected as bizarre by most people who hear them—and the few who do accept the new ideas are often equally open to other ideas that ultimately prove fruitless. Thus, creative ideas require a teacher who is able to bind the early believers together into a mutually supportive community that is able to withstanding the ridicule and mockery of its neighbors, even at a personal cost. Steiner bound his community together by offering a life-giving teaching, making it fully available to only a select few, and then warning those few that they were misunderstanding him. According to the gospels, Jesus of Nazareth did the same thing: he told his disciples that "the secret of the kingdom" had been given to them but not to outsiders, then asked why they did not understand (Mark 4:11–13).

More generally, self-reinforcement has served anthroposophy by fostering a depth of commitment in the people who start anthroposophical initiatives, and by creating a dense web of mutual support among those initiatives. In the middle decades of the twentieth century, people crossed oceans to plant new Waldorf schools or Camphill communities. It seems unlikely that they would have done so had they not seen this work as an expression of their core spiritual identities. More recently, the earliest CSAs and anthroposophical banks all emerged in communities of people whose participation in other initiatives had primed them to bring trust and solidarity to the new ventures.

The rigid boundaries created by anthroposophy's early self-reinforcement were thus, perhaps, necessary to its early development. As many students of anthroposophy point out, seeds have thick shells for a reason: their creative forces cannot survive in the world unprotected. The content of the Agriculture Course was in that vulnerable place in the years before the farmers had had a chance to find out if Steiner's ideas would actually bear fruit in practice, and so it was understandable that Steiner told the nonfarmers who had attended the course to "fix a padlock on their mouths."[99] Early Camphillers likewise created a protective sheath around people with developmental disabilities, lest they encounter violence or prejudice in the larger society.

But shells break for a reason: at some point, the creative forces cannot survive unless they mingle freely with everything else in their environment. Most of the students of Steiner with whom I spoke were convinced that the time had come, or perhaps was long past, for anthroposophy to shed its shell. One biodynamic farmer bemoaned the fact that, until recently, his farm didn't even have a sign to announce itself to the world. "I don't want to be this elite, cozy little club.... My argument has always been ... we are completely normal people. We are as normal as it gets."[100] "The biggest challenge of anthroposophy" today, explained an international leader, "is to be open-minded, open to all ways." Precisely "because Steiner has given us so much wisdom," she added, we must avoid the temptation to see ours as the only truth. Rather than getting "stuck on [Steiner's] texts, it is important to "take [anthroposophy] to the world in a living way."[101] "That is a moral question for every anthroposophist," declared Camphiller Veronika van Duin, "should I be separate from the world?" Though engagement always involves moral compromise, she insisted that it is obligatory. "If you want to be a purist, then you are not really practicing anthroposophy because you are transforming nothing."[102] Any economically isolated community, explained Seb Monteux (who, like Veronika van Duin, was raised within Camphill), faces the twin dangers of narcissism and parasitism: its members may assume they are better than their neighbors, and they may start "eating one another" for lack of interaction with other people. Healthy communities are defined by "the ideals that live within them" and not by their physical boundaries.[103]

At the Goetheanum, Jean-Michel Florin explained why anthroposophy had been slow to abandon self-reinforcing habits. In the years after World War II people felt that so much had been destroyed that it was necessary to create little "islands where we can preserve something from the destruction." That attitude was perpetuated by the generation of 1968, many of whose members saw the distinction between the capitalist mainstream and the utopian alternative in black and white terms. But contemporary environmentalists are wary of sectarianism and honor the ecological principle that "If you are not part of an organism, the organism will put you out." What's more, people bring their own spiritual experiences to biodynamics courses—talking openly about encounters with elemental beings, for example—and anthroposophy has valuable tools for making sense of such experiences.[104]

Well-meaning efforts to open up sometimes misfire. Many anthroposophical initiatives have eliminated explicit references to Rudolf Steiner or anthroposophy from their mission statements and websites in an effort to welcome people rooted in other spiritual paths—or, in some cases, to acknowledge that people of diverse spiritual paths already run the initiative. Camphill Scotland, the coordinating body for legally autonomous Camphill communities in Scotland, does not mention anthroposophy in its mission statement because not all Camphill places in Scotland work out of anthroposophy. Triodos Bank's website goes further: it contains no references to anthroposophy at all, even on pages for "history" and "frequently asked questions."[105] In a sense, this is an accurate self-representation, since Triodos loans money to Buddhist, yoga, Sikh, Pentecostal, Anglican and Catholic religious communities, as well as to environmental and social projects without any spiritual affiliation. Yet anthroposophy is embedded in Triodos's name (a reference to threefolding) and its way of doing business, and someone who learned this only after investing money might feel misled. Rudolf Steiner Foundation similarly eliminated the name "Rudolf Steiner" from its publicity after it changed its name to RSF Social Finance, to dispel the impression that it was a grant-making "foundation." Realizing the problems inherent in this approach, they began using such phrases as "spirit matters" and "inspired by the work of Rudolf Steiner" to invite potential investors to ask more questions.[106]

The leaders of anthroposophical initiatives face a catch-22: if they talk openly about anthroposophy, some hearers will experience it as proselytization; if they remain silent, some will experience it as a lack of transparency. The dilemma is embedded in a principle that many attribute to Steiner: don't answer questions that haven't been asked. Out of a desire to avoid aggressive proselytizing, they don't talk about the content of Steiner's teachings unless they are asked directly about it. "In a conversation with a social worker or someone from the Care Inspectorate," explained one Camphiller, "I would never mention forces, Ahrimanic or Luciferic or spirits or something."[107] Jean-Michel Florin elaborated: "If I explain to you what Steiner said about angels," even though you haven't asked, "what do you do with that?"[108] A founder of Triodos echoed the sentiment, explaining that "When I represented Triodos Bank to the Central Bank for example, I cannot start preaching about anthroposophy. I have to respond to the questions in a professional way." But, he added, "Someone who knows about anthroposophy can discover a lot of anthroposophy" in the way he answers the question.[109]

Other students of anthroposophy insist that it is appropriate and obligatory to answer questions that are implicit in a person's actions. In the past, said Thea Maria Carlson, the reluctance to talk openly about spiritual matters made the movement more of an "insiders' club," since outsiders couldn't figure out what it was all about. "The challenge is how to communicate what biodynamics is in a way that is both approachable and not alienating, and yet stays true to all the parts of it."[110] "When you come with your child to a [Waldorf] school," added another leader, "you've already asked the question" about the worldview underlying the school. He often tells Waldorf teachers that they have an implicit "contract" of transparency with the parents. A teacher might thus volunteer the information that "my worldview out of working with anthroposophy is that we are not in this life for the first time, that we've had multiple lifetimes, that your child coming to me may be my teacher in a previous experience and therefore I will be carrying this image of your child as this amazing being.... I will not be imposing that on you or your children in any way, but it is what is inside. It is what is driving me to ... do the best in teaching your child." This same leader added that an increasing number of Waldorf teachers are not themselves deeply grounded in anthroposophy—or perhaps they are grounded enough to have joined the Anthroposophical Society and begun a meditative practice, but not enough to give the speech just quoted, because they haven't worked with enough students to have experienced the wisdom carried from past lives.[111]

Even prominent figures in the anthroposophical movement sometimes express impatience with the inward-looking habits they see in other students of Steiner. After teaching a course at the Goetheanum, Ha Vinh Tho bemoaned the fact that Steiner's contributions are missing from so many public discussions of "the future of our planet," and blamed this on students of Steiner, who are "more concerned with internal issues of interpretation of Anthroposophy than with the burning questions of today's world." Many students of Steiner, he added, acknowledge his advice not to take anything on faith, but uphold "contents that can only be perceived by non-anthroposophists as a revelation given by an enlightened master." He then praised Otto Scharmer and Arthur Zajonc as two students of Steiner who are "well-received in any context" because they "only share with others what they have truly experienced and fully integrated themselves."[112] I would note, however, that Scharmer and Zajonc often present their experiences without mentioning Steiner, and this could contribute to the sense that Steiner's voice is missing from public conversations.

In any case, the tilt toward self-dispersal within anthroposophical initiatives has now reached such a rapid pace that it is hard to be confident that the snapshot offered in this book will still be accurate a few years after its publication. The Waldorf movement is growing with astonishing rapidity in China, where it is necessarily detached from Christian spirituality and European folk culture. Two growth areas for biodynamics are in the wine industry—which requires a soft-pedaling of Steiner's teachings about alcohol—and in India, where such groups as the International Society for Krishna Consciousness mingle biodynamic principles with traditional ayurvedic practice.

At such a time, it is hard to argue that anthroposophy needs a hard boundary to protect it from hostile outsiders. There may be still be hostile outsiders, as this chapter has demonstrated, but there are far more potential allies. In the past ten years, one Irish Camphiller told me, there has been a "massive shift." Again and again, through his work in renewable energy, he meets people who seem to possess "a full anthroposophic background" and yet have never heard of Steiner. Some practice New Age spirituality, others are devout Catholics or entirely secular—and yet they display an openness to conversations about reincarnation and uncanny insight in difficult situations.[113] Likewise, the leader who urged Waldorf teachers to share their worldviews more openly observed that much has changed since the days when his mother had to bake her own seven-grain bread because it was not sold in any stores. To continue sheltering anthroposophy from a world that actively seeks spiritual and ecological insight betrays "a lack of trust in where we are as humanity at this particular time."[114]

At the Goetheanum, a leader in the biodynamics movement summed up the consensus of most of the people with whom I spoke: "We have to do a double gesture now. The one is to deepen biodynamics ... [and] care for the spiritual sources of our movement.... And the second one is ... [to become] important partners and players and also initiators of alliances."[115] Such alliances, I suspect, will foster the continued evolution of both anthroposophy and environmentalism.

Evolution

Anthroposophy's Gifts to the Environmental Movement

Organisms evolve, ecosystems evolve, and social movements evolve. Environmentalism has changed dramatically since Rudolf Steiner gave the Agriculture Course, since Rachel Carson published *Silent Spring*, and since the first community supported farms were launched. For a century, anthroposophy and its initiatives have shaped the evolution of environmentalism, and they will likely continue to do so in the century that lies ahead. In this chapter, I will not venture to predict anthroposophy's effect on the environmentalism of the future. Instead, I will reflect more personally on the gifts that I—as a sympathetic outsider—hope anthroposophy will continue to bring to environmentalism. Though I continue to appreciate the contributions of mainstream science, the Left, and Gaian spirituality, my environmental commitments have been rebalanced by the alchemy of anthroposophy. I believe the environmental movement as a whole might benefit from a similar rebalancing.

More specifically, I see anthroposophy as the source of four significant gifts to environmentalism. These gifts are a *cosmic holism* that challenges us to attend to ever-widening circles of interconnection; a *homeopathic model of social change* that invites us to use subtle influences to heal the world; an *appropriate anthropocentrism* that allows us to experience ourselves as fully at home in the world; and a vision of *planetary transmutation* that can resist climate change while embracing biological and spiritual evolution. Cosmic holism expands the environmental imagination and counters tendencies to reduce the movement to a single issue or single activist strategy. Homeopathy reminds us that small organisms are as important as large ones in a healthy ecosystem, warding against the demand that we judge environmental practices exclusively on their capacity to scale up. Appropriate anthropocentrism protects us from the temptation to respond to ecological devastation with bitter misanthropy. And the idea of planetary transmutation prevents the ideal of conserving nature and "leaving no trace" from hardening into a stubborn resistance to evolution itself. But these gifts are valuable only as counterbalances: taken in isolation, each could be as distorted as that which it counters.

COSMIC HOLISM

By "cosmic holism" I refer to the dimensions of anthroposophy and of biodynamics that cannot be found in mainstream organics: the homeopathic preparations, the astrological planting calendar, the alchemical vocabulary, the notion that Christ's blood still lives in the soil, the ideal of the farm as a living organism, and the conviction that the farmer's spiritual striving ensures the health of the farm and the nutritional value of its produce. These reflect Rudolf Steiner's conviction that "we must extend our view to the whole Cosmos."[1] Together, they constitute a standing challenge to environmentalists to stretch our imaginations to include ever-widening webs of interconnection. One hundred years ago, cosmic holism created an imaginative space within which farmers could begin exploring the biological interconnections essential to the health of the soil; fifty years ago, it prodded gardeners to ask tough questions about DDT. More recently, cosmic holism has inspired fresh thinking about the economic, social, and cultural contexts for farming. Environmentalists need not accept all of Steiner's answers in order to draw sustenance from the surprising questions that arise from cosmic holism. What are the special contributions that persons with Down syndrome, or with autism, can make to healthy farms? What forgotten ecological truths lie buried in Ptolemy's system of planetary spheres, in Aristotle's account of the four elements, or in Paracelsus's system of medicine? What new possibilities open up when a compost pile is presented as a work of art?[2]

The environmental movement today has the resources to embrace a cosmic holism that is even wider than that offered by Rudolf Steiner. Though his system was dizzying in scope, it was limited by his preference for European culture. Yet every culture has its own cosmological traditions, its own imaginative pictures linking the carrot or the earthworm to the music of the spheres. Already in Steiner's time, Albert Howard and other pioneers of organic agriculture had their own imaginations stretched by non-Western worldviews and agricultural traditions. Today, students of anthroposophy increasingly work in partnership with representatives of other spiritual traditions. The first university-based course in biodynamics in the United States is housed at Maharishi University of Management, which also teaches a "Vedic Organic Agriculture" based on the teachings of Maharishi Mahesh Yogi. Anthroposophical proponents of seed-saving and opponents of genetically modified organisms look for leadership to Vandana Shiva. Students of anthroposophy have joined with members of the Sufi Order International to revitalize the alchemical traditions of both the West and the Muslim world.[3] In Ecuador, Finca Sagrada blends anthroposophical and shamanic spiritualities, as well as biodynamic and permacultural methods, as it seeks to "serve this sacred land in collaboration with the Elders of this Mother Earth."[4] Arthur Zajonc and Ha Vinh Tho bring decades of anthroposophical experience to their work with Buddhist organizations. Such blending reflects a rising awareness that spirituality is, by its nature, hybrid. Just as the ancient Israelites borrowed their flood story from the Mesopotamians, and the Romans modeled their deities on those of the Greeks, so too are contemporary citizens of the United States indebted to the indigenous creation stories first told on the North American continent, to the Freemasonic ideals of our founding fathers, and to the African rhythms embedded in our popular music. The cosmic holism of the future should be more conscious of its hybridity.

Whatever cosmologies environmentalists choose to embrace, we can learn much from anthroposophy's track record of navigating between a cosmic vision and pragmatic choices in the here and now. Long ago, Ehrenfried Pfeiffer identified the dilemma of discerning how to respond to a wider culture that was ready for the "biological" aspect of biodynamics but resistant to its "dynamic" (what I am calling "cosmic") challenges. "The significance of soil-life, the earth as a living organism, the role played by humus" have all "been adopted," he observed, "but with a materialistic bias, whereas an understanding of the *dynamic* side, made possible by Rudolf Steiner's pioneering indications, is still largely absent."[5] With these words, Pfeiffer sought to rebalance a one-sided situation that he himself had created, by occluding the cosmic dimension of biodynamics in his publications.

The same dilemmas face the biodynamic movement today. In North America, the codirector of the Biodynamic Association Robert Karp has been courageous in lifting up the cosmic dimensions of biodynamics for public scrutiny, by, for example, choosing such themes as "alchemy" and "spiritual agriculture" for the cover of the association's journal. The theme for the association's 2012 national conference was "sacred agriculture," which allowed both for a highlighting of the cosmic dimension of biodynamics and dialogue with farmers rooted in other spiritual traditions. In his conversation with me, Karp stressed that the biodynamics movement is able to celebrate its cosmic dimension precisely because of its track record of producing healthy farms and high-quality food. "We have to really earn our credibility by really being good at biological holism," he said. To merely preach about planetary influences, he warned, is to "stay too Platonic and ungrounded"; what is needed is research demonstrating the benefits of biodynamic preparations on "mycorrhizal fungae and the different bacteria from the forest ecosystem and the meadow ecosystem."[6] Likewise, Jean-

Michel Florin, who heads the Agricultural Section at the Goetheanum, responded to my question about biological and cosmic holism by insisting that it is "very important to have results."[7]

It is tempting to defend cosmic holism on sheer pragmatic grounds for its proven track record of stretching environmental imaginations to take a longer list of *mundane* factors into account. What difference does it make whether Mars, Jupiter, and Saturn *really* exert special influence on the farm, when it is demonstrably true that farmers who believed they do were the ones who came up with the idea of community supported agriculture? This line of pragmatic argumentation is especially potent today, as more and more corporations with dubious environmental records get involved in the growing organic sector. As Biodynamic Association codirector Thea Carlson observed, consumers turn to biodynamics today because "they are disillusioned with big agriculture and the fact that there's been kind of a corporate takeover of organics."[8] More pointedly, Tom Spaulding of Angelic Organics observed that "An organic farmer can buy a USDA-approved organic fertilizer that is really something that is an affront to the earth."[9]

But cosmic holism may not, in fact, play its imagination-stretching role if it is reduced to a mere tool for stretching the imagination. It is reasonable that some farmers might seek biodynamic certification from Demeter International merely because it is the most reliably rigorous form of organic certification. But if Demeter were to narrow its own vision to accommodate such people, it would reinforce the tendencies that lead consumers to choose corporate organics merely because they are the cheapest choices on the market. The challenge, as the organic sector grows in volume, is to preserve spaces where it can continue to broaden its vision. For Tom Spaulding—a biodynamic educator who is by no means a card-carrying anthroposophist—the secret to such preservation is an abiding sense of mystery. Biodynamic certification, he noted, requires the maintenance of a certain amount of wild space on each farm. While touring the oak savanna at Angelic Organics with farmer John Peterson, he asked "Why in the history of this farm didn't those get cut down?" Peterson replied, "Because we don't know what is there." Attention to "biological interdependentness" alone, Spaulding elaborated, doesn't help us "honor the things that are beyond our knowledge.... [We] need a way of honoring those and holding a space for the presence of those things that are unknowable."[10]

SOCIAL HOMEOPATHY

If the gift of cosmic holism is to widen the environmental imagination, anthroposophy's second gift invites environmentalists to narrow their vision by appreciating small and subtle forces. Along with the literal practice of homeopathy in the biodynamic preparations comes what I would call a homeopathic model of social change—an awareness that practices that cannot or will not "scale up" can still exert powerful healing forces on society as a whole. This is a pattern that has recurred again and again. Marjorie Spock and Polly Richards did not aspire to build either a massive farm or a global movement against pesticides, but they made the fruits of their own struggle available to Rachel Carson and other activists with loftier ambitions. Similarly, the founders of the Temple-Wilton Community Farm valued high ideals more than rapid growth, but they still catalyzed a global movement simply by sharing their stories with neighbors who possessed idealism and ambition in slightly different proportions.

Early on in my research, one interview subject mentioned that just as only 1 percent of agricultural land is certified organic, only 1 percent of organic land is certified biodynamic.[11] Yet this tiny fraction exerts its subtle influence on the whole. From the beginning to the end of my research, I have been surprised to discover that foundational components of the organic network that I did not think were associated with anthroposophy actually had a significant link. My realization that biodynamic farmers were rarely given credit for initiating community supported agriculture helped launch the book, while I did not realize that Worldwide Opportunities on Organic Farms began at Emerson College until my final week of writing in the summer of 2016. For their own part, biodynamic farmers have always understood their movement in homeo-pathic terms. Comparing biodynamic farms to "'islands' of health and healing," Philip Very promised that "these islands can ray out to the neighboring lands and like a homeopathic dose help to heal the earth."[12]

One of the metaphysical presuppositions underlying homeopathic practice is that it is neither possible nor desirable to eliminate any element from an ecosystem altogether. From the anthroposophical perspective, no idea ever truly dies, because the Akashic chronicle carries a complete record of consciousness. No amount of water can wash pollution away, because water carries a physical memory of everything that has passed through it. On the other hand, nothing can be properly classified as "pollution" in itself; the only question is what proportion of a given element is most conducive to the overall health of the system. This presupposition shapes anthroposophical practice at every level: from the reluctance of biodynamic farmers to eliminate specific pests, to the skepticism that many anthroposophists feel about vaccines, to the willingness of anthroposophical scientists to draw insights from Paracelsus and Goethe as well as Darwin and Haeckel.

Importantly, the logic of homeopathy does not automatically translate into specific environmental policies. To say that a healthy ecosystem requires a balance of diverse elements does not answer the question of which elements need to be strengthened and which need to be inhibited. To find value in both Goethe and Darwin does not determine whom to emphasize in a given moment! What anthroposophy does engender, though, is a consistent skepticism of monocultural, or one-size-fits-all, practices in agriculture and in ethics. Environmentalism needs this skepticism. While most environmentalists reject literal monocultures—thousand-acre fields devoted to a single strain of corn or soybeans—the movement is as prone to monocultural logic as any other segment of humanity. Organic standards that categorically forbid petrochemical inputs, farmers' markets that rigidly exclude nonlocal products, and aspirations for "zero carbon" lifestyles all mirror corporate agriculture's monocultural thinking. Many students of anthroposophy quietly resist absolutist styles of activism—even, for example, to the extent that most biodynamic farmers opt out of Demeter certification! This tendency may cause them to be perceived as lacking in environmental commitment, when in fact they model a subtly different form of activism. It is the difference, perhaps, between mounting a massive campaign to persuade university endowments to divest from fossil fuels, and creating green energy investment funds like those offered by the anthroposophical banks—with collaboratively negotiated interest rates so low that no university would invest in them.

The anthroposophical alternative is needed, because absolutism carries significant dangers. For individuals with a pragmatic cast of mind, absolutist prescriptions are inherently off-putting: thus many farmers who want to do right by the planet resist going organic because they can't imagine living without one specific antibiotic. Some consumers are paralyzed by the perceived need to choose among rival absolutes, such as local versus organic versus fair trade. Another problem is that monocultural solutions do not engender the imaginative suppleness we may need to respond to environmental challenges that have not yet emerged. A technological breakthrough in clean energy, for example, might meet the most rigorous standard of anticarbon activism but render us vulnerable to the rapid depletion of other resources. Most generally, monocultural activism often rests on a Kantian foundation that is contrary to the obvious ecological facts. Kant famously counseled that we should follow only those ethical principles that we are willing to see applied to everyone, and many advocates of veganism and carbon neutrality apply that rule with admirable consistency. But an ecosystem in which buffalo and prairie grass and wolves and earthworms all adhered to principles appropriate to the others could not thrive.

To be clear, I am *not* suggesting that anthroposophy's homeopathic approach is superior to the absolutisms of veganism or carbon neutrality. Absolutism has its own necessary place in the ecological ecosystem. It focuses attention on the most pressing problems, and it can even function homeopathically: a tiny number of vegans, for example, have

inspired millions of people to eat lower on the food chain. The homeopathic approach has its own weaknesses, such as a tendency toward
complacency or toward investing great energy into quixotic projects.
These weaknesses would be magnified if anthroposophy were the dominant force within environmentalism.

The power of homeopathy is evident in anthroposophy's willingness
to play a "leavening" role in larger social processes. This thought can
be traced to Jesus's parables about yeast, mustard seeds, salt, and other
small substances with big effects. Rudolf Steiner taught that "the great
mission of Anthroposophy" was to become "a leaven in every part of
life."[13] Robert Karp, echoing Steiner, has argued that activists should
"try to discern and give shape" "to what is already emerging or trying
to emerge in the world," noting that this "approach should resonate
with organic and sustainable farmers who often speak of the need to
cooperate *with* nature rather than to aggressively impose ideas and
methods *onto* nature."[14] I heard it expressed more poignantly by another
farmer, who mused on the unrecorded fruits of his four decades of biodynamic research on various Camphill farms. If someone had been following "alongside who could have jotted it down and taken the correct
pictures," he speculated, that evidence might "have gone somewhere."
But from an anthroposophical perspective, he went on, it *had* gone
somewhere anyhow. "Whatever we've done and offered up to the other
side is available now in the Akashic chronicle.... As long as the right
things have been done at some point, they'll come down when the right
time comes again."[15] I would add, more mundanely, that plants sprouted
from the seeds he saved are still growing today.

APPROPRIATE ANTHROPOCENTRISM

That farmer's emphasis on the importance of individual spiritual activity touches on anthroposophy's third gift. In its unabashed anthropocentrism, anthroposophy holds out a compelling hope that humans can live
in harmony with the ecosystems that surround us. From the perspective

of anthroposophical cosmology, human evolution began long before this particular planet materialized and will continue long after it ceases to exist. The earth is simply the vessel for the current phase of the human story. But the consequence of this is not that the earth is made subordinate to humanity's spiritual ambition. Instead, it is identified so fully with humanity that human well being cannot be imagined apart from the health of the planet.

This constructive anthropocentrism shows up in several dimensions of anthroposophical practice. First and foremost is the insistence on the farmer's spiritual development. This is not encapsulated in the standards governing biodynamic certification, as that would violate the anthroposophical principle that spiritual activity requires perfect freedom. But it is an integral component of biodynamic training programs and of countless workshops at biodynamic gatherings. Any farmer engaged in biodynamics, however casually, experiences a standing invitation to deeper spiritual practice.

There is no single template for *how* farmers should be spiritually engaged in their work. A generation ago, Heinz Grotzke portrayed farming as a sort of universal vocation, promising biodynamic farmers a chance to "experience the varying moods of student, teacher, artist, architect, and priest."[16] At Camphill Grangebeg, Tobias Pedersen explained to me that each morning he spends some quiet time picturing his fields, focusing on the surrounding wildlife, as well as on the livestock that spend time there; on the elemental beings, soil, and plants; and on "some of the difficulties the field might be having." He then "offer[s] it up to the angels to see whether I can get some form of answer, something that might help it." Most days he accompanies this meditation with a physical visit to each field.[17] Other farmers rely on Rudolf Steiner's "basic" (or "subsidiary") exercises, simple practices for achieving conscious control of mental processes. Whatever their particular practice, moreover, most biodynamic farmers are comfortable describing their work as a process of "Christianizing the earth." "It is not possible," explained Camphiller Vicky Syme, "just to connect with the land and the Christ forces there if one isn't following a personal pathway." For her, it is as simple as the old dictum that "you are what you eat": only food produced with spiritual practices will nourish both spirit and body. "You have to really experience it and work on the land.... There's a very individual connection to the Christ and in turn how we work with the land. What works for me doesn't necessarily work for someone else, and it depends where you are in your own ecosystem."[18]

This emphasis on the farmer's personal path has a double implication for the spread of biodynamics. On the one hand, it limits how quickly the movement can spread. While farmers often embrace organic certification without any inner conviction, merely because of the price premium, biodynamics proliferates one farmer at a time. On the other hand, biodynamics exerts an especially powerful attraction for young people—including many with no family background in farming—who see farming as part of a spiritual or ecological vocation. "A lot of farmers," observed Thea Carlson, "are wanting to find more meaning in their work, and can see that there is something in biodynamics that is more ... than following some set of rules."[19]

While anthroposophy's emphasis on spiritual development leads some people to intense identification with the vocation of farming, it inspires others to bring an ecological consciousness to artistic or entrepreneurial vocations. Camphiller Steve Lyons, for example, interpreted the rise of social entrepreneurship in relation not only to the environmental movement but also to the process of individualization that Steiner regarded as central to human evolution today. Because humans are "much more individualized" than we once were, "we don't relate to the earth and the natural world in the way that people used to." This is troubling to many people, but it is an illusion to think that the problem can be solved merely by stepping backward into group consciousness. Authentic environmentalism has to "go through the individualizing of human consciousness.... That's the challenge for our time, Steiner says, to find a way back to each and find a new relationship, based on our individuality, with the earth."[20]

Anthroposophy's emphasis on individual human development sets it apart from environmental spiritualities that stress "reverence for nature," understood as an intrinsic value just as it is and apart from human intervention. Camphiller Andrew Plant described this as the difference between the "Franciscan" and "Benedictine" streams within Christianity. "Saint Francis would have said, nature is beautiful, don't touch it. Let the birds come to you.... And the ecology movement is like that. Man is the only creature who fouls his own nest. If it wasn't for people, everything would be fine.... Beauty and harmony, and don't muck it up." Students of anthroposophy, by contrast, emulate the Benedictine monks who have always "worked the earth ... tilled the soil, grown orchards and so on." This implies that humans are actually capable of "doing the good, not just wishing the good or not doing anything in case it is bad."[21] Another practitioner of biodynamics explained his own faith in the human capacity for "doing the good" by unpacking the two parts of the word "biodynamics." "Bio" implies "respect to nature," and this means going "without fertilizers, without chemistry, without genetically modified procedures and so on." But "dynamic means this is not enough. We need to go further and to bring something back out of our cultural sphere as humans to nature." Ultimately, biodynamics involves a "double gesture" that seeks "to protect the wisdom of nature" but also to bring nature "nearer ... to what we are in the better sense of ourselves."[22]

Steve Kaffka exemplified this tension between anthroposophical and preservationist approaches to nature in a humorous anecdote from his time at Alan Chadwick's garden in Santa Cruz. He was giving a tour of Alan Chadwick's garden to Sierra Club president David Brower. Kaffka began, "The Garden at one time looked just like this chaparral-covered hillside. Now look at how wonderful it is," and Brower muttered that "the chaparral-covered hillside looked just fine to him." For Kaffka, this was evidence of a basic divergence between preservationists and those who, like Chadwick, saw nature as "a place to transform and create."[23]

Anthropocentrism also reflects a realistic assessment of how deeply symbiotic much of nature already is with humanity. "I would say farms are about the biggest thing going on the planet, in terms of land acreage," John Peterson pointed out. Certainly there are also mountains and deserts, but in order "to save the planet you have to take care of the farms first." For this reason, Peterson values those passages in Steiner that work against sentimental views of "nature," such as the teaching that at the end of each incarnation the soul must be purged of its "last inclinations to the sensory physical world" in order to return to "its own element."[24] "A lot of people love themselves because of how they love nature," he observes, and getting over such "sentimentalizing" may be necessary for the spiritual development of both people and land.[25]

The anthroposophical approach to human activity within nature is nicely encapsulated in a folk tale that was published in a Christian Community journal and then republished in *Bio-Dynamics* in the 1970s. It concerns a group of dwarfs who kidnap humans and force them to dance with them until dawn. A peasant named Guilcher discovers that the dwarfs leave him alone so long as he carries a plowing fork with him, and he is determined to understand why. So he voluntarily joins the dance, which is danced repetitively to the words "Monday, Tuesday, Wednesday." When Guilcher introduces a variation by singing "Thursday, Friday, Saturday," the dwarfs respond with overwhelming joy, promising to make him either rich or beautiful. Despite his personal poverty, Guilcher chooses beauty, and the dwarfs heal his humped back. His changed appearance excites the envy of a greedy tailor who, upon hearing the story, tries to add Sunday to the dwarfs' verse—and receives Guilcher's hump as a reward! Finally, Guilcher teaches them to complete the verse with "and so the week had rest," and this proves to be the charm that liberates them from enslavement to the dance. The point of the story was that "Nature ... expects something from human beings. Alone, she is not 'finished.'" But the human who wants to add to nature must do so as an artist, giving freely to her rather than expecting a material return.[26]

PLANETARY TRANSMUTATION

I suspect that for most students of anthroposophy, the bottom line is that humans simply cannot be separated from nature, just as matter cannot be separated from spirit. Humans can and should change nature, but only if we are willing to change along with it, and only if the change is spiritual as well as physical. This leads to anthroposophy's final gift to environmentalism: by placing its ecological commitments within a cosmic context of evolutionary development and planetary transmutation, it challenges such environmental values as "preservation," "sustainability," and even "resilience." For students of anthroposophy, evolutionary change is ongoing and inevitable, and the earth will eventually experience "climate change" on a scale far more dramatic than what is currently projected to result from increasing levels of atmospheric carbon dioxide. But this expectation does not lead them to be passive about carbon-related climate change. Instead, they are hard at work to ensure that the mechanistic, one-dimensional changes brought about by the concentration of carbon do not foreclose the possibilities of more authentically ecological processes of change.

To be sure, the details of Rudolf Steiner's evolutionary worldview can be discomfiting, even for devoted students. One version of the story appears in *Outline of Esoteric Science*. Human evolution, Steiner explains there, began on something called "Old Saturn"—a nonmaterial planet that should not be confused with the material Saturn that exists today, but nevertheless has a subtle connection to that planet that justifies the use of the same name. It continued on the Sun and on "Old Moon" before arriving on Earth, and it will continue subsequently in other spheres. With each change of venue, human nature added a new bodily dimension, so that on Old Saturn we had only the equivalent of a physical body, on the Sun we added the etheric body (the life force we share with plants), then the astral body (the willpower we share with animals), and finally the integrating "I" that is uniquely human. The shift to each new planet involved both a fresh start and an evolutionary step backward. Within each great cycle, moreover, are smaller cycles with their own rhythms of development and disintegration.[27]

Steiner offered another perspective on the spiritual transmutation of Earth in a lecture series that focused on the importance of keeping "Luciferic" and "Ahrimanic" elements in creative balance. In the final lecture, Steiner made the seemingly odd claim that many of the "processes active in the mineral, plant, and animal kingdoms" are rooted not in material causes but "within the human organism." He then made a claim that anticipated contemporary environmental apocalypticism: "The human will has the power to dissolve and destroy all extraneous substances and forces; and the relation between the human being and the mineral, plant, and animal kingdoms of nature today is such that our will is connected with the forces of dissolution and destruction inherent in our planet." Even though humans cannot live without engaging in destruction, Steiner warned, we must not deny that it *is* destruction. If the human will were left unchecked, "The prospect of the future would ... be far from inspiring; it would be a vista of the gradual dissolution of the earth and its ultimate dispersal in cosmic space." But, Steiner went on, human influence on the earth has another pole. "The constructive, up-building forces of the planet earth also lie in humanity itself," and are exercised especially by our sleeping intelligence. And so we must realize that "The destiny of our physical earth planet in another two thousand years will not depend upon the present constitution of our mineral world, but upon what we do and allow to be done.[28]

In lectures for Waldorf teachers, Steiner similarly challenged the scientific assumption that "minerals, plants and animals [could have] develop[ed] without man being present on the earth." On the contrary, he argued, humans had continuously channeled spiritual forces that were essential to the evolution of other beings. Comparing humanity to the yeast that makes bread rise, he asserted that "The continuous giving over of human corpses to the earth ... is a real process which works on in the earth." He appealed to the holistic principle that any complex system depends on all of its constituent elements: "It is simply untrue that the evolution of the earth with respect to its mineral, plant and animal kingdoms, would continue if man himself were not there. The process of Nature is a unified whole to which man belongs."[29]

Closely related to these cosmologies is Steiner's teaching that the blood of Christ united with the earth's soil when it was shed at Golgotha. Few biodynamic farmers would mention this in an introductory lecture or farm tour; indeed, many seem to assume that contemporary environmentalists are antithetical to Christianity. Once they are reassured that their hearer is interested in spirituality, however, many farmers will acknowledge that their deepest motivation is to participate in the Christianization of the soil that began 2,000 years ago. In my interviews, several people told me that Earth is currently in a "descending time of its evolution, it is growing older and coming apart."[30] Because humans are incarnating into a planet that is "decaying and hardening and growing more materialized," part of our destiny is to participate in the process by becoming "hardened, more materialistic, more egotistical."[31] At the same time, because of the Golgotha event, the planet is experiencing a process of spiritualization in which humans can also participate. This leaves much room for balancing complementary practices. As Christian Community priest Jens-Peter Linde put it, "one tries to be as caring to the earth as one possibly can," and "at the same time one knows that a transubstantiation of the earth in due course will also take place. One hopes that in due course means when the time is ripe and not before that."[32] Noting that people who accept the inevitability of death will nevertheless use CPR to save lives, Linde added that the creed of the Christian Community describes Christ as the being "through whom human beings attain the re-enlivening of the dying earth existence."[33] Summing it up, another farmer told me that "Biodynamics or anthroposophy in general certainly doesn't look at the planet, Earth, as being in a status quo, or that the goal would be to keep the status quo.... In anthroposophy and biodynamics everything is being looked at from a more spiritual evolution or change as well."[34]

Whatever one thinks of Steiner's picture of earth evolution, and even if one greatly prefers the standard Darwinian model, there is no denying the tension between an ethic of "sustainability" and an evolutionary worldview that affirms continual change. It is simply a fact that the earth is always changing in response to the actions of humans and other life forms. Land-based organisms could evolve only because earlier, sea-based creatures had gradually breathed oxygen into the atmosphere through photosynthesis. It makes little sense to think we could or should bring this evolutionary process to a standstill today, and of course no conservationist seriously intends this. But vocabularies of conservation, sustainability, and "zero impact" prevent us from seeing that the real choice is not between change and stasis but between monocausal change brought about by the chemical process of burning fossil fuel and polycausal evolution brought about by interrelated biological processes. Believers in planetary transmutation are free not only to be *against* the too-rapid burning of fossil fuels but also to be *for* holistic processes of change. Typically, these have social as well as biological dimensions; ultimately, they stem from a conviction that the entire cosmos is *spiritually* interconnected. Belief in planetary transmutation, in short, is an invitation not only to *love* the world just as it is but also to *participate* (with all other life forms) in its ongoing evolution.

Planetary transmutation dovetails with some of the most interesting developments in the environmental movement today. Environmental historians, for example, have shown that anthropogenic climate change is not entirely new in the twentieth century: at least since the beginning of agriculture, humans have turned forests into pastures, eliminated certain species, and enabled the spread of other species in the wake of human migration. These historians have also shown that the preservationist ethos, with its celebration of "wild" or "virgin" nature, has been tied up with imperial violence against indigenous communities, such as the original inhabitants of America's natural parks.[35] Another point of contact is with the segment of the climate justice movement that accepts the inevitability of some degree of climate change, and argues that "adaptation" and "mitigation" strategies must be developed alongside efforts to minimize the damage.

Because students of anthroposophy see humanity as capable of doing things for nature that nature cannot do for itself, their environmental ethic is in some ways similar to the "stewardship" advocated by many mainstream Christians. But their understanding of how humans are related to nature is more intimate than is the case in most models of stewardship: humans are more like a specialized organ within an organism than like a caretaker who subsists independently of the object of care. Thus, Agricultural Section leader Jean-Michel Florin stresses that "man is part of nature and not separate." Because humans can "make a lot of connections between the elements of nature," we can "help nature to go further in evolution," though we "can also destroy it." *Every* part of nature, Florin continued, has a spiritual dimension that is now at one level and will "evolve in the future to a next step," but humans have an immediate and unique capacity to recognize the spiritual dimension of animals, plants, and material elements. Indeed, we can do the same for the planet as a whole. The earth is "part of the universe and … maybe an important part," but right now it is like a seed with its evolutionary potentials mostly hidden. "In biodynamic agriculture we try to open the earth, or the soil, for connection with the cosmos, with the sky, with the stars, with the whole universe."[36]

For me, it is a bit hard to understand why the anthroposophical ethos of "spiritualizing" and "Christianizing" nature could not be used to justify genetically modified organisms, mechanized carbon sequestration, and other high-tech "enhancements" of nature. It is clear that in practice anthroposophy is *not* used to justify such things, but why not? When pushed on this question, Mark Finser, a founder of RSF Social Finance, stressed that students of anthroposophy are wary of any technology that exceeds the boundaries of human consciousness. RSF Social Finance wouldn't give a loan to a genetically modified organism corporation, even if its goal were to prevent climate change, because "We wouldn't know what the consequences are of that." Traditional plant breeding also changes nature, he acknowledged, but because it has "been going on for thousands of years," we know that it can be "done in a way that honors plants." Genetically modified organisms, by contrast, typically "only can grow for one season," and we don't yet know how that will "affect the human being."[37] Andrew Plant responded to a similar question by noting that Rudolf Steiner once said, "that the deeper you go into the subnatural world, magnetism, electricity, spaceships, whatever, the higher you have to ascend into the spiritual world, you must be so spiritually aware you can work with those forces. Otherwise you unleash them out of control, as we've done, and you mess it all up."[38] Significantly, of course, this dictum holds out the possibility that humanity might eventually achieve sufficient spiritual depth to change nature more radically. Indeed, Finser stressed that RSF Social Finance has no absolute objection to new technologies: "If someone came and said they had a way to fix carbon, take carbon out of the atmosphere that would provide much more fertility to the soil, that would be very interesting. We would be intrigued by new scientific ways of creating opportunity for the earth to be rejuvenated."[39]

The character of anthroposophical participation in earth evolution can be illustrated by an incident that occurred twenty years ago at Ruskin Mill, an anthroposophical college for young people who have learning disabilities, with a stunningly beautiful campus on the site of an abandoned textile mill. As the people of Ruskin Mill were developing their fish farm into a model of sustainable food production, they learned that they were displacing a local community of water voles. What's more, human activity was displacing water voles across England. Rather than abandon the fish farm, they decided to create a new wetland and lake farther up the valley. This was at once a gift to Ruskin Mill's human and animal neighbors, who were equally free to visit the new lake, and to Ruskin Mill's students, for whom the task of building the wetland was an educational experience. For one participant, it confirmed Steiner's teaching that in 1933 Christ began to dwell within the "etheric," that is, within the biosphere of plants, animals, and humans.

This indwelling, the participant explained, was helping human beings and Earth fulfill "our collective destiny ... to become the beings and the planet of Love." Environmental activism could thus be recognized as "a tentative foreshadowing of a newly emerging Christ consciousness."[40]

This episode is typical, both in its humble concern for an overlooked animal and in its positive attitude about human activity. While many environmentalists see the advent of the Anthropocene era as cause for mourning, students of Steiner are able to embrace it with joy and hope. Ultimately, the reason for this positive attitude may have less to do with esoteric spirituality and more to do with the simple fact that the practice of farming lies at the heart of anthroposophical environmentalism. Biodynamic farmers, and everyone who engages with biodynamics through participation in other anthroposophical initiatives, are among the small fraction of human beings today who has a tangible experience of working *with* nature, of acting in ways that change the natural world without undermining its integrity.

The gift of planetary transmutation is summed up best in a 1999 essay by Manfred Klett, a founder of Dottenfelderhof Farm, who also led the Agricultural Section of the Goetheanum. Klett began by noting that "the death of agriculture took place" during the twentieth century. Industrialization forced most farmers off the land, which resulted in widespread unemployment and left farms in the hands of "those tragic few who are left to steer machines for the sake of maximizing turnover" and "those happy few who have grasped the idea of biodynamic farming." The new environmental consciousness emerged in the wake of agriculture's death, but, Klett complained," it had "no real goal" beyond "nature conservancy and the avoidance of further destruction." The task of biodynamics was to show environmentalists that they had a creative as well as a defensive role. In the cultural sphere, they could offer "crystallization points," where practitioners of traditional crafts might meet participants in spiritual life or curative education. In the economic sphere, they could "build up local markets on an associative basis." And in the rights sphere, Klett suggested, there was a need to develop new models of ownership to reflect "the idea that the land, or better still the whole of the farm individuality, cannot be a commodity." Klett concluded that the biodynamic farm was an "embryo for the threefold social organism in our time," but I would go a step further.[41] Biodynamic farms are embryos of a world in which all people experience ourselves as integral parts of living nature, which is evolving toward greater diversity and vitality.

Anthroposophy's farm-centered vision for earth evolution, in conclusion, has much to offer every environmentalist. The simple truth is that the earth of 2100 will be vastly different than the earth of 1900. It will be a hotter planet, though we do not know how much hotter. It will be home to fewer species of plants and animals. We cannot change these facts. What we can influence are the evolutionary forces that will be changing the earth between now and 2100, and beyond. Do we want these forces to be primarily mechanical forces, such as the injection of carbon into the ocean floor and the spraying of reflective gases into the atmosphere as part of a high-tech strategy to mitigate climate change? Do we want the range of species to be limited even further, as genetic engineers seek monocultures that will maximize food production for humans on an ecologically disrupted planet? Or do we want the century ahead to be characterized by a deeper symbiotic partnership between humanity and both wild and domestic plants and animals, as we work together to restore ecological balance and gradually re-create biodiversity? If these are the things we want, we would do well to look to the biodynamic farm as an emblem of our future. It is here that farmers look closely at their cows and their corn, helping them to *be* cows and corn more authentically. It is here that wild plants and animals are welcomed as bearers of their own distinctive gifts. It is here that communities gather to learn, to celebrate festivals, and to share earth's bounty. And it is here that people are coming to *know* that our future and the future of the planet are inseparably knit together.

NOTES

INTRODUCTION

1. Helpful overviews of the environmental movement that emphasize its spiritual dimensions include Roger S. Gottlieb, ed., *This Sacred Earth: Religion, Nature, Environment* (New York: Routledge, 1996); Bron Taylor, *Dark Green Religion: Nature Spirituality and the Planetary Future* (Berkeley: University of California Press, 2010); Leslie Sponsel, *Spiritual Ecology: A Quiet Revolution* (Santa Barbara, CA: Praeger, 2012); and John Grim and Mary Evelyn Tucker, *Ecology and Religion* (Washington, DC: Island Press, 2014).

2. Trauger M. Groh and Steven McFadden, *Farms of Tomorrow Revisited: Community Supported Farms, Farm Supported Communities* (Kimberton, PA: Biodynamic Farming and Gardening Association, 1998).

3. Ben Hewitt, *The Town That Food Saved: How One Community Found Vitality in Local Food* (Emmaus, PA: Rodale Books, 2011).

4. Paul Lee, *There Is a Garden in the Mind: A Memoir of Alan Chadwick and the Organic Movement in California* (Berkeley, CA: North Atlantic Books, 2013).

5. Henry Barnes, *Into the Heart's Land: A Century of Rudolf Steiner's Work in North America* (New York: Steiner Books, 2005), 122–26; and John Paull, "The Rachel Carson Letters and the Making of *Silent Spring*," *Sage Open,* July–September 2013, 1–12.

6. Michael Schut, ed., *Food & Faith: Justice, Joy and Daily Bread* (Denver: Living the Good News, 2002).

7. Norman Wirzba, *Food & Faith: A Theology of Eating* (New York: Cambridge, 2011); Ellen F. Davis, *Scripture, Culture, and Agriculture: An Agrarian Reading of the Bible* (Cambridge: Cambridge, 2009).

8. Todd LeVasseur, Pramod Parajuli, and Norman Wirzba, eds., *Religion and Sustainable Agriculture: World Spiritual Traditions and Food Ethics* (Lexington: University Press of Kentucky, 2016).

9. *Waldorf Education Worldwide: The Development of Waldorf Education Including Anthroposophical Curative Education and Social Therapy*, trans. Johanna Collis and Martyn Rawson (Berlin: Friends of Waldorf Education, 2001).

10. For an extended anthroposophical exposition of the alchemical heritage, see Dennis Klocek, *Sacred Agriculture: The Alchemy of Biodynamics* (Great Barrington, MA: Lindisfarne, 2013)

11. Anna Bramwell, *Ecology in the 20th Century: A History* (New Haven, CT: Yale University Press, 1989), 3–21. Bramwell's argument about the sui generis politics of environmentalism is echoed in Philip Conford's exceptional histories of the organics movement in Britain: *The Origins of the Organic Movement* (Edinburgh: Floris, 2001); *The Development of the Organic Network: Linking People and Themes, 1945–95* (Edinburgh: Floris, 2011).

12. Taylor, *Dark Green Religion*.

13. Dan McKanan, *Touching the World: Christian Communities Transforming Society* (Collegeville, MN: Liturgical Press, 2007).

SEED: RUDOLF STEINER'S HOLISTIC VISION

1. The tendency to overemphasize Steiner's influence is evident in the fact that his biography has been studied far more than his movement. Students of Steiner have published at least a score of biographies, the most recent and comprehensive of which are Christoph Lindenberg, *Rudolf Steiner: A Biography*, trans. Jon McAlice (Great Barrington, MA: Steiner Books, 2012; first published in German in 1997); and Peter Selg, *Rudolf Steiner 1861–1925: Lebens- und Werkgeschichte*, 3 vols. (Arlesheim, Switzerland: Verlag des Ita Wegmans Instituts, 2012). To my knowledge the most comprehensive studies of the anthroposophical movement produced by its members are Bodo von Plato, ed., *Anthroposophie im 20. Jahrhundert: Ein Kulturimpus in Biografischen Porträts* (Dornach, Switzerland: Verlag am Goetheanum, 2003), which is a collection of individual biographies rather than a narrative history; and Rahel Uhlenhoff, ed., *Anthroposophie in Geschichte und Gegenwart* (Berlin: Berliner Wissenschafts-Verlag, 2011). There is also an excellent history of anthroposophy in the United States: Henry Barnes, *Into*

the Heart's Land: A Century of Rudolf Steiner's Work in North America (Great Barrington, MA: Steiner Books, 2005). Outsiders have written far less about anthroposophy than insiders, but in English there are two excellent, semischolarly biographies: Colin Wilson's *Rudolf Steiner: The Man and His Vision* (Wellingborough, UK: Aquarian Press, 1985); and Gary Lachman's *Rudolf Steiner: An Introduction to His Life and Work* (New York: Tarcher/Penguin, 2007). Alongside these is a single movement overview—Geoffrey Ahern, *Sun at Midnight: The Rudolf Steiner Movement and the Western Esoteric Tradition* (Wellingborough, UK: Aquarian Press, 1984)—that is heavily weighted toward Steiner's biography and writings. The German academic Helmut Zander recently published both a five hundred–page biography, *Rudolf Steiner: Die Biografie* (Munich: Piper, 2011), and a two-volume study entitled *Anthroposophie in Deutschland* (Göttingen: Vandenhoeck and Ruprecht, 2007, 2008). Despite the title, the latter is concerned primarily with the historical background of Steiner's ideas, though several chapters include epilogues covering events after Steiner's death.

2. Steiner, "Agriculture Course," trans. George Adams, GA 327, lecture 1. In addition to publishing books, Steiner gave hundreds of lecture series that were published in official and unofficial editions. To avoid confusion, each of his works has been assigned a bibliographical number, prefaced by the initials GA. English translations are available in searchable but unpaginated format at the Rudolf Steiner Archive, www.rsarchive.org. German texts can be found at the Freie Verwaltung des Nachlasses von Rudolf Steiner, http://fvn-archiv .net/. In quoting Steiner's lectures, I will generally cite the title, translator, GA number, and chapter or lecture number.

3. Newcomers to anthroposophy are encouraged to start with five "basic" books, all of which have been translated into English more than once. The most recent translations, which I will cite instead of the versions included in the Rudolf Steiner Archive, are *Intuitive Thinking as a Spiritual Path: A Philosophy of Freedom,* trans. Michael Lipson, GA 4 (Great Barrington, MA: Steiner Books, 1995); *Theosophy: An Introduction to the Spiritual Processes in Human Life and in the Cosmos,* trans. Catherine E. Creeger, GA 9 (Great Barrington, MA: Steiner Books, 1994); *How to Know Higher Worlds: A Modern Path of Initiation,* trans. Christopher Bamford, GA 10 (Great Barrington, MA: Steiner Books, 1994); *An Outline of Esoteric Science,* trans. Catherine E. Creeger, GA 13 (Great Barrington, MA: Steiner Books, 1997): and *Christianity as Mystical Fact,* trans. Andrew Welburn. GA 8 (Great Barrington, MA: Steiner Books, 1997). Those who wish to read Steiner's most influential writings in a single volume should obtain Robert McDermott, ed., *The New Essential Steiner* (Great Barrington, MA: Lindisfarne, 2009).

4. Andrew Plant (long-time participant in the Camphill Movement), interview, July 2013. Unless otherwise noted, the interviews are by the author. After conducting interviews, I allowed individuals to review the text in which they are quoted and decide whether they wished to be quoted by name or anonymously.

5. Among scholars working from within the anthroposophical movement, Robert McDermott has been keen to balance the stress on Steiner's uniqueness with an acknowledgment of his context. See Robert McDermott, ed., *American Philosophy and Rudolf Steiner: Emerson, Thoreau, Peirce, James, Royce, Dewey, Whitehead, Feminism* (Great Barrington, MA: Lindisfarne, 2012); McDermott, *Steiner and Kindred Spirits* (Great Barrington, MA: Steiner Books, 2015).

6. Good overviews of these traditions include Antoine Faivre and Jacob Needleman, eds., *Modern Esoteric Spirituality* (New York: Crossroad, 1992); and Arthur Versluis, *Magic and Mysticism: An Introduction to Western Esoteric Traditions* (Lanham, MD: Rowman and Littlefield, 2007).

7. Steiner, "Preliminary Remarks," *Basic Issues of the Social Question*, trans. Frank Thomas Smith, GA 23.

8. Steiner, "Agriculture Course," lecture 6.

9. Steiner, *Autobiography: Chapters in the Course of My Life: 1861–1907*, trans. Rita Stebbing, GA 28 (Great Barrington, MA: Steiner Books, 2006), 263.

10. Steiner, "Anthroposophy and the Social Question," trans. Harry Collison, GA 34, part 1.

11. Steiner, "Social Question," GA 34, part 3.

12. I refer especially to the works of Helmut Zander and the responses of scholars affiliated with the Anthroposophical Society: Zander, *Rudolf Steiner*; Zander, *Anthroposophie in Deutschland;* and Uhlenhoff, *Anthroposophie in Geschichte und Gegenwart.*

13. Rudolf Steiner, 1925 preface to *Outline of Esoteric Science*, 6–7.

14. Colin Campbell, "The Cult, the Cultic Milieu and Secularization," in *The Cultic Milieu: Oppositional Subcultures in an Age of Globalization,* ed. Jeffrey Kaplan and Heléne Lööw (Walnut Creek, CA: AltaMira, 2002), 12–25.

15. Email correspondence with Michael Babitch and Stephen Usher, March 2016.

16. *Anthroposophical Leading Thoughts,* trans. George and Mary Adams, GA 26.

17. Robin Schmidt (director of Forschungsstelle Kulturimpuls at the Goetheanum), interview, September 2013.

18. Mark Finser (a founder of RSF Social Finance), interview, October 2013.

19. Ehrenfried Pfeiffer, preface to Rudolf Steiner, "Agriculture Course." Pfeiffer contributed this recollection to a German symposium that was published as "Rudolf Steiner, by His Pupils," *Golden Blade* 10 (1958). I cite the version on the Rudolf Steiner Archive website.

20. Peter Selg, *The Agriculture Course, Koberwitz, Whitsun 1924: Rudolf Steiner and the Beginnings of Biodynamics* (Forest Row, UK: Temple Lodge, 2010), 23–25.

21. Pfeiffer, preface.

22. Ibid.

23. Rudolf Meyer, "Memories of Koberwitz, Whitsun 1924," *Anthroposophical Quarterly* 4, no. 1 (Spring 1959): 10–13.

24. Steiner, "Agriculture Course," lectures 1, 4, 6, and 7.

25. Ibid., lectures 4, 5, and 8.

26. Ibid., lectures 2 and 8.

27. Ibid., lectures 2 and 5.

28. Ibid., lecture 4.

29. Ibid., lectures 1 and 4.

30. Albert Howard, *The Waste Products of Agriculture: Their Utilization as Humus* (London: Oxford University Press, 1931).

31. "History of Organic Farming," *Wikipedia,* accessed March 12, 2014, https://en.wikipedia.org/wiki/History_of_organic_farming. For a more complete account of organic agriculture's beginnings, see G. Vogt, "The Origins of Organic Farming," in *Organic Farming: An International History,* ed. W. Lockeretz (Oxfordshire, UK: CAB International, 2007), 9–29.

32. Steiner, "Agriculture Course," lecture 1.

33. Ibid., lecture 2.

34. Ibid., lecture 3.

35. Ibid., lecture 4.

36. Ibid., lectures 5 and 6.

37. Ibid., lecture 6.

38. Wolf Storl, *Culture and Horticulture: The Classic Guide to Biodynamic and Organic Gardening,* rev. ed. (Berkeley, CA: North Atlantic, 2013), 35; Dennis Klocek, *Sacred Agriculture: The Alchemy of Biodynamics* (Great Barrington, MA: Lindisfarne, 2013), 21–25.

39. Steiner, "Agriculture Course," lectures 1, 5, and 6.

40. Steiner, *How to Know Higher Worlds,* 56, 59.

41. Rudolf Steiner, "The Mystery of Golgotha," in *The Christian Mystery,* trans. James Hindes and ed. Christopher Bamford GA 97 (Hudson, NY: Anthroposophic Press, 1998), 48–58.

ROOTS: BIODYNAMICS AND THE ORIGINS
OF ORGANIC AGRICULTURE

1. John Paull, "The Secrets of Koberwitz: The Diffusion of Rudolf Steiner's Agriculture Course and the Founding of Biodynamic Agriculture," *Journal of Social Research & Policy* 2, no. 1 (July 2011): 19–21; Herbert H. Koepf and Bodo von Plato, *Die biologisch-dynamische Wirtschaftsweise im 20. Jahrhundert: Die Entwicklyngsgeschichte der biologisch-dynamischen Landwirtschaft* (Dornach, Switzerland: Verlag am Goetheanum, 2001).

2. Koepf and von Plato, *Die biologisch-dynamische Wirtschaftsweise,* 24–30, 58–59.

3. G.A.M. Knapp, "Spirit in Matter, *The Work of I Kolisko,*" *Journal for Anthroposophy* 26 (Autumn 1977): 6–18.

4. Wilhelm Spiess, "The Influence of the Stars on Earthly Substances," *Anthroposophical Movement* 4, no. 42 (October 16, 1927): 238–39.

5. Quoted in Caroline von Heydebrand, "Anthroposophy, Science and Education," *Anthroposophical Movement* 4, no. 6 (February 6, 1927): 44–46 (a review of Lili Kolisko, *Physiologischer Nachweis der Wirksamkeit kleinster Entitaten bei 7 Metallen* [Dornach, Switzerland: Philosophisch-Anthroposophischer Verlag, 1926]).

6. Alla Selawry, *Ehrenfried Pfeiffer: A Pioneer in Spiritual Research and Practice: A Contribution to His Biography,* trans. Joe Reuter (Spring Valley, NY: Mercury Press, 1992), 9–10, 47–48.

7. Ehrenfried Pfeiffer, *Formative Forces in Crystallization* (London: Rudolf Steiner, 1936), 9–11, 15–16, 18–19. This book is a condensed translation of two works published in German in 1930 and 1931.

8. Pfeiffer, *Formative Forces,* 24–39.

9. Selawry, *Ehrenfried Pfeiffer,* 49–50.

10. Günther Wachsmuth, foreword to Pfeiffer, *Formative Forces,* xi–xiv.

11. Selawry, *Ehrenfried Pfeiffer,* 38–40.

12. "Announcement from the Experimental Group of Anthroposophical Agriculturists," *Anthroposophical Movement* 4, no. 6 (February 6, 1927): 47.

13. Koepf and von Plato, *Die biologisch-dynamische Wirtschaftsweise,* 59.

14. Paull, "Secrets of Koberwitz," 22–23.

15. Rudolf von Koschutzki, "Anthroposophy and Agriculture," *Anthroposophical Movement* 4, no. 12 (March 20, 1927): 92–95.

16. Ehrenfried Pfeiffer, "The Work of the Agricultural Experimental Group," *Anthroposophical Movement* 5, no. 5 (January 29, 1928): 34.

17. Erhard Bartsch, "The Present Position in Agriculture," *Anthroposophical Movement* 5, no. 9 (March 4, 1928): 69–71.

18. "Sins against Nature," *Anthroposophical Movement* 4, no. 23 (June 5, 1927): 179–81.

19. A. Usteri, "Factory, Forest and Farm," *Anthroposophical Movement* 4, no. 40 (October 2, 1927): 213–14.

20. "News of the Research Group of Anthroposophical Agriculturists," *Anthroposophical Movement* 4, no. 5 (January 30, 1927): 38–39.

21. Pfeiffer, "Agricultural Experimental Group," 34–35.

22. Demeter, "History," *What Is Demeter?*, accessed August 1, 2016, www .demeter.net/what-is-demeter/history.

23. Alan Brockman, "Comment: Standards in Food Production," *Anthroposophical Quarterly* 17, no. 3 (Autumn 1972): 60.

24. "Waldorf Education: Expansion in the Twentieth Century," in *Waldorf Education Worldwide*, 26.

25. Bodo von Plato, ed., *Anthroposophie im 20. Jahrhundert: Ein Kulturimpus in Biografischen Porträts* (Dornach, Switzerland: Verlag am Goetheanum, 2003), 983–84.

26. Evelyn Speiden Gregg, "The Early Days of Bio-Dynamics in America," *Bio-Dynamics* 119 (Summer 1976): 27.

27. "The Threefold Community ... What brought it about?" This undated typescript was apparently part of a newsletter, evidently by Ruth Pusch, that was based on Charlotte Parker's booklet "A Short History of the Threefold Community" and interviews with Parker and Gladys Barnett Hahn. Threefold Community Archives, drawer labeled "Threefold History," hanging folder labeled "Obituaries," folder labeled "Threefold History SV."

28. Gregg, "Early Days," 26–30.

29. John Paull, "The Betteshanger Summer School: Missing Link between Biodynamic Agriculture and Organic Farming," *Journal of Organic Systems* 6, no. 2 (2011): 15.

30. Adolf Hitler, *Völkischer Beobachter*, March 15, 1921, trans. Stephen E. Usher.

31. "Waldorf Education: Expansion in the Twentieth Century," in *Waldorf Education Worldwide: The Development of Waldorf Education Including Anthroposophical Curative Education and Social Therapy*, trans. Johanna Collis and Martyn Rawson (Berlin: Friends of Waldorf Education, 2001), 26.

32. "The Executive Board's Letter to Adolf Hitler," in T.H. Meyer, *The Development of Anthroposophy since Rudolf Steiner's Death: An Outline and Perspectives*

for the Future, compiled and edited by Paul V. O'Leary, trans. Matthew Barton (Great Barrington, MA: Steiner Books, 2014), 228–31.

33. G. Vogt, "The Origins of Organic Farming," in *Organic Farming: An International History,* ed. W. Lockeretz (Oxfordshire, UK: CAB International, 2007), 22–23; Anna Bramwell, *Ecology in the 20th Century: A History* (New Haven, CT: Yale University Press, 1989), 195–208; Peter Staudenmaier, *Between Occultism and Nazism: Anthroposophy and the Politics of Race in the Fascist Era* (Leiden: Brill, 2014); Anna Bramwell, *Blood and Soil: Richard Walther Darré and Hitler's "Green Party"* (Abbotsbrook, UK: Kensal Press, 1985); Uwe Werner, *Anthroposophen in der Zeit des Nationalsozialismus (1933–1945)* (Munich: Oldenbourg, 1999).

34. Meyer, *Development.*

35. Peter Selg, *Spiritual Resistance: Ita Wegman 1933–1935* (Great Barrington, MA: Steiner Books, 2014).

36. Ehrenfried Pfeiffer, *Bio-Dynamic Farming and Gardening: Soil Fertility Renewal and Preservation,* trans. Fred Heckel (London: Rudolf Steiner, 1938; New York: Anthroposophic Press, 1938). The German edition is *Die Fruchtbarkeit der Erde: Ihre Erhaltung und Erneuerung* (Basel: Verlag Zbinden and Hügin, 1938).

37. Pfeiffer, *Bio-Dynamic,* iii, 15, 65, 103.

38. Ibid., 24–35, v, 5. Though both the English *earth* and the German *Erde* can mean either the soil or the planet, the context makes clear that Pfeiffer intends the latter because he writes that no single farm can stop "the sickening of the whole earth." However, Pfeiffer did refer to the living *soil (Boden)* more often than the living earth. See *Die Fruchtbarkeit der Erde,* 9.

39. Pfeiffer, *Bio-Dynamic,* 81–82.

40. Ibid., 1–5.

41. Ibid., 143–63. Pfeiffer's method differed from scientific norms in one important way: because the instructions for making the preparations were not public, other scientists could not re-create Pfeiffer's experiments.

42. Ibid., 187–90.

43. Ibid., 210–11, 215.

44. Ibid., 58, 11.

45. Ibid., 23.

46. Steiner, "Agriculture Course," lecture 5.

47. Pfeiffer, *Bio-Dynamic,* 22.

48. Ibid., vi, 45–46, 162.

49. Vogt, "Origins," in Lockeretz, *Organic Farming,* 14–16.

50. Albert Howard, *An Agricultural Testament* (London: Oxford, 1940), 159–60; Albert Howard, *The Waste Products of Agriculture: Their Utilization as Humus* (London: Oxford University Press, 1931).

51. Howard, *Agricultural Testament*, ix.

52. Howard, *Agricultural Testament*, 27, x; Steiner, "Agriculture Course," lecture 5.

53. Howard, *Agricultural Testament*, 1–4, 17–18, 33, 19–20, 104.

54. Ibid., 171–80, 184–85, 197–98, 220–21.

55. Ibid., 18, 196, 189, 22, 185.

56. Ibid., 161.

57. Ibid., 37, 104–15.

58. Viscount Lymington, *Famine in England* (London: Witherby, 1938), 19, 42, 49, 52.

59. Paull, "Betteshanger," 18–19.

60. Rebecca Kneale Gould, *At Home in Nature: Modern Homesteading and Spiritual Practice in America* (Berkeley: University of California Press, 2005).

61. Jeffrey D. Marlett, *Saving the Heartland: Catholic Missionaries in Rural America, 1920–1960* (DeKalb: Northern Illinois University Press, 2002).

62. Conford, *Origins*, 166–67; Mike Tyldesley, "Proposals and Activities for a Threefold Social Order in Britain, c. 1920–c. 1950," accessed July 20, 2016, https://s3-eu-west-1.amazonaws.com/articles-and-essays/Tyldesley-Threefold-Social-Order.pdf.

63. Lord Northbourne, *Look to the Land* (London: Basis Books, 1940), 98.

64. John Paull, "Lord Northbourne, the Man Who Invented Organic Farming, a Biography," *Journal of Organic Systems* 9, no. 1 (2014): 31–53; Paull, "Betteshanger," 13–26.

65. Northbourne, *Look*, 3.

66. Ibid., 100–101, 9, 97, 154, 21, 79.

67. Ibid., 8, 190.

68. Ibid., 19–20, 48, 51–52.

69. Ibid., 25–26, 32, 118, 135, 140, 143–45, 185.

70. Ibid., 104–5, 187.

71. Ibid., 84–85, 180.

72. Ibid., 173.

73. Ibid., 166–67, 28, 81, 169, 88.

74. Ibid., 75, 181.

75. Lord Northbourne, *Looking Back on Progress* (Lahore, Pakistan: Ever Green Press, 1983), 7–8. (This edition notes that the text was copyrighted in 1970.)

76. Northbourne, *Looking Back,* 10, 22.

77. Ehrenfried Pfeiffer, "Prosperity—Security—The Future," *Bio-Dynamics* 1 (Summer 1941): 5.

78. Northbourne, *Look,* 191.

79. Eve Balfour, *The Living Soil* (London: Faber and Faber, 1943), 21, 143, 135–36.

80. Ibid., 143, 169–72, 49.

81. Ibid., 190, 193–95.

82. Ibid., 107, 55–56, 52.

83. Eve Balfour, introduction to Ehrenfried Pfeiffer, *Soil Fertility, Renewal and Preservation* (Peredur, East Grinstead: Lanthorn Press, 1947), 12–13. Balfour's introduction was reprinted in *Bio-Dynamics* 5, no. 2 (Spring 1947): 22–24.

84. Eve Balfour, "Towards a Sustainable Agriculture: The Living Soil" (talk given at an International Federation of Organic Agriculture Movements [IFOAM] conference, Switzerland, 1977), accessed August 5, 2016, http:// journeytoforever.org/farm_library/balfour_sustag.html.

85. J.I. Rodale, "Introduction to Organic Farming," *Organic Farming and Gardening* 1, no. 1 (May 1942): 3.

86. Ehrenfried Pfeiffer, "Introduction to the Bio-Dynamic Techniques," *Organic Farming and Gardening* 1, no. 1 (May 1942): 8–9.

87. Gregg, "Early Days," 32–36; Barnes, *Into the Heart's Land: A Century of Rudolf Steiner's Work in North America* (Great Barrington, MA: Steiner Books, 2005), 209–11; Richard B. Gregg, "Kimberton Farms," *Bio-Dynamics* 3, no. 1 (Summer 1943): 32–33.

88. Waldemar A. Nielsen, *Golden Donors: A New Anatomy of the Great Foundations* (Piscataway, NJ: Transaction, 2001), 168–76.

89. Ehrenfried Pfeiffer, *A Modern Quest for the Spirit,* compiled with an introduction by Thomas Meyer, trans. Henry Goulden (Chestnut Ridge, NY: Mercury Press, 2010); William Kracht (physician and current leader of the Fraternitas Rosae Crucis), email exchange with the author, spring 2016.

90. Joseph Kip Kosek, *Acts of Conscience: Christian Nonviolence and Modern American Democracy* (New York: Columbia, 2009), 223–24.

91. Richard B. Gregg, "The Winter Lecture Course at Kimberton Farms Agricultural School," *Bio-Dynamics* 2, no. 1 (Spring and Summer 1942): 35–37; Evelyn Speiden Gregg, "The Early Years of Bio-Dynamics in America (Part II)," *Bio-Dynamics* 120 (Fall 1976): 7–18; Barnes, *Into the Heart's Land,* 212.

92. Pfeiffer, "Prosperity," 1–5.

93. Ehrenfried Pfeiffer, "Bio-Dynamic Farming and Gardening," *Bio-Dynamics* 1, nos. 3–4 (Winter 1941): 1–6.

94. E. Riese, F. Bessenich, and E. Pfeiffer, "Dynamic Forces Practically Applied," *Bio-Dynamics* 1 (Winter 1941): 7–11.

95. J. Schultz, "Cosmic Rhythms," *Bio-Dynamics* 1 (Winter 1941): 21–25.

96. "The Bio-Dynamic Sprays," *Bio-Dynamics* 3, no. 1 (Summer 1943): 1–9.

97. Virginia Moore, "The Weed Problem," *Bio-Dynamics* 3, no. 1 (Summer 1943): 15.

98. Moore, "Weed Problem," 14–16.

99. William James McCauley, "Why the Farmer's 'Pay' Is Low," *Bio-Dynamics* 3, no. 2 (Winter 1944–45): 8–13.

100. Gregg, "Early Days," 30.

101. Gregg, "Bio-Dynamics in America (Part II)," 21–22.

102. Evelyn Speiden Gregg, "The Early Years of Bio-Dynamics in America (Part III)," *Bio-Dynamics* 121 (Winter 1977): 16–23; Barnes, *Into the Heart's Land,* 213–18.

103. Barnes, *Into the Heart's Land,* 218–29.

104. Ehrenfried Pfeiffer, "Are There Too Many People in the World?", *Golden Blade* 1 (1949): 31.

105. R. M. Querido, "Man and the Earth," *Anthroposophical Quarterly* 5, no. 2 (Summer 1960): 13–16.

106. Henry Barnes, "Journal for Anthroposophy," *Journal for Anthroposophy* 1 (Spring 1965): 1.

107. Hermann Poppelbaum, "The Dignity of the Earth," *Journal for Anthroposophy* 2 (Autumn 1965): 5–8.

108. Barnes, *Into the Heart's Land,* 112–31.

109. John Paull, "The Rachel Carson Letters and the Making of *Silent Spring,*" *Sage Open* (July-September 2013): 1–12.

110. John Davy, "Menace in the Silent Spring," *Observer,* February 17, 1963; rept. in John Davy, *Hope, Evolution, and Change: Selected Essays* (Stroud: Hawthorn Press, 1985): 221–27. Citations refer to the 1985 edition. Vivian Griffiths, "How 'Silent Spring' Came to Britain," *New View* 70 (January–March 2014): 3–5.

111. Marjorie Spock, "North America under a Light Sky," *Golden Blade* 23 (1971): 121–22, quoted in Barnes, *Into the Heart's Land,* 126.

112. Barnes, *Into the Heart's Land,* 125.

113. Marjorie Spock, "Rachel Carson—In Memoriam," *Bio-Dynamics* 71 (Summer 1964): 2.

114. Paull, "Rachel Carson Letters," 8–9.

BRANCHES: ANTHROPOSOPHICAL INITIATIVES

1. "Earth Day: The History of a Movement," accessed March 14, 2014, www.earthday.org/earth-day-history-movement.

2. Wendell Berry, *A Continuous Harmony: Essays Cultural and Agricultural* (New York: Harcourt Brace Jovanaovich, 1972), 6. See also Berry, *The Unsettling of America: Culture & Agriculture* (San Francisco: Sierra Club Books, 1977); and E. F. Schumacher, *Small Is Beautiful: A Study of Economics as if People Mattered* (London: Blond and Briggs, 1973).

3. Bodo von Plato, ed., *Anthroposophie im 20. Jahrhundert: Ein Kulturimpus in Biografischen Porträts* (Dornach, Switzerland: Verlag am Goetheanum, 2003), 985.

4. Port Huron Statement, accessed August 3, 2016, www.h-net.org/~hst306/documents/huron.html.

5. Wouter J. Hanegraaff, *New Age Religion and Western Esotericism: Esotericism in the Mirror of Secular Thought* (Leiden: E.J. Brill, 1996), 19, 10.

6. For a comparison of Steiner's views with those of his anarchist contemporaries, see Guido Giacomo Preparata, "Perishable Money in a Threefold Commonwealth: Rudolf Steiner and the Social Economics of an Anarchist Utopia," *Review of Radical Political Economics* 38 (2006): 619–48.

7. Owen Barfield, *Poetic Diction: A Study in Meaning* (London: Faber and Gwyer, 1928); and Barfield, *Worlds Apart: A Dialogue of the 1960s* (Middletown, CT: Wesleyan University Press, 1964).

8. Michael Spence, *The Story of Emerson College: Its Founding Impulse, Work and Form* (Forest Row, UK: Temple Lodge, 2013). The United States today is home to three similar colleges: Sunbridge Institute in New York, the Center for Anthroposophy in New Hampshire, and Rudolf Steiner College California.

9. Henry Barnes, *Into the Heart's Land: A Century of Rudolf Steiner's Work in North America* (Great Barrington, MA: Steiner Books, 2005), 89–97, 188–200. See also Kevin Dann, *Across the Great Border Fault: The Naturalist Myth in America* (New Brunswick, NJ: Rutgers, 2000).

10. Barnes, *Into the Heart's Land*, 194–200.

11. Herbert H. Koepf, "What Is Bio-Dynamic Agriculture?," published in German by the Freie Hochschule for Geisteswissenschaft Goetheanum and then in English translation by William Brinton and Marjorie Spock as a

special issue of *Bio-Dynamics* 117 (Winter 1976); Herbert H. Koepf, *The Biodynamic Farm: Agriculture in the Service of the Earth and Humanity* (New York: Anthroposophic Press, 1989).

12. Koepf, "What Is Bio-Dynamic Agriculture?"

13. Maria Thun, "Nine Years Observation of Cosmic Influences on Annual Plants," *Bio-Dynamics* 115 (Summer 1975): 16–22.

14. Koepf, "What Is Bio-Dynamic Agriculture?," reprinted in *Biodynamics*, Summer/Fall 2007, 27–29.

15. Barnes, *Into the Heart's Land,* 219–20.

16. Trevelyan quoted in Frances Ferrer, *Sir George Trevelyan and the New Spiritual Awakening* (Edinburgh: Floris, 2002), 32.

17. Ferrer, *Trevelyan,* 65–66.

18. George Trevelyan, "Shropshire Myth and Legend," *Golden Blade* 5 (1953): 75.

19. George Trevelyan, "Spiritual Awakening in Our Time," in *A Vision of the Aquarian Age,* 1977, accessed August 3, 2016, www.sirgeorgetrevelyan.org.uk /books/thtbk-VAA02.html.

20. Peter Tompkins and Christopher Bird, *The Secret Life of Plants* (New York: Harper & Row, 1973), 370–71.

21. "Organic Food Production," accessed August 3, 2016, www.ecovillage findhorn.com/findhornecovillage/organic.php.

22. Paul A. Lee, *There Is a Garden in the Mind: A Memoir of Alan Chadwick and the Organic Movement in California* (Berkeley, CA: North Atlantic Books, 2013), 24.

23. "A Chronology of the Life of Alan Chadwick," accessed May 7, 2014, www.alan-chadwick.org/html%20pages/chronology.html. This publication cites a conversation between Chadwick and Greg Haynes as the source for the claim that Chadwick was fourteen at the time of his encounter with Steiner. This would have been 1923, one year before Steiner gave the Agriculture Course. Steiner was already advising farmers at this time, so it is plausible that Chadwick would have been exposed to Steiner's general philosophy of agriculture but not to the specific indications related to preparations.

24. Quoted in *Alan Chadwick: A Gardener of Souls,* accessed May 7, 2014, www .alan-chadwick.org/.

25. Lee, *Garden in the Mind,* xi.

26. Ibid., 17.

27. Ibid., 14, 29.

28. Ellen Farmer, "Stephen Kaffka: Pioneering UCSC Farm and Garden Manager, Agronomist," in *Cultivating a Movement: An Oral History Series on*

Sustainable Agriculture and Organic Farming on California's Central Coast, accessed January 13, 2016, http://escholarship.org/uc/item/99x87166#page-3.

29. Lee, *Garden in the Mind,* 31–34.

30. Ibid., 38.

31. Alan Chadwick, "The Vision of Biodynamics" (lecture, Urban Garden Symposium, 1974), accessed January 13, 2015, www.alan-chadwick.org/html%20 pages/lectures/urban-gardening-symposium/urban-garden-symposium-1974-part1.html.

32. Lee, *Garden in the Mind,* 54.

33. Chadwick, "Vision of Biodynamics"; "Alan Chadwick Lectures at the Urban Garden Symposium," 1975, accessed January 13, 2016, www.alan-chadwick.org/html%20pages/lectures/urban-gardening-symposium/1_index_urban-garden-symposium.html.

34. Farmer, "Kaffka."

35. "Herbert Koepf Meets Alan Chadwick," accessed August 3, 2016, www .alan-chadwick.org/html%20pages/personal_memories/kaffka_memories /Herbert-Koepf.html.

36. Farmer, "Kaffka."

37. Lee, *Garden in the Mind,* 61, 114–16; Sharon Cadwallader, *Whole Earth Cookbook* (New York: Houghton Mifflin, 1972).

38. Lee, *Garden in the Mind,* 141, 62, 140, 175; Edward Espe Brown, *The Tassajara Bread Book* (Boulder, CO: Shambhala, 1969); Edward Espe Brown, *Tassajara Cooking* (Boulder, CO: Shambhala, 1974); Deborah Madison with Edward Espe Brown, *The Greens Cookbook: Extraordinary Vegetarian Cuisine from the Celebrated Restaurant* (New York: Bantam, 1987).

39. Informal conversation with Carol and Tim Flinders, fall 2013; Laurel Robertson, Bronwen Godfrey, and Carol Flinders, *Laurel's Kitchen: A Handbook for Vegetarian Cookery and Nutrition* (Tomales, CA: Nilgiri Press, 1976).

40. Wendy Johnson, quoted in Lee, *Garden in the Mind,* 142. See also Wendy Johnson, *Gardening at the Dragon's Gate: At Work in the Wild and Cultivated World* (New York: Bantam Books, 2008).

41. Lee, *Garden in the Mind,* 167–69.

42. Ibid., 184, 188.

43. Live Power Community Farm, accessed March 15, 2016, www .livepower.org/about-the-farm/.

44. Osmosis Day Spa Sanctuary, accessed March 15, 2015, www.osmosis.com/.

45. Camp Joy Gardens, accessed March 15, 2015, http://campjoygardens .org/.

46. Joseph Beuys, *What Is Money? A Discussion,* with Johann Philipp von Beth-mann, Hans Binswanger, Werner Ehrlicher, and Rainer Willert, and with an afterword by Ulrich Rösch (Forest Row, UK: Clairview Books, 2010), 15–16, 24–25.

47. Ibid., 58–59, 43.

48. Interview with a leader of the Anthroposophical Society, September 2013.

49. Sherry Wildfeuer (editor of the *Stella Natura* calendar at Camphill Kimberton Hills), interview, April 2014.

50. Michael Babitch (Camphiller), interview, April 2014.

51. John Bloom (vice president of organizational culture at RSF Social Finance), interview, October 2013.

52. John Peterson (biodynamic farmer), interview, November 2013.

53. Lincoln Geiger (Temple-Wilton Community Farm), interview, June 2014.

54. Interview with the leader of an anthroposophical initiative, May 2014.

55. Interview with the leader of an anthroposophical initiative, June 2014.

56. Veronika van Duin (daughter of Camphill cofounder Barbara Lipsker and a long-time Camphiller), interview, July 2013.

57. Interview with a third-generation follower of Rudolf Steiner, October 2013.

58. Ehrenfried Pfeiffer, preface to Rudolf Steiner, "Agriculture Course."

59. Interview with a leader at Hawthorne Valley, June 2014.

60. H.H. Koepf, "To Reawaken Awareness of Nature," *Bio-Dynamics* 82 (Spring 1967): 12–18.

61. Karl Ege, "An Evident Need of Our Times," in *An Evident Need of Our Times: Goals of Education at the Close of the Century,* ed. Karl Ege (Hillsdale, NY: Adonis Press), 36–39.

62. Karl Ege, "The Rudolf Steiner Farm School," in Ege, *Evident Need,* 45–51.

63. Craig Holdrege (Nature Institute director), interview, July 2014; The Nature Institute, accessed August 24, 2015, http://natureinstitute.org/educ /index.htm.

64. Craig Holdrege, *The Giraffe's Long Neck: From Evolutionary Fable to Whole Organism* (Ghent, NY: Nature Institute, 2005); Craig Holdrege, *Thinking Like a Plant: A Living Science for Life* (Great Barrington, MA: Lindisfarne, 2013).

65. Craig Holdrege and Stephen L. Talbott, *Beyond Biotechnology: The Barren Promise of Genetic Engineering* (Lexington: University of Kentucky Press, 2008), 19.

66. Hawthorne Valley Farmscape Ecology Program, accessed August 24, 2015, http://hvfarmscape.org/.

67. Anna Duhon, Claudia Knab-Vispo, and Conrad Vispo (Farmscape Ecology Program co-coordinators), interviews, July 2014.

68. Ibid.

69. Theodor Schwenk, *Sensitive Chaos: The Creation of Flowing Forms in Water and Air,* trans. Olive Whicher and Johanna Wrigley (London: Rudolf Steiner Press, 1965), 10.

70. Quote in *Understanding Water,* accessed July 31, 2016, www.livingwater flowforms.com/research.htm.

71. Tobias Pedersen (Camphiller at Camphill Grangebeg), interview, August 2013.

72. Jennifer Greene (founder of the Water Institute in Blue Hill in Maine), interview, May 2014.

73. Water Research Institute of Blue Hill, accessed August 24, 2015, www .waterresearch.org/about.html.

74. *Orion Magazine,* accessed March 14, 2016, https://orionmagazine.org /about/mission-and-history/.

75. Barnes, *Into the Heart's Land,* 340–42.

76. This appears in H. A. W. Myrin, "The Myrin Institute, Inc.," *Proceedings of the Myrin Institute* 1 (1954): 5; and on the institute's website, accessed July 29, 2016, www.myrin.org/about.html.

77. Quoted in Barnes, *Into the Heart's Land,* 344.

78. M. G. H. Gilliam, editorial in *Orion Nature Quarterly* 1, no. 1 (June 1982): 1.

79. Laurens van der Post, "Man's Search for Self," *Orion Nature Quarterly* 1, no. 1 (June 1982): 4–9.

80. John N. Cole, "Our Unnatural Cities," *Orion Nature Quarterly* 1, no. 1 (June 1982): 10–14.

81. Bernard E. Rollin, "Beyond Kindness: Animals and Moral Theory," *Orion Nature Quarterly* 1, no. 1 (June 1982): 16–23.

82. Eric Utne, "Eric Utne Goes Back to School," *Utne Reader,* September–October 2000, accessed August 5, 2016, www.utne.com/politics/practice-what-you-teach.aspx?PageId = 1.

83. "An Emerging Culture," special supplement, *Utne Reader,* May–June 2003.

84. Claus Sproll, "Letter from the Publisher: Witnessing an Emerging New Consciousness," *Lilipoh* 81 (Fall 2015).

85. John Dalton, "Welcome Aboard," *New View* 1 (Autumn 1996): 3.

86. Ibrahim Abouleish, *Sekem: A Sustainable Community in the Egyptian Desert*, trans. Anna Cardwell (Edinburgh: Floris Books, 2005), 65; Sekem, accessed August 5, 2016, www.sekem.com/.

87. Abouleish, *Sekem*, 147–48.

88. This prize was established in 1980. Other recipients include such allies of anthroposophy as George Trevelyan; Green Party founder, Petra Kelly; and permaculture initiator Bill Mollison.

89. The Right Livelihood Award, accessed March 15, 2016, www .rightlivelihood.org/perlas.html; The Philosophy of Freedom, accessed March 25, 2016, http://philosophyoffreedom.org/node/3995

90. Jesaiah Ben-Aharon, *America's Global Responsibility: Individuation, Initiation, and Threefolding* (Great Barrington, MA: Lindisfarne, 2004), 122.

91. Presencing Institute, accessed March 15, 2016, www.presencing.com /presencing.

92. C. Otto Scharmer, *Theory U: Leading from the Future as It Emerges* (Cambridge: Society for Organizational Learning, 2007). See also Eugene Schwartz, "Anthroposophy and Waldorf Education: Of Prophets and Profits," accessed March 16, 2016, https://millennialchild.wordpress.com/article/anthroposophy-and-waldorf-education-of-11omw7eus832b-15/.

93. Claus Otto Scharmer, "The Blind Spot of Leadership: Presencing as a Social Technology of Freedom," accessed March 15, 2016, www.ottoscharmer .com/sites/default/files/2003_TheBlindSpot.pdf.

94. Thea Maria Carlson (codirector of the Biodynamic Association), interview, November 2013.

95. Andreas Schad (biodynamic farmer), interview, April 2014.

96. Interview with a biodynamic farmer, June 2014.

97. Interview with a biodynamic farmer, July 2013.

98. Craig Gibsone and Jan Martin Bang, *Permaculture: A Spiritual Approach* (Findhorn, UK: Findhorn Press, 2015), 111–13, 45–47, 20–21, 57–67.

99. Interview with a biodynamic farmer, July 2013.

100. Thea Maria Carlson, interview, November 2013.

101. Federation of Worldwide Opportunities on Organic Farms Organizations, accessed July 29, 2016, www.wwoof.net/history-of-wwoof/; Sue Coppard, "Peer to Pier: Conversations with Fellow Travelers," accessed July 29, 2016, http://viewfromthepier.com/2011/05/27/sue-coppard-wwoof/.

102. Quoted in H. H. Koepf, "The Goetheanum and Bio-Dynamics," *Bio-Dynamics* 115 (Summer 1975): 4–5.

103. Heinz Grotzke, "The Future after the First Fifty Years," *Bio-Dynamics* 112 (Fall 1974): 5–6.

104. Interview with a farmer at Hawthorne Valley, July 2014.

105. Interview with a farm educator at Hawthorne Valley, July 2014.

106. Abode of the Message, field visit by the author, spring 2015.

107. CRAFT, accessed August 21, 2015, www.craftfarmapprentice.com /links.php.

108. Thea Maria Carlson, interview, November 2013.

109. Interview with a biodynamic farmer, June 2014.

110. Thea Maria Carlson, interview, November 2013.

111. BINGN Apprenticeship Program, accessed March 15, 2016, www.bingn .org/.

112. Interview with a farmer and a farm educator at Hawthorne Valley, July 2014.

113. Interview with a farmer at Hawthorne Valley, July 2014.

114. Yggdrasil Land Foundation, accessed July 29, 2016, www.yggdrasil landfoundation.org/.

115. Interview with a leader at the Goetheanum, September 2013; Stephen R. Lloyd-Moffett, *The Soul of Wine: Finding Religion in the Fruit of the Vine* (unpublished manuscript).

116. Rachel and Steffen Schneider (biodynamic farmers, Hawthorne Valley), interview, July 2014.

117. Ibid.

FLOWERS: NEW ECONOMIES FOR ENVIRONMENTALISM

1. RSF Social Finance, accessed July 29, 2016, http://rsfsocialfinance.org /news/?c=blog.

2. Global Alliance for Banking, accessed July 29, 2016, www.gabv.org/our- banks. These figures make Triodos and GLS the third and fourth largest banks in the Global Alliance for Banking on Values. The two larger banks, Crédit Coopératif in Switzerland and Vancity in Canada, were among the hundreds of credit unions founded in the late nineteenth century and in the 1940s, respectively, and were not initially motivated by environmental ideals. Each has about three times the assets of Triodos. The two largest banks in the United States, J.P. Morgan Chase and Bank of America, each has more than $2 trillion in assets.

3. Gary Lamb, *Associative Economics: Spiritual Activity for the Common Good* (Edinburgh: Floris, 2010).

4. Rudolf Steiner, "Anthroposophy and the Social Question," trans. Harry Collison, GA 34. The original title of this essay was "Geisteswissenschaft und soziale Frage"; the translator's use of "anthroposophy" to translate "Geisteswissenschaft" reflects a fairly common practice in translations of works published by Steiner prior to the founding of the Anthroposophical Society.

5. Steiner, "Social Question," part 2.

6. Steiner, "Social Question," part 3.

7. Steiner, "An Appeal to the German Nation and to the Civilized World," appendix to *The Renewal of the Social Organism,* trans. E. Bowen-Wedgewood and Ruth Mariott, GA 24.

8. Quoted in Lindenberg, *Rudolf Steiner: A Biography,* trans. Jon McAlice (Great Barrington, MA: Steiner Books, 2012; first published in German in 1997), 533.

9. Robin Schmidt (director of Forschungsstelle Kulturimpuls at the Goetheanum), interview, September 2013; Mark Finser (a founder of RSF Social Finance), interview, October 2013.

10. Emil Leinhas, "Industrial Enterprises in the Anthroposophical Society," *Anthroposophical Movement 5,* no. 4 (January 22, 1928): 29–31.

11. Leinhas, "Industrial Enterprises," 31.

12. Finser, interview, October 2013.

13. Urs Pohlman (Goethean scientist and founder of Ananné), interview, September 2013; other interviews with anthroposophical leaders.

14. Software AG, accessed August 3, 2016, www.softwareag.com/us/solutions/default.asp#business.

15. "Götz Werner," www.basic-income.net/downloads/Werner.pdf ; *International Trade News,* "Every Company Has the Customers It Deserves," accessed August 3, 2016, www.internationaltradenews.com/interviews/every_company_has_the_customers_it_deserves/.

16. For a general history of social banks, see Roland Benedikter, *Social Banking and Social Finance: Answers to the Economic Crisis* (New York: Springer, 2011), 68–73.

17. "Ernst Barkhoff," in Bodo von Plato, ed., *Anthroposophie im 20. Jahrhundert: Ein Kulturimpus in Biografischen Porträts* (Dornach, Switzerland: Verlag am Goetheanum, 2003), 49–51.

18. "Ernst Barkhoff"; Mark Finser, interview, October 2013; Robin Schmidt, interview, September 2013; Urs Pohlman, interview, September 2013; Siegfried

Finser, *Money Can Heal: Evolving Our Consciousness* (Great Barrington, MA: Steiner Books, 2006), 165.

19. Interview with a founder of Triodos Bank, September 2013.

20. Finser, *Money Can Heal*, 168–69; Mark Finser, interview, October 2013.

21. Finser, *Money Can Heal*, 176.

22. Mark Finser, interview, October 2013.

23. Finser, *Money Can Heal*, 176.

24. Finser, *Money Can Heal*, 176–83; Mark Finser, interview, October 2013.

25. John Bloom (vice president of organizational culture, RSF Bank), interview, October 2013.

26. Ibid.

27. Finser, *Money Can Heal*, 172–74.

28. Mark Finser, interview, October 2013.

29. John Bloom, interview, October 2013.

30. Finser, *Money Can Heal*, 170–74.

31. John Bloom, interview, October 2013.

32. Finser, *Money Can Heal*, 172–74.

33. Mark Finser, interview, October 2013.

34. Ibid.

35. Benedikter, *Social Banking*, 45–46; accessed August 3, 2016, Global Alliance for Banking, www.gabv.org/; Mark Finser, interview, October 2013.

36. Interviews with anthroposophical leaders, September 2013; Contraste, accessed August 3, 2016, www.contraste.org/oekobank.htm.

37. Benedikter, *Social Banking*, 47.

38. Interview with an anthroposophical leader, September 2013.

39. Mark Finser, interview, October 2013.

40. John Bloom, interview, October 2013.

41. Mark Finser, interview, October 2013.

42. Benedikter, *Social Banking*, 3.

43. Mark Finser, interview, October 2013; John Bloom, interview, October 2013; Triodos office, Bristol, UK, visit by the author, summer 2013.

44. RSF Social Finance, accessed July 31, 2016, http://rsfsocialfinance.org/; Triodos Bank, accessed July 31, 2016, www.triodos.com/en/about-triodos-bank/; GLS Bank, accessed July 31, 2016, www.gls.de/privatkunden/english-portrait/.

45. Bloom, interview.

46. Triodos Bank, "Know Where Your Money Goes," accessed May 19, 2014, www.triodos.com/en/about-triodos-bank/know-where-your-money-goes/.

47. Mark Finser, interview, October 2013.

48. Ibid.

49. Bloom, interview, October 2013.

50. Mark Finser, interview, October 2013; BALLE, "History," accessed August 3, 2016, https://bealocalist.org/history.

51. B Lab Corporation, accessed August 3, 2016, www.bcorporation.net /what-are-b-corps; Mark Finser, interview, October 2013.

52. Local Harvest's comprehensive database listed 6,728 CSAs in July 2016, about 85 percent of which were farms (the rest were entities offering CSA services on behalf of farms). This count is up from 2,932 in 2007 and 4,571 in 2012, suggesting steady growth. My own informal experimentation suggests that these numbers are roughly accurate: perhaps 10 percent of currently active CSAs are not included in the database, and perhaps 10 percent of the listed farms do not have their own currently active websites. By contrast, the United States Department of Agriculture's report of 12,617 farms that "marketed products through community supported agriculture" in 2012 is not credible. The USDA data do not show the dramatic growth that is evident to observers, and they report large numbers of CSAs even in states where there are very few. Most likely their census question was misunderstood by some farmers, especially in areas where community supported agriculture is not well known. See Local Harvest, accessed July 18, 2016, www.localharvest.org/csa/; US Department of Agriculture, *2012 Census of Agriculture*, table 43, accessed July 18, 2016, www.agcensus.usda.gov/Publications/2012/Full_Report/Volume_1,_Chapter_ 2_US_State_Level/st99_2_043_043.pdf; Steve McFadden, "Unraveling the CSA Number Conundrum," *The Call of the Land: An Agrarian Primer for the 21*st *Century,* accessed July 18, 2016, https://thecalloftheland.wordpress.com/2012/01 /09/unraveling-the-csa-number-conundrum/.

53. *European Handbook on Community Supported Agriculture: Sharing Experiences,* accessed July 18, 2016, http://urgenci.net/wp-content/uploads/2015/03 /CSA4EUrope_Handbook.pdf.

54. Peter Blaser, "The Basic Concepts Underlying the Development of the Farm and Farming Community: Niederried since 1961," *Bio-Dynamics* 119 (Summer 1976): 16–24.

55. Wolfgang Stränz, "Buschberghof CSA, a Multifunctional Farm Successful for More Than 20 Years," *Forum Synergies,* May 18, 2010, accessed 18 July 2016, www.forum-synergies.eu/bdf_fiche-experience-23_en.html.

56. "Thoughts on a Spiritual History of Agriculture: A Report of Two Lectures Given by Manfred Klett," *Biodynamics* 160 (Fall 1960), accessed July

18, 2016, www.waldorflibrary.org/articles/703-thoughts-on-a-spiritual-history-of-agriculture.

57. Dottenfelderhof Farm, accessed July 18, 2016, www.dottenfelderhof.de /dottenfelderhof/unser-hof.html; and Arthur Zajonc, "Social Dimensions of Agriculture: Interview with Clifford Kurz," *Journal for Anthroposophy* 46 (Winter 1987): 33.

58. Hal Ginge, "Agricultural Financing," *Anthroposophical Review* 3, no. 3 (Autumn 1981): 9–10.

59. Jan VanderTuin, "Zürich Supported Agriculture," *RAIN* 14, no. 2 (Winter/Spring 1992), accessed 18 July 2016, www.rainmagazine.com/archive/1992 /zsa01312014.

60. Zajonc, "Social Dimensions," 33–34.

61. Armand Ruby, "Profiles of Biodynamic Communities in New England," *Journal for Anthroposophy* 46 (Winter 1987): 42–47.

62. Trauger Groh and Steven McFadden, *Farms of Tomorrow: Community Supported Farms, Farm Supported Communities* (Kimberton, PA: Bio-dynamic Farming and Gardening Association, 1990), 43–49; Temple-Wilton Community Farm, "History of the Farm," accessed August 3, 2012, www.twcfarm.com /description.

63. Temple-Wilton, "History of the Farm."

64. Groh and McFadden, *Farms of Tomorrow*, 71–73.

65. Jean-Paul Courtens, "Biodynamics and Roxbury Farm," 2006, accessed July 18, 2016, http://sfc.smallfarmcentral.com/dynamic_content/uploadfiles /942/Biodynamics%20and%20Roxbury%20Farm%202.pdf, accessed 18 July 2016; and http://www.roxburyfarm.com/.

66. John Bloom, interview, October 2013.

67. John Peterson (founding farmer at Angelic Organics), email communication with the author, July 2014; John Peterson, "Glitter & Grease—'I Don't Believe It,'" accessed November 2014, www.angelicorganics.com/ao/index .php?option = com_content&task = view&id = 125&Itemid = 324.

68. "Angelic Organics Mission," accessed November 2014, www.angeli corganics.com/Angelic_Organics___Chicago_CSA/Angelic_Organics___ Mission_and_Principles_of_a_Chicago_CSA.html.

69. John Peterson, interview, November 2013.

70. Peterson, email communication.

71. Tom Spaulding (founding executive director of Angelic Organics Learning Center), interview, November 2013; Tom Spaulding, email communication with the author, September 2014.

72. Tom Spaulding, interview, November 2013.

73. Stonyfield Farm, accessed March 2014, www.answers.com/topic /stonyfield-farm-inc.

FRUIT: THE BROADER ECOLOGY OF CAMPHILL

1. Rudolf Steiner, *Curative Education: Twelve Lectures for Doctors and Curative Teachers,* trans. Mary Adams, GA 317.

2. Friedwart Bock, ed., *The Builders of Camphill: Lives and Destinies of the Founders* (Edinburgh: Floris, 2004).

3. Karl König, "The Three Great Errors: A Chapter in Community Living," *Cresset: Journal of the Camphill Movement* 3, no. 1 (Michaelmas 1956): 6–16.

4. Michael Babitch, email communication with the author, September 23, 2014.

5. C.A. Mier, "Agriculture and the Village Community," *Cresset: Journal of the Camphill Movement* 3, no. 1 (Michaelmas 1956): 24–27.

6. Andreas Schad (farmer at Camphill Special School in Pennsylvania), interview, April 2014.

7. Interview with a Camphiller, April 2014; Marcus van Dam, "A Healthy Way of Life," accessed July 31, 2016, www.camphillresearch.com/content-stuff /uploads/2015/09/Marcus-Van-Dam.pdf.

8. Pat Thompson, "An Open Letter Outlining One Farming Community's Resistance to MAFF," *New View* 20 (July–September 2001): 2–4.

9. Petter D. Jenssen, Tore Krogstad, and Trond Moehlum, "Wastewater Treatment by Constructed Wetlands in the Norwegian Climate: Pretreatment and Optimal Design," in *Ecological Engineering for Wastewater Treatment: Proceedings of the International Conference at Stensund Folk College, Sweden, March 24–28, 1991,* ed. Carl Etnier and Björn Guterstam (Gothenburg, Sweden: Bokskogen, 1991), 227–38; Will Browne and Petter D. Jenssen, "Exceeding Tertiary Standards with a Pond/Reed Bed System in Norway," *Water Science and Technology* 51, no. 9 (2005): 299–306.

10. Martin Sturm (farmer at Camphill Clanabogan), interview, August 2013.

11. Ibid.

12. Ibid.

13. The Camphill Community, "Biogas Plant at Ballytobin," accessed April 11, 2014, www.seai.ie/Renewables/Bioenergy/Biogas_plant_at_Ballytobin .doc.

14. Ben Hewitt, *The Town That Food Saved: How One Community Found Vitality in Local Food* (Emmaus, PA: Rodale Books, 2011).

15. Hannah Schwartz and Seneca Gonzalez (Camphillers at Heartbeet Lifesharing), interviews, August 2014.

16. Ibid.

17. Seneca Gonzalez, interview, August 2014.

18. Hannah Schwartz, interview, August 2014.

19. Interviews with Camphillers, April 2014.

20. Diedra Heitzman (Camphiller at Camphill Kimberton Hills), interview, April 2014.

21. Angelika Monteux (Camphiller at Camphill School Aberdeen), interview, July 2015.

22. Interview with a Camphiller, July 2013.

23. Bruce Bennet (Camphiller at Tiphereth Camphill), interview, July 2013; Bruce Bennet, email communication with the author, October 2015.

24. Diedra Heitzman, interview, April 2014.

25. Interviews with Camphillers, August 2013.

26. Vicky Syme (Camphiller at Camphill Grangebeg), interview, August 2013.

27. Interview with a Camphill artist, July 2013.

28. Interview with a Camphiller, July 2013.

29. Interview with a Camphiller, August 2013.

30. Interview with a Camphiller, July 2013.

31. Interview with a Camphiller, August 2013.

32. Interview with a Camphiller, July 2013.

33. Lost Garden of Penicuik, visit by the author, June 2016, accessed July 18, 2016, www.lostgarden.co.uk/.

34. Simon Beckett (Camphiller at Camphill Newton Dee), interview, June 2013.

35. Tobias Pedersen (farmer at Camphill Grangebeg), interview, August 2013.

36. Interview with a Camphiller at Heartbeet, August 2014.

37. Jan Bang (Camphiller and intentional community researcher), informal conversation, 2013; Jan Martin Bang, *Ecovillages: A Practical Guide to Sustainable Communities* (Gabriola Island, BC: New Society Publishers, 2005).

38. Findhorn Foundation, "Care Farming at Findhorn," accessed August 1, 2016, www.findhorn.org/2015/12/care-farming-at-findhorn/.

39. Interview with a Camphiller, July 2013.

40. Tom Marx (Camphiller at Tigh a' Chomainn Camphill), interview, July 2013.

41. Jens-Peter Linde (Christian Community priest), interview, July 2013.

ECOLOGY: THE BOUNDARIES OF ANTHROPOSOPHY

1. Herbert H. Koepf, "Bio-dynamic Agriculture throughout the World," *Anthroposophical Review* 3, no. 3 (Autumn 1981): 3.

2. Rudolf Steiner, "The Psychological Foundations of Anthroposophy: Its Standpoint in Relation to the Theory of Knowledge," April 8, 1911, Schmidt Number S-2412, http://wn.rsarchive.org/Articles/GA035/19110408p01.html.

3. Johann Wolfgang von Goethe, "The Experiment as Mediator of Object and Subject," trans. Craig Holdrege, *In Context* 24 (Fall 2010): 19–23, accessed August 4, 2015, http://natureinstitute.org/pub/ic/ic24/ic24_goethe.pdf; Rudolf Steiner, *The Theory of Knowledge Implicit in Goethe's World Conception,* GA 2; Rudolf Steiner, *Goethe's Conception of the World,* GA 6.

4. Steiner, *Intuitive Thinking as a Spiritual Path: A Philosophy of Freedom,* trans. Michael Lipson, GA 4 (Great Barrington, MA: Steiner Books, 1995); Owen Barfield, *Saving the Appearances: A Study in Idolatry* (London: Faber and Faber, 1957).

5. David Eyes, "What Is Goethean Science?," accessed April 7, 2014, www.awakenings.com/jcms/anthroposophy-and-goethean/35-general-anthroposophic-and-goethean/45-goethean-science.html.

6. Interview with a Goethean scientist, September 2013.

7. Paul A. Lee, *There Is a Garden in the Mind: A Memoir of Alan Chadwick and the Organic Movement in California* (Berkeley, CA: North Atlantic Books, 2013).

8. Interview with a Goethean scientist, October 2013.

9. Anna Bramwell, *Ecology in the 20th Century: A History* (New Haven, CT: Yale University Press, 1989), 40.

10. Rudolf Steiner, Preface to the 1923 edition, *Riddles of Philosophy,* GA 18.

11. Bramwell, *Ecology,* 39–52; Oliver A.I. Botar, "Defining Biocentrism," in Oliver A.I. Botar and Isabel Wünsche, eds., *Biocentrism and Modernism* (Farnham, UK: Ashgate, 2011), 20–21.

12. H. Heitler, "Life and Nuclear Forces," *Anthroposophical Quarterly* 2, no. 2 (Summer 1957): 2–7.

13. Jonathan Forman, "Human Ecology," *Bio-Dynamics* 80 (Fall 1966): 18–22.

14. "Garrity Urges Stress on Ecology," *Bio-Dynamics* 72 (Fall 1964): 4–5.

15. Herbert Koepf, "The Matter That Matters," *Bio-Dynamics* 80 (Fall 1966): 2–4.

16. H.H. Koepf, "Three Lectures on Bio-Dynamics," *Bio-Dynamics* 88 (Fall 1968): 1–6.

17. John Davy [pub. under John Waterman], "Bacon, Rudolf Steiner, and Modern Science," *Golden Blade*, 1962, rept. John Davy, *Hope, Evolution, and Change: Selected Essays* (Stroud: Hawthorn Press, 1985): 36–46. Quotations are from the 1985 edition.

18. John Davy, "Time to Stop the Plunder," *Observer*, November 17, 1968, rept. Davy, *Hope*, 234–39.

19. John Davy, "Wisdom and the Life of the Earth," *Golden Blade*, 1971, rept. Davy, *Hope*, 1–10.

20. John Davy, "Man and the Underworld," *Golden Blade*, 1980, rept. Davy, *Hope*, 12–26.

21. Carsten J. Pank, "Silent Spring: Ten Years After," *Bio-Dynamics* 104 (Fall 1972): 10–11.

22. Charles Davy, "Letter to the Editor," *Anthroposophical Quarterly* 23/1 (Spring 1978): 24.

23. Paul Carline, "Creationists and Darwin: A War on Science," *New View* 39 (April–June 2006): 8–16.

24. "Who We Are," accessed January 15, 2016, www.mandaamin.org.

25. Diana Coole and Samantha Frost, *New Materialisms: Ontology, Agency, and Politics* (Durham, NC: Duke University Press, 2010).

26. Interview with a Goethean scientist, September 2013.

27. Interview with a farmer at Camphill Glencraig, July 2013.

28. Edith Lammerts van Buren, Johannes Wirz, and Jelle van der Meulen, "The Tension between Biotechnology and Anthroposophy," *New View* 1 (Autumn 1996): 28–29,

29. David Heaf, "What Has Biotechnology Got to Do with Anthroposophy," *New View* 2 (Winter 1996): 28–29.

30. "Statement on Genetic Engineering by the Demeter Standards Committee of the Biodynamic Agricultural Association," *New View* 15 (April–June 2000): 28.

31. Rosemary Radford Ruether, "Motherearth and the Megamachine: A Theology of Liberation in a Feminine, Somatic and Ecological Perspective," in *Womanspirit Rising: A Feminist Reader in Religion*, ed. Carol P. Christ and Judith Plaskow (New York: Harper, 1979), 44–45.

32. Sallie McFague, *Life Abundant: Rethinking Theology and Economy for a Planet in Peril* (Minneapolis: Fortress, 2001), 21.

33. "The Challenge of Rudolf Steiner," directed by Jonathan Stedall (Cupola Productions, 2010), DVD.

34. Tom Spaulding (biodynamic educator), interview, November 2013.

35. Hans Thomas Hakl, "'Occultism is the Metaphysic of Dunces': The Conflation of Esotericism, Irrationalism, and Fascism in Postwar Germany," in *Esotericism, Religion, and Politics,* ed. Arthur Versluis, Lee Irwin, and Melinda Phillips (Minneapolis: North American Academic Press, 2012), 1–40.

36. Rudolf Steiner, *Intuitive Thinking,* 163–72.

37. Steiner, *An Outline of Esoteric Science,* trans. Catherine E. Creeger, GA 13 (Great Barrington, MA: Steiner Books, 1997), 120, 145. I am grateful to Diedra Heitzman for calling my attention to these passages.

38. Christopher Bamford, *The Voice of the Eagle: The Heart of Celtic Christianity John Scotus Eriugena* (Great Barrington, MA: Lindisfarne, 2000), 47. The 869 council, recognized as authoritative by Roman Catholics but not by the Eastern Orthodox, includes a canon affirming that "man has one rational and intellectual soul" and anathematizing the view that "he has two souls." Mainstream historians do not ascribe as much significance to this event as do students of Steiner, though they would agree that threefold anthropology was common in the early church and less common in the Middle Ages. H.J. Schroeder, *Disciplinary Decrees of the General Councils: Text, Translation and Commentary* (St. Louis: B. Herder, 1937), 157–76.

39. Steiner, "Agricultural Course," lecture 8.

40. Andrew Marshall (farmer), interview, July 2013.

41. George Corrin, "Down-Grading the Kingdoms of Nature," *Anthroposophical Quarterly* 11, no. 2 (Summer 1966): 32–35.

42. This is the first practice criticized on People for Legal and Nonsectarian Schools, accessed August 5, 2016, www.waldorfcritics.org/. The prohibition is rooted in Goethe's theory of color, which also influenced Steiner's spiritual interpretation of racial differences.

43. Peter Staudenmaier, "Anthroposophy and Ecofascism," accessed January 15, 2016, www.waldorfcritics.org/articles/Staudenmaier.html. I cite these quotations because Staudenmaier's thoroughgoing research forms the basis for a large share of English-language criticism of anthroposophy. His article, originally published in 2000 in a Norwegian humanist journal, appears in its original form on many websites critical of anthroposophy. Staudenmaier subsequently revised the essay ("Anthroposophy and Ecofascism," accessed

January 15, 2016, http://social-ecology.org/wp/2009/01/anthroposophy-and-ecofascism-2/) to replace the quoted passages with references to anthroposophy's "patently racist elements and its compromised past." Staudenmaier's academic publications display still more nuance and contain insights that students of anthroposophy would do well to consider.

44. Peter Staudenmaier, *Between Occultism and Nazism: Anthroposophy and the Politics of Race in the Fascist Era* (Leiden: Brill, 2014), 101–45.

45. Rudolf Steiner, *How to Know Higher Worlds: A Modern Path of Initiation*, trans. Christopher Bamford, GA 10 (Great Barrington, MA: Steiner Books, 1994), 16–19.

46. Ibid., 24–25, 62.

47. Ibid., 88–89.

48. Ibid., 89.

49. Ibid., 191.

50. Steiner, *Outline of Esoteric Science*, 247–75.

51. Staudenmaier, *Between Occultism and Nazism*, 27.

52. Rudolf Steiner, *Fall of the Spirits of Darkness*, trans. Anna R. Meuss, GA 177, lecture 5; Kevin Dann, *Across the Great Border Fault: The Naturalist Myth in America* (New Brunswick, NJ: Rutgers, 2000), 166–68. Steiner's account of how Atlantean experimentation led to the rise of modern nations bears some similarity to Elijah Muhammad's account of the origins of the white race.

53. Steiner, "Colour and the Human Races," trans. M. Cotterell, GA 349. This lecture, which is widely quoted by critics of anthroposophy, was not available on the Rudolf Steiner Archive until May 15, 2016, presumably because of its offensive content.

54. Staudenmaier, *Between Occultism and Nazism*, 64–65, 69.

55. Steiner, "Colour and the Human Races."

56. Steiner, *The Mission of Folk Souls*, GA 121, lecture 4.

57. This is Peter Staudenmaier's view, which he supports by citing similar passages in other lectures. Staudenmaier, *Between Occultism and Nazism*, 56–62.

58. George Kaufmann Adams, introduction, *Souls of the Nations* (London: Anthroposophical Publishing Company, 1938), accessed August 5, 2016, http://wn.rsarchive.org/RelAuthors/AdamsKaufmannGeorge/SoulNation/SouNat_index.html.

59. Peter Selg, *Spiritual Resistance: Ita Wegman 1933–1935* (Great Barrington, MA: Steiner Books, 2014).

60. Sergei Prokofieff, "On the Anniversary of Rudolf Steiner's Death," in Sergei O. Prokofieff and Peter Selg, *Crisis in the Anthroposophical Society,* trans. Willoughby Ann Walshe (Forest Row, UK: Temple Lodge, 2013), 76.

61. Gerard Kerkvliet, "Rudolf Steiner Recognized as an Opponent of Anti-Semitism and Nationalism," accessed January 15, 2016, http://uncletaz.com/steinerrace.html; and Richard House, "A Refutation of the Allegation of Racism against Rudolf Steiner," *New View* 31 (Spring 2004): 51–53. The passage about the mulatto baby, which is not available in English translation, appears in Rudolf Steiner, *Über Gesundheit und Krankheit,* GA 348 (Dornach: Rudolf Steiner Verlag, 1997), 189, http://fvn-archiv.net/PDF/GA/GA348.pdf.

62. Staudenmaier, "Anthroposophy and Ecofascism." This passage appears in both versions of the article.

63. "Christian-Jewish Relations: Declaration of the Evangelical Lutheran Church in America to the Jewish Community," accessed August 5, 2016, www.jewishvirtuallibrary.org/jsource/anti-semitism/lutheran1.html.

64. Peter Selg, "The Identity of the General Anthroposophical Society," in Prokofieff and Selg, *Crisis,* 43–44. Selg has also been bitterly critical of the collaborationist behavior of the official society during the Nazi years.

65. To the extent that this is Staudenmaier's position, it may reflect his association with Murray Bookchin's Institute for Social Ecology, which has long advocated for an anarchist version of environmental activism that is embedded in anticapitalist, antiracist, antisexist, and broadly antihierarchical struggles. Bookchin has been a caustic critic of deep ecology and of "cultural" strands of anarchism that seek to transcend the left-right dichotomy.

66. Bron Taylor, *Dark Green Religion: Nature Spirituality and the Planetary Future* (Berkeley: University of California Press, 2010), 10.

67. Gaia Trust, accessed August 1, 2016, http://gaia.org/.

68. Rudolf Steiner, "The Fourfold Man of Earth," *Cosmic Memory,* GA 11.

69. Steiner, "Agriculture Course," trans. George Adams, lecture 4.

70. The Pfeiffer Center, accessed August 1, 2016, www.pfeiffercenter.org/index.aspx.

71. The Weston A. Price Foundation, accessed August 1, 2016, www.westonaprice.org/.

72. Bockemühl, "Poppelbaum," in Bodo von Plato, ed., *Anthroposophie im 20. Jahrhundert: Ein Kulturimpus in Biografischen Porträts* (Dornach, Switzerland: Verlag am Goetheanum, 2003), 609–13; Hermann Poppelbaum, "Man and the Animal Kingdom," *Anthroposophical Movement* 4, no 7 (February 13, 1927): 51–55.

73. Hermann Poppelbaum, "The Consciousness of Higher Animals," *Anthroposophical Movement* 5, no. 24 (June 17, 1928): 189.

74. Hermann Poppelbaum, *Man and Animal: Their Essential Difference* (London: Anthroposophical, 1960), 131.

75. Interview with a Goethean scientist, May 2014.

76. Interview with a Goethean scientist, July 2014.

77. Richard Karutz, "African Legend of the Cow," *Anthroposophical Movement* 5, no. 19 (May 13, 1926): 145–48.

78. Michael Babitch (Camphiller), email communication with the author, March 28, 2016.

79. Ernst Lehrs, "The True Relation between Man and Animal," *Anthroposophical Quarterly* 3, no. 3 (Autumn 1958): 11–13.

80. Virginia Gilmer, "Endangered Species and Man's Animality," *New View* 2 (Winter 1996): 14–15.

81. Michael Ronall, "Sustainable Caring in Everyday Life," in *Stella Natura: Working with Cosmic Rhythms Biodynamic Planting Calendar,* ed. Sherry Wildfeuer (Kimberton, PA: Camphill Village Kimberton Hills, 2015).

82. Douglas Sloan, *The Redemption of the Animals: Their Evolution, Their Inner Life, and Our Future Together* (Great Barrington, MA: Lindisfarne, 2015), 90–117.

83. Ibid., 121, 141.

84. Abigail Zoltick, "Forgiveness for the Farmer," in Wildfeuer, *Stella Natura.*

85. Interview with a biodynamic farmer, June 2014.

86. George Corrin, "Comment: 'The Dear Earth … ,'" *Anthroposophical Quarterly* 16, no. 1 (Spring 1971): 18.

87. Thea Maria Carlson (member of the Biodynamic Association in America), interview, November 2013.

88. Interview with a Goethean scientist, July 2014. For Margulis, see Tom Wakeford and Martin Walters, eds., *Science for the Earth* (New York: Wiley), 19–36.

89. Interview with a Camphiller, July 2013.

90. Andrew Marshall (biodynamic farmer), interview, July 2013.

91. Steffen Schneider (Hawthorne Valley farmer), interview, July 2014.

92. Rachel Schneider (Hawthorne Valley farm educator), interview, July 2014.

93. Interview with a Goethean scientist, July 2014.

94. Steiner, *Outline of Esoteric Science,* 125.

95. Interview with biodynamic farmer, June 2014.

96. "Statutes of the Anthroposophical Society," accessed June 10, 2015, http://wn.rsarchive.org/Articles/Statut_index.html.

97. "Statutes of the Anthroposophical Society."

98. Rudolf Steiner, "Awakening to Community," trans. Marjorie Spock, lecture 1, January 23, 1923.

99. Steiner, "Agriculture Course," lecture 8.

100. Interview with a biodynamic farmer, June 2014.

101. Interview with an anthroposophical leader, September 2013.

102. Veronika van Duin (Camphiller), interview July 2013.

103. Seb Monteux (Camphiller), interview, July 2013.

104. Jean-Michel Florin (coleader of the Section for Agriculture of the Anthroposophical Society), interview, September 2013.

105. Triodos Bank, accessed June 10, 2015, www.triodos.com/en/about-triodos-bank/.

106. Mark Finser (a founder of RSF Social Finance), interview, October 2013.

107. Gilbert Fonteyn (Camphiller), interview, June 2013.

108. Florin, interview.

109. Interview with an anthroposophical leader, September 2013.

110. Carlson, interview.

111. Interview with a leader in the anthroposophical movement, October 2013.

112. Learning Happiness in Bhutan, "Rudolf Steiner 100 Years Later," accessed March 15, 2013, http://havinhtho.blogspot.com/2013/05/rudolf-steiner-100-years-later.html.

113. Martin Sturm (Irish Camphiller), interview, August 2013.

114. Interview with a leader in the anthroposophical movement, October 2013.

115. Interview with a leader in the biodynamics movement at the Goetheanum, September 2013.

EVOLUTION: ANTHROPOSOPHY'S GIFTS
TO THE ENVIRONMENTAL MOVEMENT

1. Steiner, "Agriculture Course," lecture 1.

2. Horst Kornberger, "Kompost Down Under," *New View* 15 (April–June 2000): 26–27.

3. Peter Lamborn Wilson, Christopher Bamford, and Kevin Townley, *Green Hermeticism: Alchemy and Ecology* (Great Barrington, MA: Lindisfarne, 2007).

4. Sacred Land Farm, accessed January 15, 2016, www.fincasagrada.com/.

5. Ehrenfried Pfeiffer, preface to Rudolf Steiner, "Agriculture Course."

6. Robert Karp (codirector of the Biodynamic Association), interview, November 2013.

7. Jean-Michel Florin (head of the Agricultural Section at the Goetheanum), interview, September 2013.

8. Thea Carlson (codirector of the Biodynamic Association), interview, November 2013.

9. Tom Spaulding (Angelic Organics), interview, November 2013.

10. Ibid.

11. If anything, these estimates overestimate both the organic and the biodynamic movements. Laura Reynolds reports that in 2010, 37 million hectares of farmland were certified organic, 0.9 percent of the total: "Certified Organic Farmland Still Lagging Worldwide," *Worldwatch Institute,* www.worldwatch.org/certified-organic-farmland-still-lagging-worldwide. However, National Geographic estimated in 2005 that 40 percent of the global land surface (approximately 5.4 billion hectares) is used for agriculture as a whole: James Owen, "Farming Claims Almost Half Earth's Surface, New Maps Show," *National Geographic News,* December 9, 2005, http://news.nationalgeographic.com/news/2005/12/1209_051209_crops_map.html. If this is correct, organics accounts for just over two-thirds of 1 percent. And the 150,000 hectares certified by Demeter International account for only 0.5 percent of the organic total. www.demeter.de/demeter-international/worldwide-network. Of course, much of the land that is farmed using organic and biodynamic practices is uncertified. All websites were last accessed August 2, 2016.

12. Philip Very, "Biodynamics as an Ecological Influence," *Bio-Dynamics* 99 (Summer 1971): 6.

13. Rudolf Steiner, "Anthroposophy and the Social Question," trans. Harry Collison, GA 34, part 1.

14. Robert Karp, "Toward an Associative Economy in the Sustainable Food and Farming Movement," *Biodynamics* (Spring 2008): 25; Karp, email communication, July 2015.

15. Interview with a farmer and biodynamic researcher, summer 2013.

16. Heinz Grotzke, "The Future after the First Fifty Years," *Bio-Dynamics* 112 (Fall 1974): 4–5.

17. Tobias Pedersen (biodynamic farmer at Camphill Grangebeg), interview, August 2013.

18. Vicky Syme (Camphiller), interview, August 2013.

19. Carlson, interview, August 2013.

20. Steve Lyons (Camphiller), interview, July 2013.

21. Andrew Plant (Camphiller), interview, July 2013.

22. Interview with a practitioner of biodynamics, summer 2013.

23. Ellen Farmer, "Stephen Kaffka: Pioneering UCSC Farm and Garden Manager, Agronomist," in *Cultivating a Movement: An Oral History Series on Sustainable Agriculture and Organic Farming on California's Central Coast,* accessed January 13, 2016, http://escholarship.org/uc/item/99x87166#page-3.

24. Rudolf Steiner, *Theosophy: An Introduction to the Supersensible Knowledge of the World and the Destination of Man,* trans. Henry B. Monges, rev. ed. (Gilbert Church, 1971), GA 9, chapter 3, part 2.

25. John Peterson, interview, November 2013.

26. Gottfried Richter, "The Christian and the Creature," *Bio-Dynamics* 112 (Fall 1974): 25–28.

27. Rudolf Steiner, *An Outline of Esoteric Science,* trans. Catherine E. Creeger, GA 13 (Great Barrington, MA: Steiner Books, 1997).

28. Rudolf Steiner, "The Influences of Lucifer and Ahriman," trans. D.S. Osmond, GA 191 and 193, lecture 5.

29. Rudolf Steiner, *The Study of Man: General Education Course,* trans. Daphne Harwood and Helen Fox, GA 293, lecture 3.

30. Steve Lyons, interview, July 2013.

31. Andrew Plant, interview, July 2013.

32. Jens-Peter Linde (Christian Community priest), interview, July 2013.

33. Jens-Peter Linde, email communication with the author, July 2015.

34. Interview with a biodynamic farmer, November 2013.

35. William Cronon, ed., *Uncommon Ground: Toward Reinventing Nature* (New York: W. W. Norton, 1995).

36. Jean-Michel Florin, interview, September 2013.

37. Mark Finser (a founder of RSF Social Finance), interview, October 2013.

38. Andrew Plant, interview, July 2013.

39. Mark Finser, interview, October 2013.

40. Alex Fornal, "Sustainable Development: The Challenge of the New Environmentalism," *New View* 17 (Fourth Quarter 2000): 15–18.

41. Manfred Klett, "The Biodynamic Farm: An Embryo for the Threefold Social Order in Our Time," *Golden Blade* 51 (1999): 33–48.

INDEX

science: anthroposophy and
mainstream, 178–190; and Balfour,
Lady Eve, 54–56; and Chadwick,
Alan, 86, 88–89; and
environmentalism, 176; Goethean,
20, 98–101, 105, 112, 114, 115, 168,
179–190, 207, 210–213; and Howard,
Albert, 43; and Koepf, Herbert,
80–82; and Myrin Institute, 102–103;
and Northbourne, Lord, 49–53, 178;
and Pfeiffer, Ehrenfried, 26–27,
37–38, 61, 184; and Poppelbaum,
Hermann, 65, 207; and Querido,
René, 65; and Sloan, Douglas,
209–210; spiritual, ix, 20, 28, 29, 53,
179–180, 196, 206, 238–240; and
Steiner, Rudolf, 4, 6, 12, 16, 17, 19–20,
25, 104, 179–184, 190
sectarianism, 76, 214–224
SEKEM, 106–107
self-reinforcing and self-dispersing
spiritualities, 7–11, 71–77, 214–224
sensitive crystallization, 26–27
Shepard, Mark, 112
Shiva, Vandana, 99, 109, 227
Shouldice, Rod, 147
Sloan, Douglas, 209–210
socialism, 5–6, 45–46, 49, 55, 74, 76,
122–123, 125, 154, 200
Solomon, Paul, 90
Spaulding, Tom, 229–230
Speiden, Evelyn, 31, 58, 60
Spock, Marjorie, xi, 24, 66–69, 101, 230
Spring Valley. See Threefold
Community
Sproll, Claus, 104–105
Stearns, Tom, 163–164
Stedall, Jonathan, 192
Steffen, Albert, 33–35, 77, 196
Stegemann, Ernst, 12, 24–25
Steiner, Marie, 33–35, 52, 80, 196
Steiner, Rudolf, ix, 1–22; and
Agricultural Experimental Circle,
24–28; and alchemy, xiii; and
Anthroposophical Society, 33–35, 126,

214–219; and associative economics,
121–129, 132–133, 140–142, 155; and baby
booomers, 92–96; and Balfour, Lady
Eve, 54–56, 71; and Barfield, Owen,
78; and basic exercises, 81, 234; and
Chadwick, Alan, xi, 85–88, 259n23;
on Christ, 13, 21, 243–244; critics of,
177, 195–204; and curative education,
153–154; on dualism and monism,
192–195; and evolution of anthroposophy, 71, 75–76; and fascism, xiv,
31–33, 195–196; and Gaianism, xiii,
xiv, 205–206; 213; and Haeckel, Ernst,
183; and Howard, Albert, 41–44; and
Koepf, Herbert, 81–82; and Kolisko,
Lili, 25; and Lebensreform, 40; and
Lilipoh, 105; and Myrin Institute, 102;
and Northbourne, Lord, 47–53, 178;
and Perlas, Nicanor; and Peterson,
John; and Pfeiffer, Ehrenfried, 11–13,
25–26, 35–39, 57, 61, 96; and planetary
transmutation, 238–241; and
Poppelbaum, Hermann, 65–66; and
racism, 33, 195–204; and Rosicru-
cianism, 59; and Scharmer, Otto, 109;
and Schumacher, E. F., 187; and
science, 4, 6, 12, 16, 17, 19–20, 25, 104,
179–184, 190; and sectarianism, 76,
214–222; and Sloan, Douglas,
209–210; and social homeopathy, 233;
and subnature, 243; and
threefolding, 121–127, 142; and
Trevelyan, George, 83–84; and
Waldorf schools, 30, 121, 239–240
Stonyfield Yogurt, xi, 151–152
Sturm, Martin, 160–162
Stusser, Michael, 90
Sufism, 93, 115, 227
Sullivan, Kerry and Barbara, 147
Syme, Vicky, 168, 234–235

Talbott, Stephen, 98–99
Tamera Ecovillage, 101
Taylor, Bron, xiv, 205, 211
Teilhard de Chardin, Pierre, 5, 84

Milton Keynes UK
Ingram Content Group UK Ltd.
UKHW010102161223
434462UK00007B/551